HOW
TO
KNOW
THE
BIRDS

Also by this author

Smithsonian Field Guide to the Birds of North America

American Birding Association Field Guide to the Birds of Colorado

Atlas of the Breeding Birds of Nevada

Let's Go Birding!

HOW
TO
KNOW
THE
BIRDS

The Art & Adventure of Birding

TED FLOYD

ILLUSTRATIONS BY
N. JOHN SCHMITT

Washington, D.C.

Published by National Geographic Partners, LLC
1145 17th Street NW Washington, DC 20036

Library of Congress Cataloging-in-Publication Data
Names: Floyd, Ted, 1968- author. | Schmitt, N. John, illustrator. | National
    Geographic (Firm), publisher. | National Geographic Society (U.S.)
Title: How to know the birds : the art & adventure of birding / Ted Floyd ;
    illustrated by N. John Schmitt.
Description: Washington, D.C. : National Geographic, [2019] | Includes
    index.
Identifiers: LCCN 2018037630 (print) | LCCN 2018038686 (ebook) | ISBN
    9781426220043 (ebook) | ISBN 9781426220036
Subjects: LCSH: Bird watching--United States--Juvenile literature. |
    Birds--United States--Nomenclature--Juvenile literature.
Classification: LCC QL682 (ebook) | LCC QL682 .F56 2019 (print) | DDC
    598.072/34--dc23
LC record available at https://lccn.loc.gov_2018037630

Since 1888, the National Geographic Society has funded more than 13,000 research,
exploration, and preservation projects around the world. National Geographic Partners
distributes a portion of the funds it receives from your purchase to National Geographic
Society to support programs including the conservation of animals and their habitats.

Get closer to National Geographic explorers and photographers, and connect
with our global community. Join us today at nationalgeographic.com/join

For information about special discounts for bulk purchases, please contact National
Geographic Books Special Sales: specialsales@natgeo.com

For rights or permissions inquiries, please contact National Geographic Books
Subsidiary Rights: bookrights@natgeo.com

Illustrations: N. John Schmitt
Design: Sanaa Akkach and Nicole Miller

Printed in the United States of America

18/QCF-PCML/1

for Jack Solomon and Paul Hess

It is nature sympathy, the growth of the heart,
not nature study, the training of the brain,
that does most for us.

—Neltje Blanchan

CONTENTS

INTRODUCTION

The Experience of Birding

T HAD BEEN a long day, and I needed to get out of the house. I needed
to go birding. So I grabbed some gear and was on my way. I wore
binoculars, of course, and a hat. I brought a small digital camera,
too, and my phone.

My birding companion that summer evening was my preteen son,
and our destination was a small city park within easy walking distance of
our home in the Denver metro area. A weak cold front had passed through
earlier in the day, bringing with it a bit of rain. But the unsettled weather
was clearing out now. A rainbow, not much of one, rose up from the
rooftops beyond the park.

We got to our favorite spot in the park, an unkempt tangle of Russian
olives by the edge of an old fishing pond. Right away, we found what we
were looking for. Bushtits! *We love Bushtits.* They arrived in our neighborhood about a decade ago. The species is expanding northward, likely
driven by habitat change and the general warming and drying of the
climate. That's worrisome, but we are also cheered by the adaptability
and resourcefulness of these oddly named birds.

We heard them before we saw them. That's how it is with Bushtits,
tiny creatures that chirp and twitter constantly as they forage in dense
vegetation at or slightly above eye level. The adult Bushtit looks like a
dirty cotton ball with a toothpick for a tail. The eyes of the adult male
are dark and gentle, the eyes of the adult female yellow and fierce and
staring. But these weren't adults, at least not most of them. These were
recently fledged young, by and large, distinguished by their loosely
textured feathers, relatively short tails, and swollen yellow gapes. If

mom looks fierce and dad looks gentle, then junior is frankly sorry-looking. Baby birds, especially baby songbirds like Bushtits, appear dopey and dejected.

My son leapt into action. Actually, his movements were rather more stealthy. Pointing a smartphone directly ahead, he walked slowly and steadily toward the roiling mass of Bushtits. The birds were indifferent to his presence, allowing him to approach close enough to obtain smartphone photos, video, and audio. Let that sink in for just a moment. He did those things *with a phone.* I'm old enough that I can remember when telephones, black and shiny, hung from the wall or sat on a desk or nightstand. There was a time, not all that long ago, when it would have seemed peculiar indeed to disconnect the phone and take it birding. And it would have been stranger still to have imagined that mobile phones would someday become central to the experience of birding.

After a couple of minutes, a troupe of Blue Jays, adults and young, brash and boisterous, descended upon the Russian olive grove, driving out the Bushtits. Four Blue Jays, to be exact. As to the number of Bushtits, we lowball-estimated the total at 15. We're not sure, but we think *two* family groups were involved. Bushtits exhibit "cooperative breeding," the technical term for what is basically avian cohousing. My son tapped the data into a birding app, and we continued on our way.

Approximately two hours and two and a half miles later, we were back home. Check that: precisely 1 hour, 52 minutes, and 4.054 kilometers, according to the all-knowing birding app. We uploaded our digital media—of Bushtits, Blue Jays, and other birds, 45 species to be exact—to eBird, the wildly popular website for creating and sharing checklists of bird sightings. My son calls it eBorg, a nod to eBird's dominance in birding today. One of his smartphone audio clips, documenting the vocalizations of fledgling Bushtits, was scientifically notable, so we uploaded it to Xeno-Canto, a crowdsourced digital library of birdsong based out of the Netherlands. And we uploaded our favorite photos and video to Facebook. A particularly winsome photo of a particularly sad-looking baby Bushtit went viral. It earned "likes" and "loves" from birders in Malaysia, India, and elsewhere. I don't think it's an exaggeration to say that we had preached the gospel of birding to the whole wide world.

Thus concluded our little getaway, our Sunday evening stroll in the park.

THIS IS A BOOK ABOUT BIRDS, of course, but it is also a book about humans. I've been a birder—someone who watches and wonders about birds—for close to 40 years, and, in case you missed it, I am struck by how much birding has changed over the course of my lifetime, especially in the past 10 to 15 years. I'll take it a step further. I am increasingly persuaded that birding today is altogether different from what it used to be.

Back in 1980, when I first started to self-identify as a birder, you could get by with binoculars (or field glasses, as some folks still called them), a field guide (there were two main choices at the time), and a notebook (for writing it all down). Going to the library was common, taking photos was rare, and recording birdsong was practically unheard of. It was a time when we used telephones, stationary objects in homes and offices, for talking to one another—and for no other purpose.

For the next quarter century, the pace of change was incremental. We started to go online; we dabbled in digital photography; we exchanged our landlines for flip phones, and, in due course, our flip phones for smartphones. And, then, somewhere between 2005 and 2010, we reached a tipping point. I can't identify a particular trigger. Smartphones were a biggie, of course, but I suspect the proliferation of inexpensive digital cameras was just as important. Apps, blogs, and online social media have been huge; same goes for the photo sharing sites, multimedia checklists, and online libraries designed specifically with the bird lover in mind. We have accumulated a critical mass of new resources for bird study. And in so doing, we have arrived at a substantially revised conception of what it means to be a birder.

Call it the post-birding era. Or don't. I'm not seriously advocating the name change. But I do believe that it is important to distinguish between who we are today and who we used to be.

THE YEAR WAS 1949. Two of the giants of nature study in the 20th century had just come out with new books. In the foreword to *A Sand County Almanac,* Aldo Leopold issued his famous dictum that "there are some who can live without wild things, and some who cannot." Leopold penned those words on March 4, 1948, seven weeks before he would die fighting a wildfire. And on November 1, 1948, Roger Tory Peterson described birding as "an antidote for the disillusionment of today's world, a world beset by pressures it has never before known." That assessment would appear in the preface to Peterson's *How to Know the Birds,* a work whose title I knowingly and respectfully adopt for the present volume.

What impresses me about both formulations is their emphasis on the distance between wild places and human spaces, a distinction that taps into the deepest veins of the Western worldview, with its Platonic insistence that everything have its place and purpose, that it be *this* thing or *that* thing. I hasten to state that I intend no criticism of Leopold and Peterson, two of the greatest influences on my own thinking. They understood the currents of their time as few others did, and they applied that understanding to tremendous pedagogical effect. They did a world of good. But they were the products of, and the prophets for, an earlier age.

Fast-forward to the present time. We say that we live in the Anthropocene Epoch, a time in which human influence and agency permeate every erstwhile natural environment on Earth. The new discipline of urban ecology has enjoyed a generally favorable reception, and the older disciplines of human ecology and cultural ecology have been repurposed for the current age. Particularly exciting for me as a birder has been our massive reassessment in recent decades of the avian mind: Birds solve problems and adapt to changing environments; they have culture and emotion, and even awareness of self and others. They are vastly more human than we ever knew.

We who watch birds today embrace a holistic outlook on the world around us. We share spaces, simultaneously natural and artificial, with wildlife. Our human lives are governed by ecological principles. We have blurred the old distinction between subject and object, between the observer and the thing observed. The birds we watch are possessed of mind and heart, and perhaps even soul and spirit, in ways we'd never appreciated. The bird lover of today proclaims the great truth that we're all in this thing together.

Which reminds me of a bird my son and I saw at the park on that summer evening a little while ago.

It was an American Avocet, an adult female. The avocet is a shorebird, a relative of the plovers and sandpipers, generally brown birds that muck around in the mud. Avocets are mud muckers, but they are not brown. They are spectacular, their heads as orange as the setting sun, their wings strikingly black and white. They're large birds, around 18 inches stem to stern. The legs are a dusky chalk-blue, and the bill, all black and impossibly thin, bends upward; it looks like a surgical instrument. Avocets are noisy around the nest. Like this one.

I said she was a female. I could tell that because of the bird's bill. The female avocet's bill is more sharply upturned than the male's. But the real reason I knew is because I'd gotten to know this particular bird. So had my son. So had the whole community. She was an old friend. She was family.

She'd had a rough go of it. Earlier in the year, she'd laid her eggs along the shore of the shallow fishing pond. The pond flooded, the eggs floated off, and the avocet nested again, this time on higher ground—right along the heavily trafficked trail around the pond. The new eggs hatched on Father's Day. I was there just hours, perhaps only a few minutes, after it happened. Mom was nowhere to be found. Dad did all the work, ushering his newborn fluffball charges across the trail and down to the water's edge. But Mom returned from her unexplained absence and soon thereafter joined Dad in the care and keeping of the baby avocets.

Don't take my word for it. Ask anybody, any human being who shared space with those avocets. Perfect strangers paused to share stories about the birds. Somebody had put a stake near the nest, plus a handwritten exhortation not to disturb the birds; avocets lay their eggs on bare ground, where they are extremely susceptible to accidental trampling. On one of my visits to the park, I saw a man studying the male as he incubated the eggs. The man's jacket was emblazoned with the word SECURITY. Was he an official protector of the avocets? I'd like to think so.

The day of fledging was a day of rejoicing. The neighborhood email list was abuzz with chat about the hatchlings. People posted about the avocets to the state listserv, an electronic bulletin board for birders. They uploaded photos to Facebook and Instagram; they logged data for eBird. The entire planet knows about these avocets.

This is birding at the present time, a shared experience, cooperative and communitarian. "The medium is the message," prophesied Marshall McLuhan well before the dawn of the internet. Nature study in the digital age is more informed, more technological, and more interactive than ever before.

My son and I went to the park with the express intent to share a story—with each other, of course, but also with you and with the rest of the world. We bypassed Leopold's injunction against those "who can live without wild things," and we perfectly inverted Peterson's conviction that birds are "an antidote for the disillusionment of today's world." Call us ambitious, even immodest, but we believe that the story of birds and people, complexly intertwined, is a story for all of us, regardless of our lot in life, regardless of our expertise or lack thereof, regardless of whether or not we self-identify as birders. Birding today is the story of connections and commonalities, not escape or antidote.

"Being a millennial," quips the contemporary nature writer Frank Izaguirre, "I think in #hashtags, but I can never get enough bird-based storytelling in any form." We go online these days, and we are gathered round the campfire. We tweet and post, and we are become minstrels and troubadours. We are bards and tribal elders, and we fill the world wide web with our blank verse and burlesques, our just-so stories, and sometimes our epic poetry. In recasting nature study as communitarian and experiential, we have reclaimed the ancient art of storytelling.

≪◇≫

"YOU MAY BE SURE there was joy in the household," exalts a master storyteller by the name of Neltje Blanchan, relating her own account of discovering newly hatched birds. Blanchan's story is about Chipping Sparrows, not American Avocets, but the overall narrative is much the same. The sparrows nested on the veranda of her house, "next to the front door through which members of the family passed every hour of the day." Blanchan and others watched the birds, studied the birds, and cared for the birds. Her story is full of details about nest building, egg laying, brooding behavior, nestling anatomy, and more. But the heart of the story, if you ask me, is the human dimension. Blanchan reports how people parted the twigs of a boxwood to peer in on the female

Chipping Sparrow at the nest, adding that "all of us gently stroked her from time to time."

You read about stuff like this on neighborhood email lists and in the chattier posts to birding listservs. But that's not where this account comes from. Instead, it appears in the author's magnum opus, *Birds Every Child Should Know*, published in 1907. The author announces her audacious agenda in the book's title: Every child, not just those born into power and privilege, ought to know the birds. Blanchan recalls that "a little urchin from the New York City slums was the first to point out to his teacher, who had lived twenty years on a farm, the faint reddish streaks on the breast of a Yellow Warbler in Central Park."

Birds Every Child Should Know presents a disarming blend of science and sentimentalism. So do other works from that era, notably Florence Merriam Bailey's *Birds Through an Opera Glass* (1889), Mabel Osgood Wright's *Birdcraft: A Field Book of Two Hundred Song, Game, and Water Birds* (1895), Olive Thorne Miller's The *First Book of Birds* (1899), Anna Botsford Comstock's *Handbook of Nature Study* (1911), Gene Stratton-Porter's *Friends in Feathers* (1917), and Harriet Williams Myers's *Western Birds* (1922). Those books and others like them were populist in spirit, intended for broad audiences; they were biological in outlook, implicitly, and in some cases explicitly, Darwinian; and they were mighty commercial and critical successes. And, then, in one of the stranger episodes in American intellectual history, they became largely forgotten.

Bird study was at a crossroads. "A century ago," according to the ornithological historian Rick Wright, "it was anybody's guess which direction this newborn hobby would grow in. The defining focus of American birding could have been conservation, or life history study, or aesthetics, or taxidermy, or any of the thousand and one things the human mind can do with a living object. Instead, we decided, I believe more or less consciously, to make bird-watching about identification."

With his *Field Guide to the Birds* (1934), Roger Tory Peterson powerfully advanced an emerging new paradigm for birding. His unpretentious book cut through the clutter of biology and natural history, and focused on the smallest suite of "field marks" required to identify a bird in life. This new approach was given a name, the "Peterson System," and was endowed with a mathematical elegance. By dispensing with sentimentalism and science, Peterson untied the Gordian knot of bird identification.

Other field guides followed suit, notably Chandler S. Robbins and co-authors' *Birds of North America: A Guide to Field Identification* (1966), National Geographic's *Field Guide to the Birds of North America* (1983), and David A. Sibley's eponymous *Sibley Guide to Birds* (2000). These and others have run to multiple editions and are in wide use today. They are vastly superior to their predecessor, but make no mistake about it: In their conception and execution, they are fundamentally Petersonian.

Along the way, the distinct culture of modern birding came into being. Birders aspired to expertise in the matter of field ID and competed for the longest lists of species seen. Rules were set and obeyed, conventions established and enforced, traditions observed and entrenched. I can't imagine that Peterson and his generation ever intended this, but birding by the end of the 20th century was widely viewed as exclusionary, underpinned by a caste system of skill level and expertise. There were bona fide birders, and then there was everyone else.

Yet there's a happy ending to this story.

Neltje Blanchan's universalist agenda for nature study has roared back to life. Truth be told, it never died. But I think it went underground, awaiting receptivity by a new generation of bird lovers. The internet, far from killing nature study, has rehabilitated it. Birding in the 20th century was practiced by experts and steeped in tradition, but birding today is more inclusive and extemporaneous. Birding in the digital age has become experiential and Darwinian, repudiating its Platonic heritage. And birding nowadays is accessible to anybody with a Wi-Fi connection.

The story gets better. This go-round, we haven't thrown the baby out with the bathwater—as we did when Peterson deposed the generation who preceded him. Yes, we have rejected some of the more objectionable aspects of 20th-century bird study, especially its Platonic objectification of the bird as an ensemble of field marks. But we have retained the rigor—the elegance, the precision, and, I would say, the beauty—that Peterson brought to bear on nature study, even as we have reclaimed and repurposed the holism and experientialism that he discarded.

That synthesis, or fusion, is the touchstone of birding at the present time.

ONE OF THE SPECIAL SIGHTINGS FOR MY SON AND ME at the park was a family of Say's Phoebes. Do you imagine that I'm about to tell another story? Sort of. But this time, it's a story about a thought process, an explicit formulation of how to know the birds.

A bird swooped across the nature trail and landed on a mullein stalk, facing directly away. All we could see was the bird's backside, perfectly plain gray. In a heartbeat—no, it didn't take nearly that long—I knew it was an adult Say's Phoebe. How is that even possible? Well over a hundred bird species in our area have basically gray upperparts.

I saw no field marks at all. Instead, I conceived of the bird in eco-logical and psychological space. Say's Phoebes, lovely though they may be, have this thing for junked landscapes in open spaces. My son and I had wandered to a junky part of the park, where mulleins and other weeds had taken over. A construction project was in progress, replete with mounds of earth and an all-important portable toilet. I'm dead serious: Say's Phoebes are undeniably, irresistibly drawn to outdoor restrooms. Our sighting of the bird was practically preordained.

The phoebe flew to the roof of the Porta Potty and fed a fledgling. Two others were waiting on a nearby dirt pile. Say's Phoebe, *Sayornis saya*, $n = 4$: Tap it into the eBird app. The eBird impulse derives in part from the rigor and formalism of the Peterson System. But also: Say's Phoebe! Yay! *Baby* Say's Phoebes. Woohoo! Our eBird checklist tells the story of the Say's Phoebes; the Bushtits and Blue Jays are in there, too, and so is the female American Avocet keeping vigil at the pond. Go ahead—see for yourself. Take a look at our eBird checklist, our storybook, our treasury of birdlore: *ebird.org/view/checklist/S46776303.*

We scooted down a shrubby hillside, and the phoebes were out of sight. But not yet out of earshot. The call of the adult, although not all that loud, is far-carrying and distinctive: a short pip or peep, followed by a whistle that rises rapidly and then trails off. The experience of hear-ing, but not seeing, a bird is powerful. "There is a peculiar virtue in the music of unseen birds," opined Aldo Leopold. "Songsters that sing from topmost boughs are easily seen and as easily forgotten; they have the mediocrity of the obvious."

When I wake up to birdsong, as I do every morning of my life, I am the recipient of a blessing. I can lie there, my head still on the pillow, and rattle off the names of the dozen or more bird species I am hearing. I have compiled whole eBird checklists still in bed with my eyes closed—"stationary count" protocol, of course. Birdsong is my secret decoder ring for nature. True story: Once upon a time, my father and I were lost in the Appalachian Mountains. We found our way out of the woods by recognizing the song of a particular bird, a Black-and-white Warbler, I had heard near the trailhead hours earlier. And although I'm not prepared to claim that that unseen bird saved our lives, it certainly saved us a lot of time and trouble. How to know the birds is occasionally (*very* occasionally) useful, but it is also something far grander. How to know the birds is how to know the world around us, richer and more wondrous than we ever knew, bright and beautiful and blessed.

≪◇≫

HOW TO KNOW THE BIRDS is a storybook for bird lovers. It is not a field guide in the traditional sense. Many of the accounts go into some detail about the way birds look and, just as important, the way they sound; but many others barely scratch the surface in that regard. What you *will* find in the accounts—and I've endeavored to emphasize this in every single one of them—is a big idea, a method or technique or resource, about bird study in our age. A number of the accounts conclude with an open-ended question or, at least, some measure of ambiguity; that's a reflection of the intellectual health and scientific rigor of modern birding. An even 200 accounts, or lessons, fill the pages of this book.

The birding life is a journey of exploration, of learning as you go, of innumerable micro-discoveries and occasional breakthroughs. And that's the spirit I hope to convey in *How to Know the Birds*. We're going to embark together on a birding adventure—not a bird walk like the one my son and I went on, but rather a leisurely year of witness and wonder. Along the way, we'll get to know 200 bird species, one bird at a time, one day at a time, one lesson at a time.

Our journey together will be an imaginary one, but I think it will be realistic. I consider 200 species to be a manageable total for a whole year of birding. And I regard 200 days of birding as typical—an afternoon here, a morning there, and longer stints on occasion. Most of all, I believe

it is reasonable and realistic to expect that we'll know more at the end of the year than we did at the beginning.

How to Know the Birds comprises six main sections.

We'll kick things off in January with a series of lessons that I've grouped under the rubric of "Spark Bird!" (§§1–36). A great many birders report having had an encounter with a *spark bird*, the bird that got them started. The spark bird is an epiphany, a turning point, a moment of wonder and sudden awareness, the first step in a lifelong love affair with all things avian. In this section, we entertain the most foundational question in all of birding: *What's the name of that bird?* We'll learn to name not only the different species, but also the different plumages: male versus female, juvenile versus adult, summer versus winter, etc.

Our next section, "After the Spark" (§§37–74), takes us from mid-March till late May. In this section, we delight in what might just be the two most awesome aspects of avian biology: birdsong and migration. Our understanding of these two topics has undergone substantial revision in the past couple decades, especially in the context of the digital revolution, and I hope I have conveyed some of the thrill of discovery that has been brought to bear on the matter.

Spring turns to summer, and we ask the question, "Now What?" (§§75–115). For so many of us, there comes a time in this birding life when we desire to make the jump from passive observation of birds to actually doing something. Summer is the time when birders volunteer for bird observatories, enlist in breeding bird surveys, and so forth. The warmer months are in many ways the most compelling time of the year for studying bird biology, and the lessons in this section explore courtship, nesting, molt, and more. And this is the section where we tackle head-on an issue we've danced around thus far: bird conservation.

Next there follows a section I've titled "Inflection Point" (§§116–141), corresponding to the latter half of meteorological summer. If I had to choose one stretch of the year that is least understood by birders, it would be this one. It is the time when most birds are molting—flying, and in some cases not flying (because they are rendered flightless when they molt), under the radar. Bird conservation is a major preoccupation of this section.

For fall migration, we explore the question of "What We Know" (§§142–169). The whole book seeks to address that matter, needless to say, but here we look at the specific sources of our knowledge: books and the internet, bird clubs and ornithological societies, museums and universities, and, just as important, our own independent observations and insights. We also consider the allied question of who we are; it is in this section that we delve most deeply into the character and passions of the birding community.

Finally, philosophy. I must say, I've never met a lifelong birder who isn't at least a part-time philosopher; sooner or later, birding takes a metaphysical turn, and so shall we in the final weeks of the year. In a section titled "What We Don't Know" (§§170–200), we probe the limits of current knowledge—and excitedly wonder about what comes next.

≪◇≫

I DON'T MEAN to imply that one ought to achieve mastery of birding during the span of a calendar year. Indeed, I resist altogether the idea that one ever masters birding. I'd quit birding—I'm quite serious in saying this—if I ever got to the point where there was nothing more to learn, nothing left to discover, nothing new to know. What keeps me going, more than anything else, is the promise of new knowledge about birds and new ways of understanding and appreciating the natural world.

That said, I well appreciate that so much of the birding experience is day to day. The following is a cliché, I suppose, but it applies well to birding: Learning how to know the birds requires living in the present moment and aspiring to achieve mindfulness; it is about being attuned to the idea of suchness, the way things are. An encounter with a bird is often just that: the observer and the thing observed—no more, no less. The 200 lessons in this book trace a definite thematic arc, but I hope each one has some stand-alone value, too.

One last thought before we get under way. There is a sense in which birding can be all things to all people: science, conservation, romance, adventure, discovery, and more. But if you think about it, all those things are variations on a theme: All those things are deeply human. Birding is a profoundly humanistic enterprise. And on that note, I cannot help but think of Socrates's exquisite distillation of what it means to be human: "The unexamined life is not worth living." Birding, ultimately, is about self-discovery and self-awareness, about apprehending and celebrating the experience of being alive in this world today. In the pages that follow, I'm going to chart a course for the birding life that reflects my own experiences and impressions. I hope you'll come along for the ride, but I also hope—no, I insist—that you draw on your own interests and aspirations as we journey together. If I've learned one thing in all my years as a birder, it is this: There are as many ways to engage and appreciate birding as there are bird lovers in this world. So take this book and make it your own. We're all in this thing together, but learning about birds is intensely personal.

Let's go birding!

PART ONE

SPARK BIRD!

January—February

1 SPARK BIRD!

⫷⫷⫷ ⫷⫷⫷ ⫷⫷⫷ ⫷⫷⫷ ⫷⫷⫷ ⫷⫷⫷ ⫷⫷◇⟩⟩⟩ ⟩⟩⟩ ⟩⟩⟩ ⟩⟩⟩ ⟩⟩⟩ ⟩⟩⟩ ⟩⟩⟩

Cedar Waxwing
Bombycilla cedrorum

"Wow!"

It's just a bird, you say to yourself, but unlike any you've ever seen before. Its colors and patterns are impossibly precise: pinpoint dabs of red on the wingtips and a smart yellow band across the tip of the tail; a sharp black mask over the eyes; and a fine, wispy crest. Not a feather is out of place on this supremely elegant bird. It looks hand-painted.

The bird is quite tame, allowing close approach. It's wolfing down the blood-red berries on the gnarled hawthorn tree out back. At one point, the bird flips a berry from the hawthorn—and catches it with its tiny black beak! You can't help yourself; you laugh out loud, and the bird spooks. And not just the one bird. As it flies away, it is joined by a dozen others, evidently all the same species. The birds make a shrill trilling sound as they fly off. You stand there in awe, and the compact flock departs from view.

"What *was* that bird? What *were* those birds?"

It's a Cedar Waxwing, known to ornithologists as *Bombycilla cedrorum*. You don't know it at the time, but this is your *spark bird,* the name birders give to the species that triggers a lifelong passion, bordering on obsession, with birds. The spark bird is a moment of epiphany, a conversion experience. There are "born-again birders," no joking, and many birders cleave their lives neatly in two: "before the spark" and "after the spark." Years, even decades from now, you may look back upon this encounter as a defining moment, perhaps *the* defining moment, in your life.

You quickly discover that, apparently, waxwings aren't all that uncommon. Who knew? And you get to wondering about something: What about all the other sorts of birds in your part of the world? How many species are there? What are they called? What do they look like? And how do you tell them all apart?

2 A FAMILIAR BIRD

American Robin
Turdus migratorius

APPROXIMATELY 1,000 BIRD SPECIES have been documented to occur in the wild in North America north of Mexico. The majority of those species are birds whose official names aren't generally well known beyond the birding community. But a handful are familiar to everybody. Case in point: the robin—officially, the American Robin, *Turdus migratorius*. It is the only bird in America that goes by the name robin. There are other robins in the world—for example, the European Robin, *Erithacus rubecula*; and the Japanese Robin, *Larvivora akahige*—but only one American Robin.

The adult American Robin is immediately recognized by its combination of entirely brick-red underparts and gray-brown upperparts. A few other bird species approach that general color scheme, but none is as strikingly patterned above and below. The robin is a *big* bird, among American songbirds definitely at the large end of the spectrum. Robins are tame, and they often form large flocks. And they're loud! Are they ever! The caroling of the robin is exuberant, excessive, and, more than anything else, *loud*.

Robins are common across much of North America, but don't let that fool you. The robin is one of the truly marvelous birds of our continent. Michael O'Brien, on anybody's short list of the greatest birders of all time, calls the American Robin his favorite bird. The species is at once ordinary and extraordinary. Chances are, you're within 1,000 feet of a robin *right now*. That's the ordinary part. The migrations of robins are stirring; their adaptability to different habitats is staggering; their easily observed family life is endlessly fascinating and, with no apologies for the sentimentalism, heartwarming.

Everybody knows the robin—its name, its basic color scheme, its general place in the American vernacular. Yet it takes a lifetime to really *learn* the American Robin, so varied, so wonderful. Well, we have to start somewhere. "The beginning of wisdom is to call things by their proper name," said Confucius.

3 (MOST) BIRDS ARE (FAIRLY) EASY TO ID

≪≪ ≪≪ ≪≪ ≪≪ ≪≪ ≪≪ ≪≪◇≫≫ ≫≫ ≫≫ ≫≫ ≫≫ ≫≫ ≫≫

Red-tailed Hawk
Buteo jamaicensis

D ID YOU DRIVE a car in the past week? Ride a bus or take the train? Then you probably crossed paths with a Red-tailed Hawk, the most widespread and adaptable raptor species in America. Nowhere are Red-tailed Hawks particularly abundant; they rarely form flocks, the way robins and waxwings do. Yet most neighborhoods, farmsteads, and parks have one or two Red-tails. They're big birds; they perch out in the open; and they absolutely *love* freeway lampposts. Nothing is guaranteed in birding, but if you see a big, blocky hawk along a busy byway, there's a decent chance it's a Red-tail.

Take a quick look at a Red-tailed Hawk, and you'll instantly be impressed by two things: (1) It looks like a hawk, and (2) It has a red tail. This bird is well-named. The matter of what is a hawk—the idea of "hawk-ness," if you will—is complex. We'll get to that later. But many hawks are obviously, well, hawks. As U.S. Supreme Court Justice Potter Stewart famously said, "I know it when I see it." He wasn't talking about *Buteo jamaicensis*, but he might as well have been. This is a fearsome-looking beast, with a hooked beak, sharp talons, and glowering yellow eyes. On the perched bird, the folded tail, typically obscured by the long wings, is hard to see. But when the bird takes flight, there is no doubt about it: The adult Red-tailed Hawk has a broadly, blatantly, beautifully *red* tail.

Red-tailed Hawks are highly variable, but, still, the garden-variety adult is a cinch to identify. It's the only large hawk with an extensively red tail. And it's both a reminder and an encouragement that many birds—certainly not all of them, but probably the majority of them—are straightforward to identify. Soon we'll be studying birds that *are* challenging to ID. But let's not lose track of the lesson of the Red-tail: Most birds are relatively easy to name.

4 AVIAN DIVERSITY

Black-capped Chickadee
Poecile atricapillus

I**T'S A FINE** winter morning in New York City's Central Park, and the park's Ramble is alive with birds: sparrows kicking about in the leaf litter, finches in the treetops, an unseen woodpecker tapping somewhere. A pied and inarguably cute bird pops out for a view. With its black cap, white cheeks, and black bib, it is a snap to identify. The sparrows, finches, and woodpecker present certain ID challenges, but not this one. The bird even says its name: *chick-a-dee-dee-dee*. No question about it, this bird is a chickadee.

The same scenario plays out in city parks and at backyard birdfeeders in Jacksonville, Florida, and Reno, Nevada, and just about everywhere else in the continental United States and Canada. Black cap + white cheeks + black bib = chickadee. And if there is any lingering doubt, the bird says its own name and is so darned cute.

Except for one thing.

There are different kinds of chickadees, and they are quite similar in appearance. The chickadees in New York City are Black-capped Chickadees, *Poecile atricapillus*, whereas the chickadees in Jacksonville are Carolina Chickadees, *P. carolinensis*. The chickadees in Reno are a third species, the Mountain Chickadee, *P. gambeli*. To some extent, the chickadees sort out by geography: Black-capped in the East and North, Carolina in the Southeast, Mountain in the West, and so on and so forth for all seven species of chickadees. In Pittsburgh, though, Black-capped and Carolina chickadees overlap, and in Denver, Black-capped and Mountain chickadees co-occur. Where their ranges come into contact, different species of chickadees sometimes hybridize, producing confusing intermediate individuals.

Yes, you can simply say "chickadee" and be done with it. But most birders elect not to. For one thing, there is the pure intellectual challenge of being able to sort out the chickadees. And for many birders, there is something grander: the awareness of all the behavioral and ecological diversity in America's birds, even in some of our most familiar groups, like chickadees.

5 A COMMON BUT UNFAMILIAR BIRD

Horned Lark
Eremophila alpestris

IT HAS BEEN CALLED "the most common bird you never heard of." The Horned Lark breeds on mountaintops, in low deserts, and all across the American prairie. In winter, it frequents plains, shores, and farm fields. And unlike most New World birds, it ranges widely in Eurasia. Yet most ordinary folk—normal people, nonbirders—just don't know the bird.

Horned Larks don't come to birdfeeders. They eschew parks and neighborhoods. And they're flighty, often staying hundreds of feet ahead of human intruders upon their domain. Although the act of simply seeing a Horned Lark requires little effort, the feat of correctly identifying one is something of an accomplishment. The Horned Lark is a birder's bird.

A huge part of the experience of birding is the thrill of discovery. Keep at it for a while, and you might register a bona fide ornithological discovery: a first nesting record for your state or province, for example, or a new field mark for separating one avian species from another. The vast majority of your discoveries, though, will be entirely personal: realizing that there are owls on your property, or that eagles migrate over your neighborhood each year, or that thousands of Horned Larks swarm the pastures, cornfields, and waste places around the outskirts of town.

Eventually and inevitably, the birder comes to take the Horned Lark for granted. Once you know they're there, Horned Larks are everywhere. Objectively speaking, they're as beautiful as when you first encountered them, with their ornate facial markings and tinkling call notes, rising up in front of you. But they become frankly commonplace after a while. Perhaps, but there is something else: Years, even decades, after our first encounter with the species, it is an inspiration. We never forget that initial wonder, that moment of awareness that this world of ours is full of undiscovered wonders and blessings. The example of the Horned Lark sustains us for as long as we are birders.

6 (MANY) BIRDS HAVE DISTINCTIVE COLORS

≪≪ ≪≪ ≪≪ ≪≪ ≪≪ ≪≪ ≪≪◇≫ ≫≫ ≫≫ ≫≫ ≫≫ ≫≫ ≫≫

Mallard
Anas platyrhynchos

S OONER OR LATER in the birding life, we get serious, or at least semi-serious, about the whole business of bird identification. Maybe "serious" isn't quite the right word. "Methodical" is closer to the birder's way of engaging bird ID. In the same way that athletes watch film and musicians practice scales, so birders apply certain methods to the matter of identifying birds. And birders, like athletes and musicians, ascribe special importance, bordering on devotion, to learning the fundamentals.

One of the fundamentals is surely color. Flip through the pages of a field guide, and probably the first thing you'll notice is the spectacular diversity of colors displayed by even closely related birds. Ducks, for example. Especially on their heads. And *especially* on the heads of male ducks, called drakes.

The most familiar of all ducks is the Mallard, known to hunters as the Greenhead. The etymology of the word "Mallard" is something of a mystery; our best guess is that it derives from a word meaning "wild drake." The meaning of Greenhead, meanwhile, is crystal clear: The bird's head is green, gloriously so in good light. Other birds have green heads—female tanagers and buntings, along with various hummingbirds of both sexes—but the Mallard takes the cake. Another duck, the Common Merganser, has an entirely green head, but it is a duller green. Anyhow, you would never confuse drake Mallards and mergansers; that's because their bills are utterly different. The merg's bill is deep coral-red all over, whereas the Mallard's is unambiguously, uniformly, solidly yellow.

There you have it: Entirely bright green head + bright yellow bill = drake Mallard. There's much more to the Mallard than the green-and-yellow color combo; it quacks, it swims, it waddles about. We'll get to behavior and other identification cues. For now, though, the first and perhaps foremost lesson in bird ID: Look at the colors on birds, especially on the head, and especially on the male.

7 PAY ATTENTION TO PATTERN

Song Sparrow
Melospiza melodia

QUICK! THINK OF a truly colorful bird! Did a tanager or a hummingbird come to mind? A Painted Bunting, perhaps, or a Roseate Spoonbill? Chances are, you did not conjure the image of a sparrow. The 50-some species of sparrows in the United States and Canada tend to run in shades of brown. Throw in a few rufous and gray highlights, and you have your standard-issue American sparrow.

Birders of a certain age refer to sparrows and other small brown birds as LBJs, short for little brown job (and presumably allusive to the initials of a certain U.S. president in the 1960s). In many cases, sparrow ID requires that we assess field marks other than color. Sparrows, maybe more than any other group, challenge us to make use of the all-important field mark of *pattern*.

Consider the Song Sparrow, one of the most widespread of all bird species on the continent. Although there are many regional variants (called subspecies), Song Sparrows are all basically the same: They're brown. Some are dark brown, some are light brown, and many are just plain brown, but, you get the picture: Song Sparrows are brown.

To separate the Song Sparrow from other sparrows, look at how the brown is distributed, or patterned, across the bird's body. Song Sparrows have brown streaks below, instantly ruling out a couple dozen species of plain-breasted sparrows. The streaks are coarse, so we're not dealing with one of the sparrow species with fine streaking. And the streaks coalesce in a central spot, or stickpin, on the breast. Now we're down to two or three species. Next up: the coarse stripes on the face. The bird is a Song Sparrow.

Regarding the bird's color, we never got past "LBJ." Focusing instead on pattern, we quickly worked our way down from 50+ species to the one and only Song Sparrow. For sure, there is more to the Song Sparrow than its brown streaking. (As you might have surmised, it has a terrific song!) But a rapid assessment of the bird's plumage pattern got us the right ID.

8 SIZE MATTERS

<<< <<< <<< <<< <<< <<< <<<○>> >>> >>> >>> >>> >>> >>> >>>

Common Raven
Corvus corax

BLACK MAY BE the absence of color, but it also an indicator of feather strength. Black plumage gets its color, or lack thereof, from the pigment melanin—or, more precisely, from a class of pigments called melanins. Melanins confer mechanical strength, resistance to bacteria, UV protection, and other advantages. All else being equal, black coloration is good for birds.

Mainly or entirely black plumage has evolved multiple times. But if there is one group of birds that is quintessentially black, it is the crows and ravens in the genus *Corvus*. Five species of *Corvus* occur regularly in North America north of Mexico, and all five are utterly and completely black: all their feathers, along with all their so-called bare parts (basically, eyes, bill, and feet). Henry Ford would have loved the genus.

If you'll allow the metaphor, the Common Raven is the Humvee of the genus *Corvus*. It is by far the largest "corvid" in North America. Not only that, it is North America's largest "passerine"—the name given to an immense group of perching birds, or songbirds. But let's not stop there: The Common Raven is the largest passerine on the planet.

To put things in perspective, the Common Raven is larger in all respects than the Red-tailed Hawk, a decently large raptor. It is longer from bill to tail, its wingspan is greater, and it weighs more. The raven is 15 times more massive than the American Robin, a good-size passerine, and 200 times more massive than the Golden-crowned Kinglet, one of our smallest passerines. Compared to other corvids, the Common Raven is more than twice the mass of the Chihuahuan Raven of the Desert Southwest and close to three times heavier than the widespread American Crow.

Size matters, it is said. That may or may not be true in human affairs, but it applies well to bird ID. What the Common Raven lacks in color it more than compensates for in size.

9 SHAPE MATTERS

Mourning Dove
Zenaida macroura

I N GOOD LIGHT and at close range, the Mourning Dove is a thing of beauty: warm pearly-buff all over, with vinaceous and greenish highlights on the neck. The eye is surrounded by a thin circle of baby blue, and the wing coverts are marked with black spots. By all means, take the time to savor the view of a Mourning Dove; it's worth it.

At the same time, don't freak out if you can't get close enough to discern the iridescence on the neck or the blue orbital ring around the eye. In a typical encounter with the species, we don't see those things. In many instances, in fact, we can't make out color or pattern at all. Instead, we see a bird flying past at first light, or we glimpse a bird on a wire, or we note a bird perched on a housetop. All we see is a silhouette of a decidedly medium-size bird effectively devoid of any plumage markings. What are we to do?

The Mourning Dove, like so many other bird species, has a distinctive shape. It is slender overall, with an oddly small head and a long, tapered tail. This characteristic shape is readily apparent on the perched bird, and it really comes to life on the bird in flight; that's because the tail, narrow and pointed, is especially prominent as the bird flies past.

Body shape is undeniably subjective. A bird may appear slim and lanky when relaxed, but rather rotund when balled up in the cold. Of course, that subjectivity applies to our perception of anything else on a bird: its overall size, its plumage patterns, its colors, and so forth. And many shape-based field marks—for example, bill size and leg length—are remarkably consistent. A Mourning Dove, say, will almost always appear short-legged and slender-billed. Learn body shape! It is mildly to hugely relevant for the field ID of almost all the birds in our area.

10 MASSIVE PARALLEL PROCESSING

Downy Woodpecker
Dryobates pubescens

W E HAVE SEEN that birds can be identified by color (Mallard, §6), pattern (Song Sparrow, §7), size (Common Raven, §8), and shape (Mourning Dove, §9). In most instances, though, we have to process multiple inputs (color, pattern, size, *and* shape) to obtain the desired output of the correct identification. Let's see how it works.

We have before us a bird that is colored black, white, and red. In other words, it's not a Blue Jay, an American Goldfinch, or one of hundreds of other species in our area. This is a good start! Next we note that the bird is distinctively patterned: checkered and striped, black and white all over, with a bit of red on the crown, in a manner unique to the woodpeckers. Closer assessment of pattern reveals a broad white stripe down the back, a mark shown by only two woodpeckers: Downy and Hairy. The bird looks small, suggesting Downy. Finally, bill shape: short for a woodpecker, about the same length as the distance from the back of the eye to the base of the bill. That's right for a Downy, wrong for a Hairy. Our bird is a Downy Woodpecker. QED.

There is a decided logic to the preceding, as if bird identification might be approached by means of the IF-THEN statements of a computer program. Don't laugh: The bird ID app on your phone works that way. And get a load of this: More than a century ago, widely used dichotomous keys guided the amateur naturalist step by step to the correct identification. The human brain is different, of course, a sort of massive parallel processor that integrates inputs simultaneously.

Smartphone apps, dichotomous keys, and human brains—what do they all have in common? They work best when presented with multiple inputs. It's almost always that way with the field identification of birds. And even if we could reduce bird ID to a single input, we wouldn't want to. The experience of birding would be terribly diminished.

11 SEX AND GENDER

≪≪ ≪≪ ≪≪ ≪≪ ≪≪ ≪≪ ≪≪◇≫≫ ≫≫ ≫≫ ≫≫ ≫≫ ≫≫ ≫≫

Northern Cardinal
Cardinalis cardinalis

ACROSS MUCH OF its extensive range, the Northern Cardinal is unmistakable. The adult male is unique: completely red except for a bit of black on the face, with a prominent crest and a honking red bill. What about the female? Even though she is often referred to as "duller" or "drabber," her color scheme is actually more complex than the male's. Like the male, the female cardinal is huge-billed and crested; and she has red highlights in the wings and tail; but her underparts are a warm buff-brown and her upperparts a colder gray-brown.

The Northern Cardinal exhibits strong sexual dimorphism, the name given to the situation in which males and females look different (*di* = "two" and *morph* = "shape" or "form"). In extreme cases, males and females of sexually dimorphic birds have been described to science as different species! Be wary of supposing that the phenomenon of sexual dimorphism somehow favors males. Female phalaropes are spectacular, their mates relatively plain; the female Belted Kingfisher is tricolored (orange, steel-blue, and white), the male simply bicolored (blue and white); the yellow eye of the female Bushtit is fearsome, the black eye of the male serene; and in most species of hawks and owls, the females are substantially larger than the males.

The "di" part of "dimorphism" is problematic, and so even is the "sex" part of "sexual." A sandpiper called the Ruff, rare in North America but widespread in Eurasia, has four genders, differing in size, shape, color, and pattern. We are beginning to appreciate that birds, like humans and many other behaviorally complex organisms, exhibit gender polymorphism.

What does all of this mean for bird identification? In many groups of birds, it means twice as many kinds of birds for us to look at! (Four times as many in the case of Ruffs.) That adds another dimension to the challenge of bird identification—and to the enjoyment and appreciation of wild birds.

12 AGE-RELATED PLUMAGE VARIATION

White-crowned Sparrow
Zonotrichia leucophrys

TAKE A QUICK LOOK at a White-crowned Sparrow, and you'll see how it got its name. This sparrow has a brilliant white crown, set off by two broad black stripes. The contrast is striking, and many observers rate the White-crowned as one of our most handsome sparrows. Stick with a winter flock for a little while, though, and you'll notice something a bit odd: Some of the birds aren't striped black and white on the crown. Instead, their crowns are a dull gray-buff, set off by rufous-brown stripes.

Given what we know of plumage variation in the Northern Cardinal (§11), we might reasonably infer that the two kinds of White-crowned Sparrows correspond to the two sexes. A first guess might be that the bright ones are the males, the duller ones the females. But we also saw in our study of the cardinal that that supposition (bright male, dull female) is often wrong. So maybe it's the other way around: dull male White-crowned Sparrows, bright females.

Actually, we've been barking up the wrong tree.

Male and female White-crowned Sparrows are practically identical, at least in terms of the gross plumage characteristics we tend to notice in the field. The variation we're seeing in our flock of winter White-crowns is not related to sex. It is due entirely to age. White-crowned Sparrows in their first winter are striped gray-buff and rufous-brown. In the spring of their second calendar year, they acquire their namesake white crown bordered by jet black.

In the same way that sex-related (and gender-related) plumage variation depends on the species (extreme in cardinals, negligible in White-crowned Sparrows), so age-related plumage variation must be considered on a species-by-species basis. It is patently obvious in a winter flock of White-crowned Sparrows, but comparatively muted in other sparrow species. We can take this idea even further: In some species, we can distinguish male from female not only among the adults, but also among the young birds. We'll get there!

13 SEASONAL VARIATION

<<< <<< <<< <<< <<< <<< <<◇>>> >>> >>> >>> >>> >>> >>>

Common Loon
Gavia immer

"THE LOONS! THE LOONS!" It's one of the most famous bird-related lines in film history. Truth be told, more people know the Common Loon, *Gavia immer*, from *On Golden Pond* than from real-life encounters with the species. The loons in Mark Rydell's film are birds on the breeding grounds, wailing like wolves and plumaged as if in formal dinner attire. Common Loons nest in the north woods, mainly in Canada, and typically far from major concentrations of humans.

In fall, though, they disperse broadly southward, reaching the southern United States and northern Mexico. You might see one or a handful on an inland body of water practically anywhere in the Lower 48, and you might well see hundreds along the Gulf and Atlantic coasts. But you won't see them the way Katharine Hepburn and Henry Fonda saw them in *On Golden Pond*. Winter loons are gray and smudgy, lacking the sharp contrast shown by loons in summer. And the splashes of color you see in summer—green on Common, ruby on Red-throated, violet on Pacific—are gone in winter. What's going on?

In a nutshell, loons, like so many other birds, exhibit seasonal variation in appearance. Their summer plumage differs from their winter plumage. You might also say that their breeding plumage differs from their nonbreeding plumage, but, as we shall see (§§121, 125), those terms are problematic. For now, we'll stick with summer and winter, perfectly accurate. Two questions arise: Why do loons and other birds look different in spring and summer, and how do they do it?

Easy questions, surprisingly complex answers. Let's defer the "why" question entirely for now. As to the "how" question, it depends. In the case of loons, the birds *molt* out of one plumage and into a new one. In other words, they wear two different coats of feathers—one in summer, another in winter. This is the molt strategy (§§119–124) of the Common Loon; other species apply various other strategies. And that barely scratches the surface of the challenging and fascinating topic of avian molt, a topic we'll return to extensively.

14 GEOGRAPHIC VARIATION

Yellow-rumped Warbler
Setophaga coronata

THIS BIRD IS efficiently named! Males and females, although quite different in appearance, exhibit a yellow rump, a patch of feathers where the base of the tail and the lower back come together. Adults and youngsters, also different in plumage, are conveniently marked with yellow rumps. And summer and winter birds, different in yet other ways, nevertheless share the namesake yellow rump. If you're doing the math, that's eight possible plumage combinations: two sexes, times two age classes, times two seasons. Thank goodness for the yellow rump!

There's something else. Yellow-rumped Warblers differ in a fourth way. They show strong geographic variation in plumage. In very coarse terms, eastern Yellow-rumps have white throats, whereas western Yellow-rumps have yellow throats. They are so different that they have been treated as separate species, the white-throated Myrtle Warbler versus the yellow-throated Audubon's Warbler. The differences are striking on adult males in summer, and they are usually discernible even on dull birds in winter.

Geographically distinctive populations of a species are often referred to as subspecies. The concept is simple, but the details are fiendishly complex. One treads carefully in the realm of subspecies biology. For example, it is not technically correct to refer to Myrtle and Audubon's Warblers as subspecies; rather, they correspond to subspecies groups, a distinction that trips up even professional ornithologists.

Let's back up a step. The birds called Myrtle and Audubon's Warblers clearly differ from one another. They have been classified as separate species, and they may yet again be elevated to full-species rank. Birders are to be commended for distinguishing between Myrtle and Audubon's Warblers—and between the geographically delineated populations of many other bird species. But be careful with the "subspecies" label. It often doesn't fit. You can't go wrong, though, with the biologically powerful concept of the *population*. Geographic variation is a pervasive theme in American ornithology, and we shall return repeatedly to the idea of regional differences in bird populations.

15 INDIVIDUAL VARIATION

Herring Gull
Larus argentatus

THEY'RE "SEAGULLS" IN popular parlance, evocative of swim beaches in summer and cloud-shrouded rocky coasts in fall and winter. There's nothing wrong with the word, but birders refer to them simply as "gulls," for the perfectly good reason that many of them are found far from the sea—or significant water of any sort. During the winter months, in particular, you might find gulls around landfills, pastures, and ball fields. Congregations well inland routinely reach the four digits, sometimes the five digits.

You scan the flock and you're struck by a paradox. They're all the same (all gulls, or seagulls), yet each one looks different. Especially the big dark ones. You see some general themes: dull pinkish legs, mainly blackish bills, dusky plumage overall. But *this* one is streaked blackish above, *that* one checkered brown and tan; *this* one's legs are brighter, *that* one's bill is darker; *this* one has a notably mottled breast, *that* one an obviously paler belly; and so forth and so on.

To cut to the chase, they're all Herring Gulls. Not only that, they're all first-winter Herring Gulls, hatched the summer before. They're all the same subspecies, *smithsonianus,* of the Herring Gull. Presumably, they're a mix of males and females; in first-winter gulls, the sexes do not differ in plumage. So what's the source of all the diversity in this flock?

The answer is individual variation. Gulls—especially first-winter gulls, and *especially* first-winter Herring Gulls—are notoriously variable. Think of them as human teenagers: unmistakably human teenagers, yet each one distinctive. The analogy is better than you might think, as first-winter Herring Gulls are, in a way, adolescent. If you don't have access to Herring Gulls, see if you can discern individual variation in local populations of Canada Geese, Rock Pigeons, American Robins, and House Finches.

Variety is the spice of life, it is said, and that quip inadvertently captures a great biological truth: All populations of organisms exhibit individual variation.

16 IF IT WALKS LIKE A DUCK . . .

≪≪≪ ≪≪≪ ≪≪≪ ≪≪≪ ≪≪≪ ≪≪≪ ≪≪◇≫≫ ≫≫≫ ≫≫≫ ≫≫≫ ≫≫≫ ≫≫≫

White-breasted Nuthatch
Sitta carolinensis

A BIRDER FROM ASIA, on her first visit to the Americas, sees an ovoid bird clambering about the bough of a shade tree. She shows the bird to her host, a lifelong American. "What is it?" the American asks.

"I'm not sure of the exact species," the Asian birder lets on, "but obviously it's some sort of nuthatch."

Obviously it's some sort of nuthatch. How does the visiting birder, who's never seen the species, know that? More than 99.7 percent of the world's bird species *aren't* nuthatches; somehow, the Asian tourist has immediately ruled out all those possibilities. And consider the converse: Her host, who casually but frequently notices the bird while hiking and gardening, doesn't know its name.

If it walks like a duck . . .

Seriously, that bit of folk wisdom gets at one of the fundamental strategies for bird identification. Nuthatches walk up and down tree trunks, and they do so erratically. Other kinds of birds climb trees, but none in the manner of nuthatches. Birders know that woodpeckers climb with jerky movements, that creepers ascend trunks with smoother movements, and that nuthatches are practitioners of the random walk.

You don't have to see color and pattern to recognize a nuthatch. You don't need a good read on size and shape. If you see a bird walking like a nuthatch, there's a very good chance it's a nuthatch—even if you've never seen the particular species you're looking at.

Once you've determined that you're looking at a nuthatch, the ID is a sure bet. The White-breasted is colored and patterned in ways that instantly differentiate it from the three other North American nuthatches. A quick check of the field guide or bird ID app confirms it. That's all well and good, but consider what got us so quickly to the nuthatch section: an awareness and appreciation of the unique behavior of the nuthatch family. Over and over again, we shall see that bird behavior is of supreme importance in field identification.

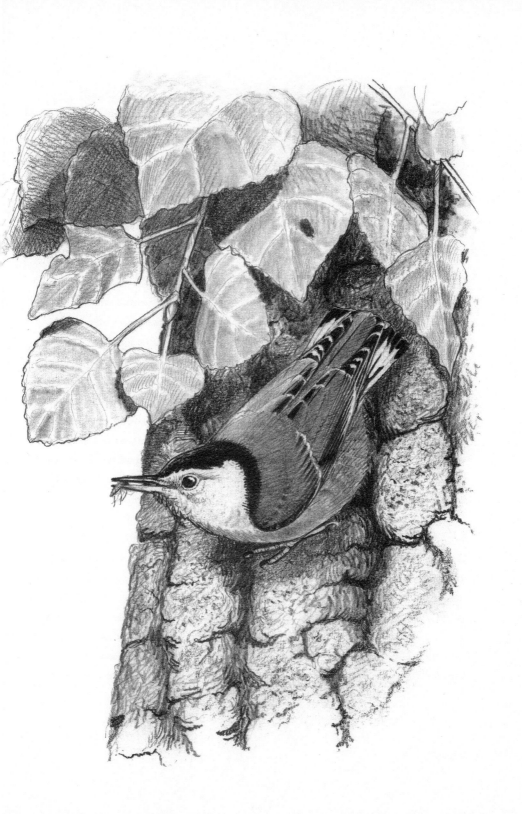

17 A COLORLESS, SHAPELESS, AMAZING BIRD

American Dipper
Cinclus mexicanus

I F YOU SENT OUT a survey asking American birders to name the most distinctive bird species on the continent, you'd get responses along the lines of Blackburnian Warbler, Bald Eagle, and Pileated Woodpecker. It's easy to see why. The adult male Blackburnian Warbler's throat is so intensely orange that it looks like it's on fire; indeed, an old name for the species is Flamethroat. The Bald Eagle, with its gleaming white head, has been called "all field mark" by one commentator. And the Pileated Woodpecker, an enormous bird with a blazing red crest, stops you in your tracks no matter how often you've seen one.

Another species that would make any birder's short list is the American Dipper, a bird practically devoid of field marks. It is round, about the size of your clenched fist, with a stubby tail and a normal bill. It is dark gray all over, showing brownish or bluish hints in good light, but appearing simply black much of the time. The bird is without form or feature. Yet it is among the most distinctive birds in America.

The American Dipper is, to use an overused word, unique. It is a songbird, yet it is aquatic. Now don't look for it on quiet fishing ponds or along the edges of babbling brooks. No, look for it *in* rushing water. Waterfalls are especially favored! This bird—perhaps a relative of the very terrestrial wrens—swims in cold streams and rivers in the foothills and mountains, frequently submerging in its search for the larvae of dragonflies and other arthropods. From time to time, it pauses on an exposed rock or piece of flotsam, where it bobs continually in quick jerks. The impression is of somebody doing knee bends. This is the "dipping" behavior from which the species gets its name. And the weirdest thing of all: It flashes its eyelids! They are pure white against the otherwise black body, tiny pulsars.

18 ID BIRDS BY MICROHABITAT

⋘ ⋘ ⋘ ⋘ ⋘ ⋘ ⋘◇⟫ ⟫ ⟫ ⟫ ⟫ ⟫ ⟫ ⟫

Green-winged Teal
Anas crecca

WHAT BIRDS ACTUALLY *do* is of the utmost importance in field identification. Nuthatches walk about randomly on tree trunks (§16), for example, whereas dippers swim in icy rivers (§17). It is exceedingly unlikely that you will ever see a dipper walking in the manner of a nuthatch, or a nuthatch swimming like a dipper.

Implicit in the preceding is that it's important to note *where* birds do what they do. If you spend enough time along streams and rivers in the West, you will find dippers and nuthatches along the same stretch of your path—but never in precisely the same place. The dipper is in the water, of course, and the nuthatch is clinging to the ample trunk of the cottonwood at the water's edge.

Tree versus water. Anybody can see the difference. But it requires greater sensitivity to discern the innumerable *microhabitat* differences that are so relevant to bird ID. To appreciate the importance of microhabitat, we'll leave behind the broadleaf riparian woodland (nuthatches, dippers) and head for a nearby fishing pond, full of ducks. Some of the ducks are loafing out on the open water; others favor the cattails near the shoreline; and still others are on dry land, foraging in the grass beyond.

We also note a tight bunch of small ducks probing industriously in the mucky microhabitat where water meets land. They give the impression of a flock of sandpipers. The light is poor, but it doesn't matter. We already have a good idea as to what these birds are. Small ducks, bunched up tight, *feeding like sandpipers on a mudflat:* Green-winged Teal.

To be sure, almost any duck *could* be on the mudflat with the teal. And any teal might well enlist with any other duck species—out in the open water or wherever. But that initial microhabitat cue set us on the path to the correct identification. "First thought, best thought," said Allen Ginsberg (and others before him), and so it often is with microhabitat cues for bird ID.

19 ID BY PHYSIOLOGICAL ECOLOGY

Least Sandpiper
Calidris minutilla

S HADES OF BROWN. That's an ungenerous but honest assessment of plumage variation in the bulk of the several dozen sandpiper species that occur annually in North America. Some of them add flourishes of black and rufous in spring and early summer, but brown and gray-brown are your basic options on most sandpipers in the colder months. Fortunately, they differ appreciably in body shape and microhabitat preference. Let's see how this works.

You're on one of our southern coasts in winter—not the actual seashore, but a mile inland, where sandpipers are spread out seemingly at random around a tidal lagoon. Their distribution is in fact anything but random. If we could wave our magic ID wand, we would know that godwits go *here*, knots *there*, and "peeps" over *there*. Speaking of peeps . . .

If sparrows are the terrestrial LBJs (§7), then the little brown sandpipers in the genus *Calidris*, often called "peeps," are their aquatic counterparts. In winter, there aren't many options to consider, but Least Sandpiper versus Western Sandpiper is a challenge across much of the southern United States. Although subtle plumage differences exist, the two species are most readily separated in winter by *simultaneous* consideration of shape and microhabitat.

Both are tiny, but the Least is ridiculously small; its scientific name, *minutilla*, conveys its diminutiveness. And although both have short bills, the Least is especially short-billed. At the same time that we are processing these differences in size and shape, we note the microhabitat preferences of the two species: out in the shallow water a ways for the Western, just out of the water's reach for the Least.

It makes all the sense in the world. The slightly smaller and shorter-billed Least is less suited for foraging in standing water, so it retreats to the sandbars and mudflats where food is more readily procured. Yes, it makes sense, but let's not sell ourselves short: In learning to ID the Least Sandpiper, we have engaged the scientific discipline of physiological ecology, the study of an organism's anatomical adaptations to its environment.

20 WATCH BIRDS FLY

American Kestrel
Falco sparverius

A MEDIUM-SIZE BIRD FLIES BY. It's decently long-tailed, but we can't really say much else about it. Is this a small hawk of some sort? A pigeon or dove? A cuckoo, even? Suddenly, the bird pulls up and does something remarkable: Its wings suddenly stiff, it's simply *hovering in midair*. To a birder unfamiliar with this behavior, it's a pinch-me-I'm-dreaming moment. How can the bird do this? Why doesn't it fall to the ground? Do the laws of physics even allow this?

To the birder who knows the species, there can be no doubting its identity. As if on cue, the bird suddenly drops to the ground—not because it's finally stalled out, but, rather, volitionally. A moment later the bird flies back up with a meadow vole, which it detected indirectly via an ultraviolet signal emitted by the prey item's urine. The bird flies up to a pole, flips its tail in a smooth motion, and proceeds to pluck the vole apart.

The bird is an American Kestrel, the smallest falcon in the United States and Canada, and we were 100 percent certain of its ID the moment it began hovering, or kiting, as the behavior is often termed. Other hoverers include hummingbirds, kingfishers, and the uncommon Rough-legged Hawk, but they do it their own way. A great many bird species are distinctive in flight, and that suggests a strategy for getting better at bird ID: When a bird inconveniently flies off, don't despair! Instead, pay attention to its flight style. A starling in flight looks nothing like a blackbird; many waterfowl are readily identified in flight; the flight of a dove is perfectly level, that of a woodpecker smoothly sinusoidal; identically plumaged crows and ravens strike different profiles on the wing; and seafaring "tubenoses" can be recognized at tremendous distances by birders familiar with how they fly. Birds in flight are marvelous to behold—and oftentimes much easier to ID than you might think.

21 LOCATION, LOCATION, LOCATION

≪≪ ≪≪ ≪≪ ≪≪ ≪≪ ≪≪ ≪≪◇≫ ≫≫ ≫≫ ≫≫ ≫≫ ≫≫ ≫≫

Tufted Titmouse
Baeolophus bicolor

AN OBVIOUS STARTING POINT in bird ID is an assessment of what a bird looks like: its colors and patterns, its size and shape. Just as important is a consideration of what the bird is doing: how it feeds, how it flies, etc. But all those things are, in many instances, an exercise in putting the cart before the horse. That's because it's often the case that the only thing you need to know is where you are. If you're birding around Houston, and you see or hear a titmouse, it is going to be a Tufted Titmouse—end of story. And if you make the haul inland to Abilene and find a titmouse, it will be a Black-crested Titmouse, practically guaranteed.

There are five species of titmice in North America, and identification by morphology and behavior is not always straightforward. But simply knowing where you are is often the *only* thing you need to make the ID. A titmouse in Colorado *has* to be a Juniper Titmouse, a titmouse in Pennsylvania *has* to be a Tufted Titmouse, and so forth. Texas, with its bounteous avifauna, harbors three species of titmice: Tufted in the East, Black-crested a bit farther west, and Juniper sparingly west of the Pecos River. There is some overlap, and the look-alike Tufted and Black-crested titmice hybridize where their ranges abut. But the general principle holds: Tufted Titmice *here*, Black-crested Titmice *there*, and watch out for hybrids where the species come into contact.

Birds have wings, of course, and many species are more or less prone to vagrancy—to wandering far off course. By and large, though, birds are found where the field guide range maps show them. "Location, location, location," the realtors say, and the same applies to birding. Know where birds occur: Tufted Titmice in Houston and Beaumont, but not in Abilene and Brownsville—and for that matter, all over Louisiana, but never in New Mexico. It's as important as any field mark.

22 THE VALUE OF LOCAL EXPERIENCE

⫷ ⫷ ⫷ ⫷ ⫷ ⫷ ⟨⟩ ⟩⟩ ⟩⟩ ⟩⟩ ⟩⟩ ⟩⟩ ⟩⟩ ⟩⟩

Ring-necked Duck
Aythya collaris

CONSULT A RANGE MAP for the Ring-necked Duck, and you'll see that the species occurs in winter pretty much from sea to shining sea across the southern two-thirds of the Lower 48 states. However, the Ring-necked Duck is not uniformly distributed across that wide swath of latitude. You need to look for it where there is standing water, and the water has to be deep enough to accommodate the species' proclivity for diving. But that's about it; the Ring-necked Duck is a diet generalist, favoring crayfish and mollusks, but also perfectly willing to eat submerged vegetation, insect larvae, worms, and just about anything else it can find down there.

The curious thing, though, is that Ring-necks emphatically *don't* occur on every pond and reservoir in a particular park or preserve. One pond might harbor a hundred or more, while another, not even a quarter mile away, is devoid of ducks. How can we know which pond or ponds have the flocks, and which ones don't? Well, we could be scientific about it, and ask questions about water temperature, food availability, and so forth. Those are valid approaches, but let's not lose sight of a particularly straightforward and powerful way of knowing: experience.

If you bird your local region long enough, you start to learn things like: *This pond has Ring-necked Ducks until the water freezes up.* Or: *When it's really cold, Ring-necks find their way to this stretch of the river.* And just as valuable: *For whatever reason, this reservoir never seems to have ducks of any sort.* You can learn this stuff by zooming in on eBird range maps; you can learn it from other birders in your area; and, best of all, you can learn it from the sum of your own experiences, winter upon winter.

Birds have habits. Know those habits, and you'll greatly increase your chances of getting the bird—whether you're doing a Big Day or leading a field trip, whether you're conducting an ornithological survey or simply birding for pure enjoyment.

23 TIMING IS EVERYTHING

≪≪ ≪≪ ≪≪ ≪≪ ≪≪ ≪≪ ≪≪◁▷≫ ≫≫ ≫≫ ≫≫ ≫≫ ≫≫ ≫≫

Anna's Hummingbird
Calypte anna

A HUMMINGBIRD ZIPS BY. What species is it? If you're in Vancouver, British Columbia, you have two main choices: Rufous and Anna's. If you're there in the dead of winter, you have just one choice: Anna's. Now if you're from St. Louis or Toronto, it may come as a surprise that Anna's Hummingbirds are routine in winter as far north as Vancouver. That's because you know that your hummingbird (the Ruby-throated Hummingbird) migrates south in late summer and doesn't return until well into the spring. Other widespread North American hummingbirds—the Broad-tailed, the Black-chinned, and the aforementioned Rufous—are likewise migratory. Indeed, the Rufous is, in a certain sense, the most migratory bird species of all! It migrates farther, relative to its body length, than any other bird on Earth. Among North American hummers, though, the Anna's is an outlier, being sedentary across much of its range.

When you look at range maps, whether online or in your field guide, be sure to ponder the question of seasonality as well as geography. And consider that patterns of seasonality are rarely uniform across the ranges of widely distributed bird species. Case in point: the feisty, vocal, red-headed Anna's Hummingbird. In its core range in the West Coast region, the species is largely resident, the term given by ornithologists to bird populations that generally stay put throughout the annual cycle. But Anna's Hummingbirds do disperse a bit in the winter, with regular movements east into the Great Basin and the Mojave Desert and, with a counterintuitive flourish, north along the coast to Juneau, Alaska.

The vast majority of American birds exhibit seasonal movements of some sort. Some are the stuff of legend: the nonstop flight of the Ruby-throated Hummingbird across the Gulf of Mexico and the Rufous hummer's long-distance excursions between central Alaska and southwestern Mexico. Others, like the short-distance dispersal of the Anna's Hummingbird, are comparatively subtle. Regardless of the distance traversed, these seasonal movements, or lack thereof, are valuable cues to a bird's ID.

24 LOCAL MOVEMENTS

≪≪ ≪≪≪ ≪≪≪ ≪≪≪ ≪≪≪ ≪≪≪ ≪≪◇≫≫ ≫≫≫ ≫≫≫ ≫≫≫ ≫≫≫ ≫≫≫ ≫≫

American Tree Sparrow
Spizelloides arborea

WHAT DOES IT mean to say that a bird is a winter resident of a given state or province? It doesn't literally mean that the species takes up residence from the winter solstice till the spring equinox. At mid-latitudes in North America, winter-resident land birds tend to arrive in autumn and depart in spring. That's still pretty imprecise. For any particular species, though, we can usually be surprisingly confident about the timing of arrivals and departures.

If American Tree Sparrows winter in your area, then it is likely the case that they are the last of the sparrows to arrive in autumn. The main arrivals around 40° north latitude aren't until early November, well after other sparrow species—White-throated, Swamp, and others—have set up shop for the winter. And tree sparrows withdraw early. At the same latitude, most are gone by the end of March, and reports after mid-April are notable (or erroneous).

During their several months with us in the winter, tree sparrows are fussbudgets, always on the move. Not surprisingly, the quest for food determines individual birds' movements, but so does something else: snow. Not snow cover per se, but actual falling snow. An experimental study from the 20th century showed that several bird species, including the American Tree Sparrow, are induced to take flight when the first few flakes start to fall. Tree sparrows may also undergo more sustained wintertime dispersal within their core range. The reasons for this aren't clear, but may involve some interplay between food availability and the late-winter onset of the species' spring feather molt. Intriguingly, these movements take place at least partly at night; on still winter nights in January and February, see if you can hear the pure, piercing flight calls of tree sparrows dispersing.

Full-on spring and fall migrations of tree sparrows and other species, often involving flights of hundreds or thousands of miles, understandably catch our attention. But movements *within* a season, although more subtle, are often significant—and typically complex and dynamic.

25 LEARN "S&D"

⋘ ⋘ ⋘ ⋘ ⋘ ⋘ ⋘ ◇ ⋙ ⋙ ⋙ ⋙ ⋙ ⋙ ⋙

Hermit Thrush
Catharus guttatus

BIRDERS CALL IT "S&D," shorthand for "status and distribution," the calculus of a species' occurrence in time and space. S&D can be expressed via range maps and seasonal bar graphs and even mathematical equations, but nothing beats the power of the written word: "The only spot-breasted thrush that winters in the United States."

Six species of spot-breasted thrushes—five in the genus *Catharus,* plus the Wood Thrush in the genus *Hylocichla*—breed in the United States and Canada, but only the Hermit Thrush routinely winters here. Know that bit of S&D, and you have learned how to identify spot-breasted thrushes in winter. It's that simple. During migration and the breeding season, though, it's not as straightforward.

The Hermit Thrush comprises three main populations, technically referred to as subspecies groups. In a nutshell, they are (1) a Pacific slope group, (2) an interior West group, and (3) everything else: Midwest, Appalachians, Eastern Seaboard, and a good deal of Canada. Migration timing and overall migratory strategies differ among the three populations. The details aren't important for now, but the bigger point stands: Know these differences, and you greatly improve your chance of getting the ID right with migrating thrushes as well as birds on the breeding grounds.

In the same way that all birds have feathers and wings, so all birds have S&D. Think of S&D as a field mark—subject to variation, of course, and not infallible. And bear in mind that S&D is as much temporal as spatial, a point that often gets lost. Needless to say, it's critical to know which species of *Catharus* thrushes migrate through your area; that's the spatial component of S&D. But it's just as essential to have knowledge of their temporal distribution. Thus, in late summer and autumn in much of the Midwest: Veeries and Swainson's Thrushes first, Gray-cheeked Thrushes later, Hermits last of all.

Look at the bird, for sure. But also look at a calendar and a map. That's the essence of birding by S&D.

26 BY ANY OTHER NAME

Red-breasted Merganser
Mergus serrator

B
IRDS, LIKE PEOPLE, have names. We can extend the analogy further: Most, although not all, North American birds have a "first name" and a "last name," or a "family name." And so it is of course with most, although not all, of the persons we encounter in daily living. We've now made the acquaintance of 25 birds, and 24 of them comply with this naming scheme: Cedar Waxwing (§1), American Robin (§2), Red-tailed Hawk (§3), and so forth. The only outlier thus far has been the mononymous Mallard (§6), the avian equivalent of Beyoncé or Cher. But even the Mallard is often referred to as the Mallard Duck, or, in certain technical applications, the Northern Mallard.

The analogy goes only so far. When we say "Red-breasted Merganser," we're not talking about a particular individual. Instead, we apply the name to a whole population of birds, as if they were all the human residents of a particular city or all the persons in a specific demographic cohort. "Red-breasted Merganser" is more like "New Yorker" or "Baby Boomer" than "John Smith" or "Jane Doe." It is the name given to a *species*—in the case of the Red-breasted Merganser comprising about 500,000 individuals worldwide.

By convention, the name is capitalized. We might refer to a mixed-species flock of lowercase mergansers; and it is perfectly fine to employ the hunter's descriptive "sawbill," also lowercase. But when we write the name with capital letters, we affirm the precepts of ornithological science: Capitalization denotes that the bird is an individual of the species given the name Red-breasted Merganser.

A question remains: Why is it called Red-breasted Merganser, as opposed to, say, Spike-haired Sawbill or Gray-sided Seaduck? The easy answer to the question: Because professional ornithologists in the American Ornithological Society (AOS) say so. The rest of us follow suit. But we still want to know: Why did the AOS settle upon *this* name, as opposed to *that* name, for this red-breasted, spike-haired, gray-sided, saw-billed, seafaring merganser? We'll take up that matter in the next lesson.

27 STANDARD ENGLISH NAMES

Pileated Woodpecker
Dryocopus pileatus

THE BIRD'S NAME makes sense. It pecks wood. Okay, it's more of a wood whacker or wood walloper, but still. As to the pileated part, there's a Latin word, *pileum,* that, in honest-to-goodness Latin, meant something along the lines of "felt cap." In our time, the word is restricted essentially to scientific ornithology, and it is an anatomical term, referring to a region of the bird's head running from the base of the bill to the center of the nape. The male of the species in question has the most stunning pileum you're likely to see on any bird in our area. Hence, Pileated Woodpecker, an entirely sensible name.

But why *that* particular name? The pioneering colonial naturalist Mark Catesby (1682–1749) named it the Large Red-crested Woodpecker. That's a fine name: "Red-crested" is more precise than "Pileated," and the bird is impressively large. The folk names "Log-cock" and "Wood-hen" remain in currency, and it's enchanting to consider that the bird has been known, at least in some quarters, as "Stump-breaker."

The answer, we already know (§26), is that bird names are established by the American Ornithological Society (AOS). The official, AOS-sanctioned name of a bird is referred to as its standard English name. It's okay to say or write "Log-cock" or "Stump-breaker," and in certain instances it is desirable and preferable to do so. But we use the standard English name for the sake of, well, standardization. We have to call it *something*. It's not that "Pileated Woodpecker" is necessarily the most descriptive, or the most expressive, or otherwise the best, name. It serves as the bird's identifier, somewhat analogous to the Social Security number or passport number assigned to a human being.

Sure, some amount of thought and even logic goes into the establishment of standard English names. And we'll take up that matter in the lessons to follow. But, for now, let's emphasize that a name is, to a large extent, just a name.

28 SCIENTIFIC NAMES: LOVE AND LOGIC

Belted Kingfisher
Megaceryle alcyon

T
AKE A LOOK at the title of this entry. Next to the bird's sensible-looking standard English name (§27), Belted Kingfisher, you'll see another name, italicized, *Megaceryle alcyon*. This is the so-called scientific name conferred upon this species of kingfisher. Like the standard English name, the scientific name of a bird (or any other organism) is given to an entire species. And as with standard English names, scientific names comprise a "first name" and "last name," but with a twist. Literally. The group name goes *first*.

Just as "kingfisher" is the name given to a group of birds, so *"Megaceryle"* refers to multiple bird species. And just as "Belted" identifies a particular species of kingfisher, so *"alcyon"* denotes that same species. Thus our bird has two unique identifiers: Belted Kingfisher, its standard English name; and *Megaceryle alcyon,* its scientific name. It's like your Social Security number and driver's license number: two different names for the same person.

The name "Belted Kingfisher" makes sense, but what's the deal with *Megaceryle alcyon? Mega-* derives from the Greek word for "large"; *-ceryle* from the Greek word for "kingfisher," and *alcyon* also from a Greek word for "kingfisher." You get the idea: This is a large kingfisher.

Scientific names can be poetical and evocative. The curlews are called *Numenius,* Latin for "new moon," the shape of the bird's bill; the crossbills with their curved bills are *Loxia,* related to ancient auguries that were obscure or oblique; and the prairie-chickens are named *Tympanuchus* for a kind of drum used in Roman orgies. As to *alcyon,* you may have wondered whether it is related to the word "halcyon." Answer: Yes. The "halcyon days," according to ancient myth, were so calm that the apocryphal floating nests of seaborne kingfishers (no such thing) were undisturbed.

There is a certain logic to the formulation of scientific names, and we'll get into more detail on that presently (§29). But you can also enjoy them for what they are: little poetical fragments, like haiku, that enhance and enrich the stories of the birds we love to watch.

29 SCIENTIFIC NAMES: RULES AND REGULATIONS

Common Grackle
Quiscalus quiscula

Q UISCALUS? QUISCULA? What's up with that? Seriously, that's the meaning of this bird's scientific name. Both *Quiscalus* and *quiscula* are misspellings of the Latin word *quisqualis,* in essence, "What's the deal?" or "Whatever!" The species was conferred its scientific name in 1758 by the Swedish naturalist Carl Linnaeus, who had no experience with this slender and glossy blackbird in life. We're not sure why Linnaeus named it as he did, but the designation has stuck. By fiat.

When somebody gives a species a scientific name, we're saddled with that name. Forever. This is the Principle of Priority, and it is both arbitrary and essential. It's arbitrary because someone like Linnaeus—with vastly less expertise in matters quiscaline than you or me—can give it the name *quiscula,* and that, as they say, is that. But it's essential because it ensures that we're all talking about the same species, no matter how crazy the name is. And crazy these names so often are: misspelled, mistranslated, misconstrued, biologically nonsensical, and politically incorrect.

There are a great many other rules of biological nomenclature. For example: The scientific name is always binomial, comprising two names, italicized, the first word in caps, the second lowercase. Always. No exceptions. Thus, another kind of grackle, the Great-tailed Grackle, is *Quiscalus mexicanus,* with the lowercase *m,* even though we would capitalize the proper adjective in modern English. Contrary to popular belief, these names are not necessarily in Latin; so it is improper to call them Latin binomials, despite the widespread use of that misnomer. Call them, simply and descriptively, scientific names.

A parting thought. The rules of biological nomenclature are fantastically complex and recondite; we've barely scraped the tip of the iceberg here. Learn the rules and regulations if you wish. But don't lose sight of the lesson from last time (§28): Bird names are fun! Practically every scientific name has a backstory—some bit of bird lore or human interest, or a literary allusion or poetical flourish, or just plain weirdness.

30 SPLITTING SPECIES IN TWO

⋘ ⋘ ⋘ ⋘ ⋘ ⋘ ⋘◇≫ ≫ ≫ ≫ ≫ ≫ ≫

Wilson's Snipe
Gallinago delicata

L IKE MOST OTHER SNIPES in the sandpiper family Scolopacidae, the one called Wilson's is a brown ball of a bird with a remarkably long bill. The species is named for Alexander Wilson, an expat Scot who, in the late 18th and early 19th century, gained a reputation as the father of American ornithology. Look up "Snipe, Wilson's" in the index of any field guide, and you'll soon enough learn how to identify and appreciate this particular species of snipe.

Unless the book was published before 2002.

In that year, the American Ornithological Society, then known as the American Ornithologists' Union (AOU), changed the name of the species from Common Snipe to Wilson's Snipe. Wait a minute. Didn't we just say (§29) that you can't go changing species names willy-nilly? True, but that's not at issue here. What happened in 2002 is that the AOU decided that the species then known as the Common Snipe actually consists of two species. And, as we already know (§§26–29), every species *has* to have a name. So our snipe, the one that displays above wet hay meadows on summer nights, was given a new name. Two new names, actually: a new standard English name (§27), Wilson's Snipe; and a new scientific name (§28), *Gallinago delicata*.

We've skipped a step. *Why* was the snipe split into species? The simple answer is that a critical suite of factors—differences in ecology, behavior, and genetics—lined up the right way. When the AOU (or AOS, same difference) splits a species, the decision is almost always based on consideration of multiple criteria.

You might have thought of something: If a species can be split in two, can two species be lumped into one? To answer that question, we need look no further than the example of the snipe. Go way back in ornithological history—all the way to the early 20th century—and the name "Wilson's Snipe" reappears in the literature. So the Wilson's and Common snipes were lumped into one species in the early 20th century, then re-split early in our own century.

31 LUMPING SPECIES INTO ONE

Dark-eyed Junco
Junco hyemalis

LOOKS CAN BE DECEIVING. So can names. The boldly marked junco is in fact a kind of sparrow. Two species occur in our area. The Yellow-eyed Junco, basically a Mexican species, reaches the United States only in Arizona and New Mexico, but the widespread Dark-eyed Junco ranges across much of the United States and Canada.

Dark-eyed Juncos exhibit fantastic geographic variation in plumage (§14), far more than you might see in a mixed-species flock of sandpipers. The so-called "Slate-colored" juncos of the East and North are instantly differentiable from the colorful "Pink-sided" and "Gray-headed" juncos of the Interior West; a distinctive "White-winged" junco is restricted as a breeder mainly to the Black Hills of South Dakota; and the variable "Oregon" junco is itself a complex of multiple populations (subspecies).

Yet they're all one species: Dark-eyed Junco, *Junco hyemalis*. What gives?

In a nutshell, the different populations of juncos interbreed extensively where their ranges overlap. "Slate-colored" and "Oregon" juncos share genes in the Canadian Rockies; "Pink-sided" and "White-winged" juncos interbreed when given the chance; and the "Oregon," "Gray-headed," and "Pink-sided" juncos all do it, too. When genes flow more or less freely between populations, that indicates that only one species is involved. And given our current understanding of gene flow among all these juncos, we believe that there is just the single species.

It hasn't always been that way. Consult a field guide from the mid-20th century, and you'll notice at least four junco species. Go back further in time, and the number rises even higher. No more. The juncos have been lumped—into a single species, the one we today call the Dark-eyed Junco.

But they look so different! True, but the different Dark-eyed Juncos are surprisingly similar in other respects: their songs and calls; their breeding ecology; their body morphology; their migratory strategies; and, as we have just seen, their genes. As is the case with splits (§30), the AOS examines multiple lines of evidence when it lumps species into one.

32 THE ABCS (NOT) OF CHECKLIST ORDER

American Coot
Fulica americana

OPEN UP THE NEWSPAPER—or, more likely, consult your smartphone—and check out the baseball standings in the sports section. The various teams aren't listed in alphabetical order, or, if they are, it's pure coincidence. Rather, they're listed according to their winning percentages. On top of that, clusters of teams, called divisions, are grouped together. Within the baseball division called the American League East, the Yankees are at the top, let's say, followed by the Orioles and Blue Jays, with the Rays and Red Sox at the bottom of the heap. Similar orderings occur within other divisions: American League Central, National League West, etc. It's much the same with the bird species on the checklists in our apps and field guides.

Don't look for the American Coot with other "A" birds (American Robin, Ancient Murrelet) or "C" birds (cormorant, crow). Instead, look for this coal-colored commoner with other birds in its division, a so-called family of birds, the Rallidae, that includes the Virginia Rail, the Sora, the Purple Swamphen, the Common Gallinule, and the American Coot. Drop down one species below the American Coot, and you'll see the Sungrebe; it's in a different family, the Heliornithidae. Then scan above the various species of Rallidae, and you'll see a completely different assemblage, the hummingbirds in the family Trochilidae. The analogy isn't perfect, but it's also not all that far off: The Rallidae are the American League East, the Heliornithidae are the American League Central (same league, different division), and the Trochilidae are the National League West (different league altogether).

This is the key point: The birds on our checklists are sequenced according to their evolutionary relationships. Huge orders of birds are like different sports leagues; smaller families are like sports divisions; and the individual species are like the different teams. Coots (Rallidae) and Sungrebes (Heliornithidae) are in the same order (Gruiformes), while hummingbirds (Trochilidae) are in a completely different order (Apodiformes). The whole checklist is a tree of life, a linear depiction of the relationships among birds.

33 DO THE CHECKLIST SHUFFLE

Lapland Longspur
Calcarius lapponicus

FLIP OPEN TO the longspurs in the current (seventh) edition of the *National Geographic Field Guide to the Birds of North America,* known to birders simply as *Nat Geo*. Now go back a page; you're in the section on finches. But if you perform this same exercise with the sixth edition, you'll discover that the waxwings and silky-flycatchers, not finches, immediately precede the longspurs. And if you consult one of the late–20th-century editions of *Nat Geo*, you'll find the juncos right in front of the longspurs. What's behind all this change?

In a nutshell, scientists are forever updating their understanding of the evolutionary relationships among birds. As recently as the late 20th century, longspurs were thought to be in the same family (Emberizidae) as the juncos; hence their placement with juncos in the field guides from that era. Then molecular ornithologists discovered that longspurs are relatively distant from the juncos and other sparrows in the family Emberizidae (recently reassigned to the family Passerellidae), so longspurs were assigned to a new family (Calcariidae) and moved to a new spot in the checklist. And even more recently, the placement of the finches (family Fringillidae) was found to be wanting, so they were moved from near the end of the checklist to their present position right in front of the longspurs.

These checklist shuffles occasion some grumbling among birders, but they shouldn't. They reflect the inexorable march of scientific progress. As we accumulate more and better data about avian genetics, morphology, and ecology (especially genetics!), we achieve an ever clearer picture of the evolutionary relationships among birds.

Will it ever end? Will the linear sequence of birds on our checklists ever stabilize? Most ornithologists would answer that question with a qualified yes. As powerful genetic analyses are applied at the level of deep taxonomy (studies among groups of distantly related birds), one senses that we are nearing the holy grail of checklist stability. But there will always be tweaks! And the open-minded scientist is always receptive to the exciting possibility that we got it all wrong.

34 GO TO THE HEAD OF THE CLASS

American Wigeon
Mareca americana

THE AMERICAN WIGEON, being a kind of duck, appears near the top of the checklist of birds. What does it mean that wigeons and other ducks are at the front of the pack, whereas grosbeaks and orioles bring up the rear? A glib explanation is that a bird's placement on the checklist corresponds to how "primitive" it is. That would mean grosbeaks, orioles, and other songbirds are more "advanced" than wigeons and other waterfowl. There's a kernel of truth to the preceding, but it's also misleading.

Here's the deal. The songbirds, including grosbeaks and orioles, are thought to have arisen more recently in the evolutionary scheme of things than an ancient ancestor of the ducks and grouse. (You read that right. Wigeons and Wild Turkeys are conjoined in a higher-order grouping called the Galloanseres.) Thus, the relatively "modern" songbirds appear farther down the checklist. If that's all there were to it, we'd be in good shape. The problem, though, is that we frequently misapply this primitive-versus-advanced dichotomy at the species level.

American Wigeons, like humans and bacteria, are subject to the laws of biology. Regardless of their ancestry, wigeons evolved relatively recently. And they're still evolving. Same with *Homo sapiens:* We humans are members of a relatively ancient group, the primates, but our species has evolved spectacularly in the past hundred thousand years or so. And bacteria take the cake. Brand-new species metabolize airplane fuel and other resources that didn't even exist until the 20th century.

Keep in mind that evolution cannot satisfactorily be portrayed by means of a linear checklist (§32). Instead, evolution is better rendered pictorially as a tree of life, often revealing as much branching (speciation) in the ancient groups as in the recent groups. The American Wigeon, despite its placement near the head of the checklist, isn't primitive. Its color and patterns, its diverse vocalizations, its complex social system, and its many other traits are all recently evolved—and, more to the point, are still evolving.

35 OTHER APPROACHES: TAXONOMY

Ruby-crowned Kinglet
Regulus calendula

S PEND ANY AMOUNT of time around a bird banding operation (§161), and you'll hear mention of "Ricky." It's the name of an olive-green bird, a fussbudget, a fireball, a tiny bundle of feathers, known in other circles as the Ruby-crowned Kinglet. Why Ricky?

Answer: Because the Ruby-crown's banding code is RCKI (Ruby-crowned Kinglet), and birders pronounce it "Ricky." You might also hear "Whiffle" for WIFL, the Willow Flycatcher, and "Nomo" (like the baseball player) for NOMO, the Northern Mockingbird, etc. These banding codes—always four letters—are inarguably efficient, especially when you're taking notes in the field or entering data onto a spreadsheet. Who wants to write out "Northern Rough-winged Swallow" (29 characters, including spaces) or "American Three-toed Woodpecker" (30 characters) when NRWS and ATTW, respectively, will suffice? A few birders and ornithologists apply a similar scheme to the scientific names of birds: REGCAL for the kinglet's *Regulus calendula*, EMPTRA for the flycatcher's *Empidonax traillii*, and so forth. (Some of these six-letter names are rather PG-13; if you have nothing better to do . . .)

A scandalous question might occur to you: Why do we use official standard English and scientific names? Especially scientific names. In fact, some biologists have advocated scrapping the whole Linnaean system (§29) and replacing it with a bar-code system, or perhaps, in today's parlance, a QR-code system. The arguments for doing so are intriguing and, some would say, persuasive.

These alternative taxonomies—four-letter codes, six-letter codes, bar codes, and more—are just that: alternative taxonomies. For now, standard English names (§27) and scientific names (§28) are the lingua franca of our birding community. But if you're bilingual, so to speak, good for you. Your field guides, checklists, and apps say "Ruby-crowned Kinglet," but it's perfectly fine to call that restless and wide-eyed bundle of energy bopping around the banding station "Ricky." Like a real bilingual, you will enjoy an expanded outlook and perspective on the world around you.

36 OTHER APPROACHES: SYSTEMATICS

≪≪≪ ≪≪≪ ≪≪≪ ≪≪≪ ≪≪≪ ≪≪≪ ≪≪◇≫≫ ≫≫ ≫≫ ≫≫ ≫≫ ≫≫ ≫≫

Peregrine Falcon
Falco peregrinus

I F YOU TOOK a straw poll of birders and ornithologists, the Peregrine Falcon would surely be at the top of the list of the world's greatest raptors. This fastest animal on Earth is, in the eyes of many, the very essence of power and majesty. Yet it is not, in some sense, a raptor. In 2012, scientists with the American Ornithologists' Union (AOU) moved the falcons out of a grouping with the raptors and into a new assemblage including—get this—parrots and songbirds. It turns out that the mighty Peregrine is more closely related to warblers and parakeets than to eagles and condors.

The birding community received the news with a mix of amazement and resistance. Few if any birders seriously questioned the science behind the discovery (the AOS is both credible and generally conservative in its decisions), but many, understandably, asked whether it matters. In particular, birders wonder whether our field guides ought to follow the linear sequence of the AOS. The argument goes like this: The judgments of the AOS are doubtless correct, but it makes more sense to group similar birds together. Thus: unrelated swimming birds like ducks and coots; longspurs, larks, and look-alike sparrows; and the raptorial falcons and eagles.

Steve Howell, one of the most prolific and provocative of contemporary ornithologists, is a leading advocate for such an arrangement. Other ornithologists, including the authors of *Nat Geo,* are leery of Howell's approach and favor the science-based findings of the AOS. Their reasoning recalls that of the influential 20th-century scientist Theodosius Dobzhansky, who memorably quipped that "Nothing in biology makes sense except in the light of evolution." In this view, a fundamentally evolutionist outlook is required for making sense of the diversity of birdlife all around us.

Bottom line: Both approaches to systematics (the study of the relationships among species) are out there. By all means, embrace the science-based systematics of the AOS; but don't dismiss out of hand the pedagogically powerful, if culturally conditioned, insights of Howell and company.

PART TWO

AFTER THE SPARK

March—May

37 AFTER THE SPARK

<<< <<< <<< <<< <<< <<< <<<<>>> >>> >>> >>> >>> >>> >>>

Eastern Phoebe
Sayornis phoebe

GRAY-BROWN BIRD DARTS in front of us, swoops down to the canal along the trail, and snatches an insect from the water's surface. Three thoughts occur to us, more or less simultaneously, and more or less automatically: "Wow," "That's an Eastern Phoebe," and "A phoebe is a kind of flycatcher." The thoughts aren't consciously formulated, but there they are, flitting about in the cerebral cortex of the birder's brain. We see a phoebe or any sort of bird, and we do three things: We marvel at the object of our devotion (§§1–5), we name the object (§§6–25), and we ponder the meaning of the name (§§26–36).

That's a fine beginning. But let's be clear about something: It's just a beginning. We've got a ways to go.

The great contemporary natural historian Kenn Kaufman for many years penned a monthly column, "After the Spark," about all the things that happen in the years following our "conversion" to birding. Yes, the sense of wonder is still there, felicitously so; yes, field identification retains its absorbing interest for the birder; and, oh yes, the arcane principles of systematics and taxonomy continue to delight and vex us. But there's more to come.

Our phoebe gobbles down the bug, then flies up to a bridge just downstream. That gets us to thinking about something: Eastern Phoebes *really* like bridges. They also like barns, storage sheds, and other outbuildings. *Why is that?* Phoebes have been won over by artificial structures, but most other flycatchers have not. How come?

This is birding "After the Spark," more intentional and deliberate than it once was. New insights and new ways of thinking come to us every time we venture afield; we are possessed of newfound awareness and appreciation of the world around us. We begin to engage birds and other objects in nature in a manner that is, for want of a better word, personal. This is "how to know the birds." This is when the real fun starts.

38 BIRDS ARE SOMEWHAT TO EXCEEDINGLY NOISY

Red-winged Blackbird
Agelaius phoeniceus

THE SKY IS gray, and the cold drizzle could change over to snow at any moment. You're in the car, on the way from Point A to Point B, and—dang it—you're not sure if you remembered some essential item: the diaper bag, the birthday present, whatever. So you pull over on the shoulder, hop out, dart back behind the car, yank open the tailgate, and—whew—it's all there.

You breathe a literal sigh of relief, and ever so quickly glance over the bleak landscape beyond: a cornfield and some outbuildings; a couple of still bare trees; and a tiny, sorry-looking cattail marsh. It doesn't look like much, *but the place is alive!* The din of birdsong drowns out the rumbling of a tractor and even the ubiquitous road noise. You hear piercing whistles, mechanical clanking sounds, harsh trills, and pleasing gurgles. These are all the sounds of a loose assemblage of Red-winged Blackbirds.

In most habitats in America and everywhere else, birdsong dominates the landscape. Birds sing in New York and Chicago, in Phoenix and Los Angeles; they fill pine forests and hardwood swamps with song, but they also proclaim from lonely deserts, buttes, and tundra; and birds sing from practically every stretch of roadside on Earth.

In many situations, expert birders do 75 to 90 percent of their bird ID by sound. At dawn in a California redwood forest or an Appalachian ravine, that number is closer to 99 percent. And at night (§52), the figure is essentially 100 percent. *Yet the majority of birders are mildly to hugely challenged by the prospect of learning birdsong.*

It is perhaps the greatest conundrum in all of nature study. Crack open a window right now. You hear birds, don't you? But how do you know what species you're hearing? That is the fundamental question of earbirding (one word, no space or hyphen), as it has come to be known. And it is the matter to which we now turn (§§39–54).

39 THE CATCH-22 OF UNSEEN BIRDS

American Woodcock
Scolopax minor

THE AIR IS cool and calm as darkness falls. You're in a scrubby woodlot in the Midwest, and you're taking in the soundscape of the early evening. Red-winged Blackbirds are settling in at a night roost, spring peepers are going at it in a wet swale, and a Great Horned Owl is hooting in the distance. Then you hear something utterly bizarre: a loud, harsh buzz. It goes off again. And again. A pause ensues. Soon you're hearing another strange sound: endless twittering, soft yet insistent, as if high overhead, way above the treetops. For the next half hour, you keep hearing those strange sounds: the harsh buzz in the woods, the soft twittering in the sky. What *are* those sounds?

Short answer: They are the utterances of a displaying male American Woodcock. A kind of sandpiper, the woodcock breeds in dry woods—hardly the sort of place you might reasonably expect to find a shorebird. Its buzzing sound is a bit like that of a nighthawk or a goldeneye, and its aerial display can suggest a pipit or lark. Your field guide dutifully states those things, but there's the rub. How do you even know where to start? We're dealing with a forest-inhabiting sandpiper that sounds like a nightjar, a duck, and a songbird!

When we actually *see* birds, we usually have a general idea as to what we're looking at. Ducks look like ducks, sandpipers look like sandpipers, and so on. If we see an unfamiliar duck or sandpiper, we know which section of the field guide to consult. But if we hear an unfamiliar sound—the harsh *peeent!* and soft twittering of a woodcock, let's say—it's not at all obvious where in the field guide to start searching for the ID.

To learn birdsong, you need to see the bird. The preceding may seem self-evident and snarky, but, as we are going to learn in the next lesson, it is not.

40 THE ABSOLUTE BEST WAY TO LEARN BIRDSONG

Spotted Towhee
Pipilo maculatus

SPEND A COUPLE HOURS in the shrubby foothills of the western United States, and you will probably make the acquaintance of the Spotted Towhee. Spend a long day or a weekend, especially in the warmer months, and you may well encounter dozens or scores of towhees. You'll see a few of them, but you'll hear many more. That's because towhees tend to stay out of sight, skulking in the undergrowth. Out of sight, perhaps, but rarely out of earshot: Towhees are noisy!

Their basic call is a whining nasal note, relatively low-pitched; they also give a higher note, a fine buzz, especially during short flights through the thickets. Spotted Towhees feed on the ground by kicking at the leaf litter; the scratching sound of their feet is audible and often the first indication that a towhee is nearby. Finally, they *sing*. Do they ever. The song of the Spotted Towhee is unmusical but spirited, broadcast all day long. Spend the morning—or even a hot afternoon—on the breeding grounds, and you might hear the song of the towhee a thousand times.

Now for the weird part. The hard part. The uncomfortable part. A lot of birders, no matter how much time they spend in the company of towhees, seem constitutionally incapable of learning the bird's song. With the songs of towhees and most other species, it's in one ear and out the other. The problem is one of auditory memory. How do you remember the song of the Spotted Towhee?

Short answer: *Watch the bird sing*. There's something indelible about *seeing a bird sing*.

The human brain is holistic and integrative. It's okay to listen to recordings and to analyze spectrograms (and we'll get to those matters in due course), but nothing reinforces auditory memory like being there. An unseen bird, whether in real life or on a recording, is a disembodied voice, incorporeal and easily forgotten. But a dapper towhee, teed up on a snag, singing his heart out, is etched in the auditory cortex of your brain forever.

41 TRANSLATING BIRDSONG INTO ENGLISH

Eastern Towhee
Pipilo erythrophthalmus

DRINK YOUR TEA!

That, according to almost every field guide, is the song of the Eastern Towhee, the eastern counterpart of the Spotted Towhee (§40). Now if you've never heard an Eastern Towhee and go out listening for the bird that advises, "Drink your tea," you won't hear the bird. That's because the towhee's utterance sounds absolutely nothing like those three English words. You could stumble upon three random syllables in Mandarin or Finnish, and they would come much closer to *Drink your tea!* than anything in "Towhee." The introductory *Drink* note in the towhee's song is nearly 5 kilohertz, impossibly high-pitched even for the world's greatest soprano. The whole song is produced by an organ called the syrinx, simply lacking in humans.

As a matter of objective fact, Eastern Towhees don't say anything remotely resembling the English words "drink," "your," and "tea." Yet we hear the towhee, and our brains go, "Drink your tea!" How does that work?

In the same way that we recognize the rumbling of thunder or the whispering of aspen leaves, so we—at least we who are birders—recognize the song of the Eastern Towhee. And we got to that point, whether or not we recognize and appreciate it, via experience. We were there, in the moment, with the bird. We heard the song of the towhee, looked up, and, consciously or unconsciously, intentionally or unintentionally, *saw the bird singing*. Then our amazing brains got down to business, processing auditory and visual stimuli simultaneously, creating a mental image of the bird's song. It was the act of *hearing while seeing* that created the auditory memory (§40).

Then we needed words for what we were hearing. *Drink your tea!* is a memory aid. We hear the song of the towhee, as foreign and untranslatable as the sound of thunder and aspen leaves, and we hear *Drink your tea!* Hey, if it works . . . True, but something's nagging at us: If the towhee *doesn't* utter those three English words, what *is* it saying?

42 BIRDSONG WITHOUT MNEMONICS

Western Meadowlark
Sturnella neglecta

FROM THE TALLGRASS PRAIRIE of the Upper Midwest to the cholla-and-greasewood deserts of the Southwest, the song of the Western Meadowlark is one of the first signs of spring. Go out on a calm morning in late winter in appropriate habitat—practically any open area will suffice—and you will be surrounded by meadowlark song.

The song of the meadowlark is easily learned but hard to put into words. That doesn't mean folks haven't tried! According to birders in the Sunflower State, the meadowlark says *Kansas is beautiful*. Colorado birders are less enthusiastic about that mnemonic, but the proprietor of a brew pub in Denver hears *Put down another one* in the song of the Western Meadowlark. Contemporary field guides largely eschew English translations of the species' song, opting instead for descriptive terminology such as "low," "rich," "bubbly," and "gurgling."

Those terms aren't inaccurate, but neither are they particularly useful. That's because they could just as well describe the utterances of certain shorebirds, doves, and finches—not to mention backyard water features and human voices. You might as well describe the English words "screech" and "whisper" as harsh-sounding and soft-sounding, respectively. Instead, we signify those words with unique permutations of letters: *s-c-r-e-e-c-h*, etc. Even in English, with its notoriously irregular spelling, the system works reasonably well. In a phonetic language like Spanish, the system is practically failproof.

Could a phonetic system be applied to the description of birdsong? The answer is a resounding affirmative. However, the song of the Western Meadowlark—low, rich, bubbly, gurgling, and, above all else, complex—is probably not the best place to start. We need a bird whose song is simpler, perhaps just a few short whistles, if we're going to make inroads toward the goal of establishing a phonetic system for describing birdsong. And, as we'll see in a moment, America's other meadowlark fits the bill quite nicely.

43 A MUSICAL SCORE FOR BIRDSONG

Eastern Meadowlark
Sturnella magna

How might you go about learning the song of this plump denizen of farm country in the East and scrublands in the Southwest? The best way is to gain actual experience in the field, simultaneously watching and listening (§40) to a real live meadowlark. As a memory aid, you can transliterate the song elements into English or at least English phonemes (§41); one popular translation is *spring of the year,* and a popular phonemic rendering is *tee-yah tee-yair*. A more analytical approach is to describe the qualities of the bird's song (§42); *Nat Geo* cuts to the chase with "clear" and "whistled," while the Peterson guide elaborates somewhat ("two clear whistles, musical and pulled out").

Frank M. Chapman's visionary *Birds of North America* (1895), like *Nat Geo* and Peterson, describes the song; it is "a clear, plaintive whistle of unusual sweetness." But Chapman's account of the Eastern Meadowlark goes further; Chapman provides a musical score of the song of *Sturnella magna*. The song, in triple meter, starts on the E above tenor C, rambles around the upper registers of the treble clef, and ends on the D above tenor C. Elsewhere in Chapman's proto–field guide, the simple song of the Black-capped Chickadee is rendered as a soprano C dropping three half-notes to an A.

Reality check. The meadowlark doesn't really start on an E, it doesn't sing in triple meter, and it doesn't even sing the discrete notes implied by Chapman's score. In the same way that meadowlarks don't really say *spring of the year,* neither do they obey the peculiar and culturally constructed conventions of Western music. So musical scores for birdsong never really caught on, and they had pretty much disappeared from field guides before the middle of the 20th century.

All that said, Chapman was onto something. At least in the case of simple songs (Eastern Meadowlark, Black-capped Chickadee), there ought to be a way of graphically depicting what we are hearing. He was right. Problem is, the technology hadn't yet been invented.

44 HOW TO READ THE MUSIC OF BIRDSONG

≪≪ ≪≪ ≪≪ ≪≪ ≪≪ ≪≪ ≪◇≫ ≫≫ ≫≫ ≫≫ ≫≫ ≫≫ ≫≫

Northern Bobwhite
Colinus virginianus

THIS BIRD GETS its name from its song: *Bob . . . White!* The species is most commonly heard in the warmer months, but particularly amorous males start singing in early spring. According to all the field guides, the song is whistled, which, if you think about something, is odd: In what sense is the name *Bob* whistled? We're back to the problem of the Eastern Towhee (§41) and the Eastern Meadowlark (§43). The bobwhite doesn't really say "bobwhite," or anything at all approximating that word. Enter the Golden Guide.

More than a half-century ago, Chandler S. Robbins and colleagues published *Birds of North America: A Guide to Field Identification*. This little book, widely known as the "Golden Guide" (for its publisher), was instantly influential, packed with one innovation after another. Particularly innovative was the Golden Guide's inclusion of *sound spectrograms* of bird vocalizations. These spectrograms are, in essence, the "musical scores" from the proto–field guides of the era of Frank M. Chapman (§43). But there's a huge difference: Spectrograms portray birdsong as it really is, completely unlike the well-intended contrivances of Chapman and his generation.

The bobwhite spectrogram in the Golden Guide shows three discrete sound elements: a line segment at 0.7 seconds, another line segment at 1.2 seconds, and then an upswept element at 1.8 seconds. And that, believe it or not, is the song of the Northern Bobwhite. If you have experience with spectrograms, you see those three traces of ink, and your brain hears a bobwhite.

Clearly, we have a problem. The vast majority of birders do *not* have any meaningful experience with spectrograms; they see those three traces of ink, and they hear nothing. The spectrograms in the Golden Guide never caught on, something that distressed Robbins right up to his death in 2017. But that's changing. In just the past couple years, spectrograms have begun to enter the birding mainstream. We'll spend the next several lessons learning how to see birdsong in spectrograms.

45 LEARN BIRD VOCALIZATIONS ONLINE

Greater Yellowlegs
Tringa melanoleuca

SPRING COMES EARLY to the freshwater marshlands of the middle latitudes of North America. All it takes is a bit of sunshine and snowmelt for a cattail marsh to come to life with Red-winged Blackbirds, Tree Swallows, and more. Even a few shorebirds get in on the action: boldly marked Killdeer and plainly marked Greater Yellowlegs. Let's focus on the yellowlegs.

It's standing on the far side of the marsh, in an open spot that's half mud, half ice. Some ducks—Redheads and Green-winged Teal—are nearby, but our interest is squarely on the yellowlegs. It's so . . . drab. Except for those yellow legs, it's your basic gray-brown sandpiper. Suddenly, the bird flushes, calling as it puts up. Your first impression is that the sound is *loud*. Other words come to mind: shrill, sharp, piercing.

The bird circles the marsh and felicitously elects to land right near where you are standing. It's close enough for you to discern the size and shape of the bill (long, slightly upturned). The bright yellow legs really stand out now, and you can make out a white eye-ring on the bird's otherwise undifferentiated gray-brown plumage. Then it flies off, this time for good, all the while uttering those shrill, sharp, piercing notes.

What next? A fine idea would be to go online and reinforce your aural memory of the Greater Yellowlegs, and an excellent starting point would be the crowdsourced website Xeno-Canto. It's as easy as entering the species name and listening to the recordings—400,000 strong at this writing. Listen to the recordings, yes, and something else: *Watch* them. Every Xeno-Canto recording is accompanied by a spectrogram, which you can either view online or download for later study. In due course, you learn to *see* the alarm call of the Greater Yellowlegs: three notes, falling in pitch, descending through the three-kilohertz range, each about 10 milliseconds. We're not there yet. Learning to see spectrograms does take some practice.

In the meantime, a more mundane matter: What about the ducks—the Redheads and teal—still massing on the far side of the marsh?

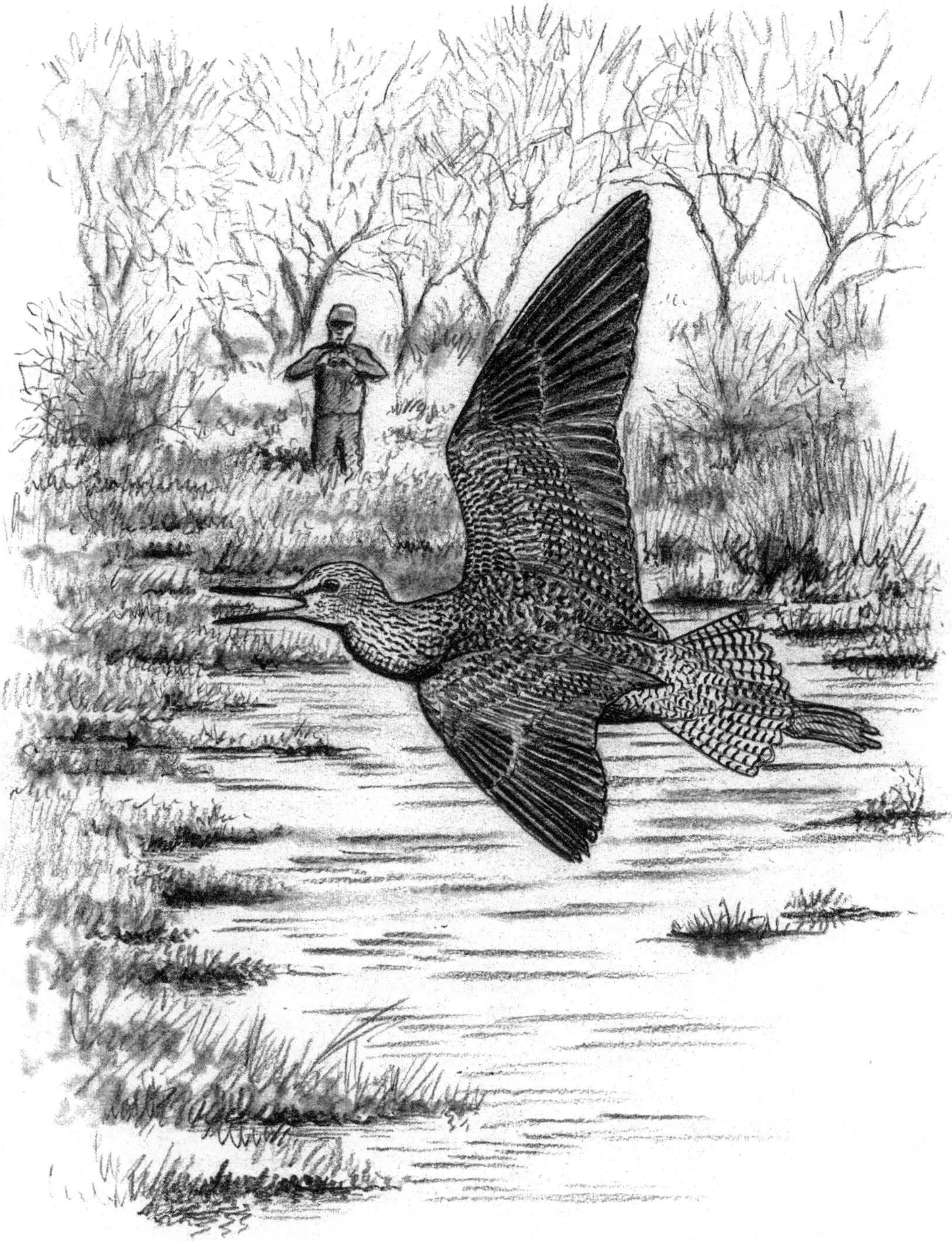

46 DUCK MUSIC

≪≪ ≪≪ ≪≪ ≪≪ ≪≪ ≪≪ ≪≪◇≫ ≫≫ ≫≫ ≫≫ ≫≫ ≫≫ ≫≫

Redhead
Aythya americana

THE AIR IS cool and humid, and you're standing by the edge of a large reservoir. You close your eyes and take in the sounds of this calm spring morning: a dog splashing around at the lakeshore, kids throwing stones in the water, and the artless banter of fishermen. And something else, faint yet far-carrying: a mournful whistling, nasal and resonant, descending in pitch. You step away from the dogs and kids and fishermen, and you hear the sound more clearly. It's coming from out on the lake, from where all those drake Redheads are thrashing about.

The chorusing of male Redheads is one of the most haunting natural sounds in America. Yet most birders are unaware of it. Part of the problem is that the sound is soft; another aspect of the problem is that the birds are typically distant; and yet another problem is that it happens for just a few weeks in early spring. We're not talking about the stentorian proclamations of cranes or the powerful arias of *Catharus* thrushes. Duck music is soft and subtle.

Duck music. That's the real problem. We don't even think of ducks as musicians. Yet many of our ducks—Redheads, for starters, but also Canvasbacks, Green-winged Teal, and scoters—are accomplished vocalists. Our outlook is changing, though, thanks to the recent emergence of crowdsourced websites of bird vocalizations (§45).

The Redhead is rarely recorded, yet the Xeno-Canto website hosts 16 uploads at this writing. They vary in quality, and only a handful are of chorusing males. Still, that's a quantum leap from a decade ago. (Xeno-Canto launched in 2005, and didn't really catch on until around 2010.) Browse the recordings on Xeno-Canto or eBird, and you quickly appreciate that duck vocalizations go way beyond the unfortunate "quack" of children's books.

It's awesome that Xeno-Canto and eBird are instructing a new generation of birders to read spectrograms, but let's not lose sight of something more basic: It's awesome that those websites have opened our minds to whole soundscapes we never knew about.

47 BACK TO THE BASICS

≪≪ ≪≪ ≪≪ ≪≪ ≪≪ ≪≪ ≪≪◇≫ ≫≫ ≫≫ ≫≫ ≫≫ ≫≫ ≫≫

White-throated Sparrow
Zonotrichia albicollis

W E'VE BEEN DANCING around something: Really, how do you *hear* sound from a spectrogram? The spectrogram of a Northern Bobwhite (§44) is obviously different from that of a Greater Yellowlegs (§45), which in turn differs clearly from that of a Redhead (§46). But that's like saying the Devanagari script of Hindi differs from the Cyrillic script of Greek and Russian. We want to go further. We want to know how to actually read the script.

Enter the White-throated Sparrow.

The spectrogram of a typical White-throat song consists of four or five perfectly straight horizontal lines. That signifies that their notes are pure whistles. They are identical, except for their placement on the spectrogram. From left to right, the first line is whistled first, the second line is whistled second, and so on. They also differ in their vertical placement: The higher lines are whistled at a higher pitch.

Spectrographically, the song of the White-throated Sparrow is very simple. Most other sparrows sing songs that are considerably more complex. And, truth be told, many White-throats ornament their songs with trills, stutter steps, and sundry other embellishments. Go to Xeno-Canto or eBird (click on "Search Photos and Sounds") and play around with the songs of White-throated Sparrows. With a bit of experience, you'll start to hear birdsong as it really is—with no need for recourse to mnemonics and other contortions. Keep at it for a while, and you'll get to the point that you can hear song in almost any spectrogram.

There's no rule that you have to learn spectrograms. In the same manner, you don't have to carry a camera in the field and analyze your every photo for subtle patterns of plumage variation and feather wear. You don't even have to use binoculars; indeed, bare-naked birding (§§174–175) has much to recommend it and seems to be catching on. That said, spectrograms have finally arrived on the birding scene. They're free, they're fun, and they're easily learned. Consider giving them a whirl.

48 MAKE RECORDINGS OF BIRDSONG

Carolina Wren
Thryothorus ludovicianus

THE SOUND IS so loud as to be literally startling. You flinch when you hear it—a rapid-fire series of rich, repetitious whistles. The bird is holed up in a dense thicket of honeysuckle and Virginia creeper, but you wait it out: Eventually a reddish-brown bird pops up, belts out that song again, and proclaims itself to be a Carolina Wren. You stick with the bird, watching it sing. By catching it in the act, so to speak, you create a powerful aural memory of the song (§40).

Then you whip out your smartphone, open the camera app, and make a video. The bird itself is rather small in the frame, but you can sort of see it: a bright brown blob amid a tangle of vegetation. The sound quality, meanwhile, is impressive; you can hear not only the steady chanting of the wren, but also the fainter calls of other species. It's almost as good as being there!

Even better than smartphones are the pocket-size digital recorders that have proliferated—and become quite economical—in recent years. A perfectly serviceable entry-level recorder is yours for under $100. Spend a little bit of time fiddling with the settings (sensitivity, low-frequency filter, mic directionality), and you'll soon be obtaining high-fidelity recordings of just about any bird vocalization. Insects, too, if you're into that.

Next: With easily downloaded freeware like Audacity or Raven Lite, you can perform basic editing. Simple stuff like trimming the recording, removing traffic noise, and amplifying the sound. And, then, if you are so inclined, upload the recording to a crowdsourced website like eBird or Xeno-Canto. In the process, you're practically guaranteed to learn how to see birdsong in spectrograms (§§44–47).

As with learning spectrograms, there's no birding rule that you have to make recordings of bird vocalizations. But doing so powerfully reinforces learning. Not only that, it preserves a special moment. Just press PLAY, and that jaunty Carolina Wren is still hollering from the thicket.

49 WHAT IS BIRDSONG?

Sora
Porzana carolina

IN THE SAME WAY that most bird species have multiple plumages (male versus female, summer versus winter, juvenile versus adult), so many birds give a variety of vocalizations. You can see what's coming next: the inevitable human need to give names to different sorts of bird sounds. To see how this works, let's visit a cattail marsh—one of the best things a birder can do at practically any season of the year, at any time of day or night.

One of the birds in our marsh is a Sora, a plump little rail that likes to hide from view. But it's not shy about saying what's on its mind! The Sora gives two main vocalizations: a descending whinny and a rising whistle. To be spectrographic about it (§§44–47), the whinny runs to more than four seconds and comprises 30+ notes, whereas the rising whistle is a single-note vocalization lasting less than half a second.

What messages does the Sora convey with these utterances? The following is simplified, but, basically, the whinny appears to function as a call and the whistle as a *song*. Songs are given primarily in the context of the breeding season, whereas calls are given year-round; unsurprisingly, the Sora's whinny may be heard in the dead of winter (or any other time of year), but the whistle is heard more often in spring and summer.

Songs are often, but not always, subjectively more complex than calls. As regards the Sora, though, most hearers would probably rate the call as the more complex vocalization. Indeed, if you bop on over to Xeno-Canto, you'll see that there is considerable inconsistency about terminology, with many contributors calling the whinny a song. Other terms are similarly problematic: "Nocturnal flight calls," for example, may be given by birds perched in broad daylight.

Categories like song and call get us only so far. We need to try to listen to what the birds are saying.

50 WHAT THE WOODPECKER SAYS

Red-bellied Woodpecker
Melanerpes carolinus

SASSY AND SHOWY, the Red-bellied Woodpecker is among the most popular birds in its range—basically, the eastern half of the United States. Part of the appeal is no doubt its striking plumage: flaming scarlet on the crown, transverse zebra stripes across the upper surface. But the bird's varied *sounds* also endear it to casual and hard-core birders alike.

All year long, both sexes give an explosive nasal note, a bit less than a tenth of a second, often doubled or trebled. It sounds a lot like the alarm of an eastern gray squirrel. This is the common call, an all-purpose declaration, the Red-belly's way of saying, "Here I am!" Starting in late winter, another vocalization is added to the mix: a wavering or trilled note, lower-pitched than the call, and longer (more than a quarter second). That song, given by territorial males until early summer, functions as a *song*. But not the only song!

The Red-bellied Woodpecker "sings" an entirely different "song," and it does so by bashing its bill into a tree 40 or more times for about 1.75 seconds. This is a nonvocal sound, technically a sonation, and such utterances are common in the bird world. It may not sound musical or tuneful to human ears, but a song it is; like the trilled vocalization, this rapid-fire series is given by males on territory. Yet another sonation is the audible pecking of a bird, male or female, while feeding. They're called wood*peckers* for a reason.

So our Red-belly makes four basic sounds: a vocal call (both sexes, year-round), a vocal song (mainly or exclusively males, late winter–summer), a nonvocal song (the drumming, males only, late winter–spring), and the nonvocal tapping or pecking of foraging birds (both sexes, all year round). The exact terms don't matter. Indeed, the word "sonation" shall not appear again in this book! But the larger point stands: Bird sounds have meaning. And we can learn what birds are saying.

51 HE SAYS, SHE SAYS

Great Horned Owl
Bubo virginianus

ONLY A HANDFUL of bird sounds are known to everyone: the quack of a duck, the squeal of a gull (or "seagull"), and the hooting of an owl. There are many owls, of course, and many of them don't hoot: Barn Owls shriek, Elf Owls yap, and Screech Owls warble. But some of them are honest-to-goodness hooters, and one of them, the Great Horned, is the hooter's hooter. The mellow hooting of this huge owl has been dubbed into the soundtrack of practically all American movies with scenes from cemeteries, haunted houses, and the woods at night.

But which sex is hooting?

The song of the Great Horned Owl—a series of irregularly spaced hoots—is given by both sexes, and it is easy to distinguish male from female. The male typically gives four or five low-pitched hoots, the female usually five to eight slightly higher hoots. What's especially nice is that the male and female often duet, making the differences obvious. With experience, though, the sex of a lone Great Horned Owl—bachelor or bachelorette, widower or widow—can be ascertained.

An objection might have occurred to you. *Females* sing? Until recently, ornithologists believed that female birds, by and large, do not sing. A few exceptions were known: the Northern Cardinal, several warblers, and the Great Horned Owl. But female song was thought to be an aberration. No longer. In recent years, it has been established that female song is pervasive.

Unsurprisingly, university ornithologists have played a leading role in documenting female song. But ordinary birders have likewise been crucial to the effort, due mainly to the proliferation of inexpensive, user-friendly, high-quality digital recorders (§48). The crowdsourced websites Xeno-Canto and eBird prompt the user to input the sex of a singing bird—and, importantly, provide a field for "sex unknown." So the next time you hear a singing bird, see if you can determine its sex—and consider recording the song and uploading it to the internet.

52 NIGHT SHIFT

⋘ ⋘ ⋘ ⋘ ⋘ ⋘ ⋘◇⟫ ⟫ ⟫ ⟫ ⟫ ⟫ ⟫ ⟫

Western Grebe
Aechmophorus occidentalis

YOU'VE HEARD OF a "night owl." Maybe you're one yourself—the sort of person who, for any of a number of reasons, is up and about during the overnight hours. Think of all the convenience store clerks and ER nurses, young parents and mewling infants, light sleepers and late-night revelers, and so many others who populate this world of ours. It's much the same in the bird world.

Owls are no doubt the best known of avian, uh, night owls, but most other birds are partially to highly nocturnal. It probably won't come as a surprise that the birds known as night-herons are nocturnal; ditto for nighthawks, which happen to be in a family of birds known as the nightjars. But many other birds work the night shift as well: Virginia Rails, Marsh Wrens, Common Yellowthroats, American Woodcocks, and Common Loons, to name just a few.

To state the obvious, it's hard to see birds at night. So birding at night is an almost strictly aural undertaking. And without the distraction of visual cues, night birders invariably report that nocturnal vocalists are peculiarly noticeable. The Western Grebe is stunning by day, with its black-tie attire and eyes like garnets—so much so that its disyllabic "advertising call" is something of an afterthought. At night, though, that far-carrying cry is a primal scream, equal parts spine-tingling and bewitching, impossible to ignore and unlikely to be forgotten.

When grebes vocalize at night, they aren't necessarily singing—at least not in the technical sense (§§49–51). Mind you, many birds do sing full-on songs at night: owls for starters, but also many species that sing by day. With our somnambulant Western Grebe, though, we may be hearing nothing more than a simple "Hello" or "Good evening." Or perhaps "Get outta here!" Another grebe is in the vicinity, and one bird is talking to another. Grebes and other birds—like so many human beings—are out at night, doing whatever they do.

53 A TOUCHY SUBJECT: HEARING LOSS

House Finch
Haemorhous mexicanus

THE HOUSE FINCH gets a bad rap. It's a doorstep bird, a garden bird, indeed, according to certain birders, a "trash bird." Across much of this finch's range, it's not even a native species: House Finches, native to the Southwest, were introduced to New York City in the 1940s. They quickly spread, driving the golden spike, as it were, with native House Finch populations well before the end of the 20th century.

The adult male is a dude, a dandy, flaming red on the breast and crown—and noisy! You can hear his boisterous song from inside a moving car with the windows up. Bring the car to a stop and roll down the windows, and the lusty singing of the House Finch attracts the attention of even the avowed nonbirder. The run-on song is twangy and herky-jerky, lacking cadence until it abruptly ends with a telltale metallic element.

The songs and other sounds of birds are meant to be heard, and the male House Finch evidently got the memo. The finch's songs—loud, long, and relatively low-pitched—are intended for conspecifics (members of the same species), but we humans are perfectly capable of listening in. And so it is with most other avian vocalizations: from the honking of geese to the cooing of doves, from the caroling of robins to the chatter of swallows. Most bird sounds are eminently audible to our human ears.

There's this notion, and it's regrettable, that you must have good hearing, whatever that means, to be a good earbirder (§38). Don't believe it! Some of the best earbirders—women and men who write influential books and papers on birdsong—have mediocre hearing. True, they can't hear the handful of especially high-pitched songs they could hear when they were younger: those of the Golden-crowned Kinglet, the Blackpoll Warbler, and a few others. But those species are acoustic outliers.

By all means, take good care of your hearing. Avoid exposure to jet engines and jackhammers, and see an audiologist every once in a while. At the same time, appreciate that earbirding is mostly about what's in your brain and heart.

54 A BEAUTIFUL BIRD

Sandhill Crane
Antigone canadensis

LET'S BE HONEST about something. There are certain birds that only a birder could love: fall warblers and winter sparrows, most gulls and terns, and all "empids" and peeps (small flycatchers and sandpipers, respectively). And we'll add to that list the Great Blue Heron, for a reason we'll return to in a bit.

There are also the sorts of birds that command all of us, birders and nonbirders alike, to stand up and take notice. The Sandhill Crane is one such bird. There are bird festivals devoted entirely to Sandhill Cranes, multiday celebrations of the species; there are crane societies, crane consortiums, and crane coalitions all across the continent; and there are more coffee-table books on cranes than even the biggest coffee table could ever hope to hold.

Why is that? What's the allure of the species? The curious thing is, a Sandhill Crane, standing at the edge of a marsh, is rather ungainly. And a flock of a hundred, foraging in the stubble of a fallow cornfield, is, well, a hundred times more ungainly. The Sandhill Crane is basically a slighter, wimpier, duller version of the Great Blue Heron.

Here's the difference. Great Blues are usually silent, and that's a good thing—because their calls are tormented, retching utterances of white noise. But the bugling of the crane is one of the ultimate emblems of the North American wilderness, in the same league as the howling of wolves and the yodeling of loons. One hears cranes, and one quickly forgets that they are gangly, bug-eyed, frog-eating kissing cousins of the coot clan.

We birders are attracted to birdsong for a variety of reasons: as a field identification aid, as an absorbing intellectual challenge, as a cutting-edge scientific matter, and more. And when we stand at attention before trumpeting cranes, we are compelled by an especially poignant and human impulse: Because birdsong is one of the most powerful and moving of all natural phenomena.

55 THE GREATEST SHOW ON EARTH

Tree Swallow
Tachycineta bicolor

THE MOMENT YOU hear it—a pleasing warble of relatively low-pitched notes, randomly rising and falling in pitch—your spirits are lifted. It doesn't matter that the sky has turned gray in the past hour; light rain is falling now, and the temperature continues to drop. All those annoyances are suddenly insignificant.

You are hearing Tree Swallows, the first of the spring. They're actually among the bad boys of the bird world: forever bickering with one another and aggressive toward other species. But you give them a pass this morning. For one thing, they are stunning: glistening-green above, snow-white below. Their species name, *bicolor*, is apt. So is their genus name: *Tachycineta* combines the Greek words for "swift" *(tachys)* and "moving" *(kineter)*. And it's true: Those Tree Swallows sure fly around fast!

As migratory species go, Tree Swallows are in the middle of the pack. Their migrations extend for "only" many hundreds to a few thousand miles. Nevertheless, they are amazing, weighing in at well under an ounce, yet capable of migrating from Mexico to the coastal plain of the Arctic Ocean. And many of them are second-calendar-year birds, hatched less than 12 months earlier. You couldn't even walk across the room when you were that age. It's even more impressive than that: Those selfsame Tree Swallows completed their first migration back in late summer of the previous year, when they were just *weeks* old! You couldn't crawl—you couldn't even sit up in your crib—at the same age.

How on Earth do they do it? We'll get there (§§56–74), but first things first. First, let's take it all in: Those zippy little emerald-backed creatures are on the wing, and they command us to pay attention *right now*. The sky is full of swallows, at least a hundred, flying north. The spectacle is as marvelous today as when we, or any human, first opened our eyes on the natural world.

56 "FOS"

Swainson's Hawk
Buteo swainsoni

THE BIG BIRD, a hawk, is perched on a wire—and that's enough of a clue. The Red-tailed Hawks present all winter don't normally watch from wires; this is probably something different. You pull the car to a stop, whip out your binoculars, glance at the object, and confirm your suspicion: a Swainson's Hawk, a light-morph adult, your "FOS," or "first of season." It's also an "FOY," shorthand for "first of year," but FOS seems to be preferred by birders—for the simple reason that, for many species, you get to do it again in the fall.

There's an undeniable joy in espying those harbingers of spring. It's a cliché, but we still smile at the sight of crocuses poking up through the snow. And even though mourning cloak butterflies overwinter as adults, there's still something bewitching about seeing one flittering about on a sunny afternoon in later winter. We've all heard about the swallows returning to Capistrano, California (they're Cliff Swallows, to be precise about it), and the buzzards (Turkey Vultures, actually) of Hinckley, Ohio, are only slightly less well known. Robins and bluebirds, too, are famous auguries of the end of winter, but problematically so: Across much of North America, they're actually present throughout the winter months! Old myths die hard . . .

The Swainson's Hawk, though, is the real deal. These birds have just returned from Argentina! That bird on the wire has just flown at least 5,000 miles. Depending on how far north you are and how far south the hawk migrated, the figure approaches 10,000 miles.

In a few days, the sighting of a Swainson's will be perfectly humdrum; the species is common in summer across the western half of the continent. But there was something special about that FOY on the wire—something that impels us to get outside and go birding on those still raw and chilly days in early April, year after year after year.

57 SPRING HAS SPRUNG

Solitary Sandpiper
Tringa solitaria

NEARLY EVERYBODY IN North America is generally aware of the phenomenon of spring migration—the chiefly northward dispersal of birds across the continent during the season of the year that follows winter and precedes summer. But what, and when, exactly, is spring?

The official answer is known to all. Spring in the northern hemisphere begins at the moment of the vernal equinox, around March 20, and runs till the summer solstice, on or about June 21. And across the mid-latitudes of the continent, spring migration is in progress, to a greater or lesser extent, throughout the entire period.

Consider the case of the spring migration of shorebirds, in particular from the vantage point of an observer far from the seacoasts. The first shorebird—a Killdeer winging its way north or an American Woodcock already on territory—may appear as early as mid-February, when winter is still going at full tilt. And the last of the shorebirds—in many regions, White-rumped Sandpipers—are still hastening north after the solstice. This is the lesson of S&D, or status and distribution (§25), and it is of paramount importance to understanding and enjoying bird migration at any time of the year.

Among shorebirds, the slim and wary Solitary Sandpiper is an exemplary spring migrant. In places like Chicago and Philadelphia, sightings before the equinox are practically unheard of. The bulk of the northbound flight of the species coincides with April showers and May flowers. For whatever reason, the Solitary Sandpiper conceives of spring in much the same way we humans do.

For whatever reason. Indeed. What *is* the reason for which this plain-Jane sandpiper's migration peaks in late April and early May, as opposed to late March, say, or early June? We're going to spend the next several lessons (§§58–62) exploring the biological basis of the timing of migration. There is an underlying logic to it all—but not without a few surprises!

58 MIGRATION TIMING: A PARADOX

Orange-crowned Warbler
Oreothlypis celata

MORE THAN 50 SPECIES of wood-warblers in the family Parulidae occur in North America north of Mexico, and all of our species are, to a greater or lesser degree, migratory. Some of them—Pine and Yellow-rumped Warblers—migrate early, mainly in April, through the mid-latitudes. The Lucy's Warbler, a tiny desert dweller, averages earliest of all, with some individuals on the move by late January. Other warblers are at the rearguard of spring migration; the peak flights of Connecticut and Blackpoll Warblers aren't until Memorial Day weekend.

The dingy Orange-crowned Warbler belongs to the early cohort, not quite as early as the Pines and Yellow-rumps, yet well in advance of even the earliest Blackpolls and Connecticuts. When Orange-crowns go through the Midwest and Rocky Mountains, there's still a chill in the air—and sometimes still snow on the ground. What's going on? What's the deal with all this variation in migration timing?

A reasonable first guess might be that the early migrants have the farthest to go—to the boreal forests of Canada and Alaska. Nope. By and large, it's precisely the other way around. The Pine Warbler is a short-distance migrant, wintering in the southeastern United States and breeding no farther north than southeastern Canada. Blackpolls and Connecticuts, in contrast, winter in South America and breed mainly across Canada—even well into Alaska in the case of the Blackpoll.

Our Orange-crowned Warbler—restless and inquisitive, despite its drab attire—fits the model perfectly. It migrates, on average, a bit farther than most Pines and Yellow-rumps (and pretty much all Lucy's), and thus migrates just a bit later in the spring.

This general pattern plays out in many other avian groups: vireos and sandpipers, *Catharus* thrushes and *Empidonax* flycatchers, and so forth and so on. To be clear, there are exceptions to the rule. But the general rule stands: Contrary to what you might think, the birds that have the farthest to go are the ones that migrate last.

59 LEAPFROG MIGRATION

Fox Sparrow
Passerella iliaca

N O MATTER HOW MUCH experience you have with the Fox Sparrow, you always do a double take on seeing one. It's so big! A Fox Sparrow, at first glance, could be mistaken for a thrush. The reddish hues of many Fox Sparrows further contribute to their thrushlike appearance.

There's something else about Fox Sparrows that can trip us up. They show tremendous geographic variation—so much so that many authorities believe that multiple species, perhaps as many as four, are involved. An observer from Nashville or Ottawa, on seeing a Fox Sparrow in San Francisco, might well imagine she's got a new sparrow, a "lifer," in her scope or bins. But her bird is "just" a West Coast Fox Sparrow, technically of the *unalaschcensis* group.

An interesting thing about these West Coast Fox Sparrows, collectively often referred to as "Sooty" Fox Sparrows, is that they themselves exhibit extensive latitudinal variation in their migration strategies. The birds that breed the farthest north (well into the Aleutians) actually winter the farthest *south*, whereas the birds that breed the farthest south (in the Puget Sound region) winter the farthest *north*. This counterintuitive phenomenon is termed the leapfrog migration strategy, and we see it repeatedly among birds breeding in America and elsewhere in the northern hemisphere. Many thrushes, warblers, and sandpipers exhibit leapfrog migrations, both within species and among species.

The leapfrog migration in Sooty Fox Sparrows was painstakingly detailed in a 1920 monograph by ornithologist Harry S. Swarth, but many other leapfrog migrations have been discovered surprisingly recently. For example, a leapfrog migration in the well-studied Golden Eagle was documented only in the 2010s. Not surprisingly, recent technologies like satellite telemetry and geolocators (§163) are proving useful in the elucidation of this and other migratory strategies. It goes without saying that bird migration has been known and appreciated since ancient times; but the actual details are still being worked out—often with unexpected results.

60 THE LOGIC OF MIGRATION: RESOURCE AVAILABILITY

≪≪ ≪≪ ≪≪ ≪≪ ≪≪ ≪≪ ≪≪◁▷≫ ≫≫ ≫≫ ≫≫ ≫≫ ≫≫ ≫≫

Osprey
Pandion haliaetus

T HE DISTINCTIVE OSPREY has one of the most cosmopolitan ranges of any bird on Earth. It can be found on every continent but Antarctica, and many individuals migrate far out at sea. You might think that a bird with so broad a distribution would be a habitat and dietary generalist, but, actually, the Osprey is a textbook case of ecological specialization. Ospreys eat fish. Only big fish. Only big, live fish that they catch for themselves. Ospreys don't scavenge, they don't steal, and they don't mess with minnows and shiners and stuff.

You might see the problem. In places like Finland and Fairbanks, big fish aren't available to Ospreys during the winter. So they migrate each autumn to warmer climes with fish-filled waters. And they return to big lakes in continental interiors shortly after the spring thaw each year. They're hardy; many Ospreys have arrived at mid-latitude water bodies by late March, when it hardly feels like spring. But they must have open water; an Osprey at a frozen lake is a fish out of water.

The migration strategies of many other bird species are closely synchronized with resource availability. Warblers and other insectivorous land birds time their spring migration so as to coincide with bud burst, which, in turn, is when caterpillars begin to emerge; newly hatched caterpillars are, on average, less toxic to birds than their older counterparts, and the hungry migrants feast on them. A particularly compelling example of this phenomenon involves the staging of several shorebird species in spectacular numbers all up and down the Delaware Bay shore in late May, when horseshoe crab eggs are super-abundant. And in the tropics, a great diversity of birds migrate up and down mountainsides in accordance with predictable annual fluctuations in the availability of fruits and nuts.

Resource availability isn't the only determinant of a bird's migratory strategy, but it's a big one. "Feed the birds," Mary Poppins exhorted us. She was a bird biologist without ever knowing it!

61 THE LOGIC OF MIGRATION: WING MORPHOLOGY

Swainson's Thrush
Catharus ustulatus

TAKE A LOOK at a Swainson's Thrush, a migrant at a stopover site, and what do you see? It's brown overall, showing a suffusion of buff if the light is good, but appearing grayer, almost colorless, if the bird is lurking in the shadows. We want a good view, so we linger with our bird till it emerges from a thicket and is standing right in front of us on the trail.

Other field marks come into view: black spots on the breast, gray-brown flanks, relatively bright spectacles, and so forth. A question arises: *Why* does the bird look this way? A thorough consideration of the matter will come later (§§181–184), but for now we'll focus on one field mark that has specific relevance to appreciating bird migration. Our Swainson's Thrush's wingtips are long and dark, nearly black. Again: *Why?*

The Swainson's Thrush is a long-distance migrant, wintering as far south as Argentina and breeding well into Alaska. And it's small, weighing in at barely an ounce. That's right, an *ounce,* not even one percent of the weight of a newborn human. In order to get from Argentina to Alaska—or just the relatively short hop from Costa Rica to Colorado—the bird needs a powerful build. Musculature and metabolism have a lot to do with it, but so does wing morphology. Hence the long wings and blackish wingtips of the Swainson's Thrush.

The long, pointed wings confer aerodynamic advantage, maximizing lift and minimizing drag. And the black pigment signifies a mechanical advantage; it is derived from one or more melanins (§8), molecules with exceptional physical strength, essential for retarding feather wear on the trans-hemispheric journey.

It's a constant theme across a great many avian groups: Long-distance fliers sport long wings with black tips. And it has practical consequences for us as birders: Differences in wing morphology are often discernible in the field, and can be of considerable usefulness in separating look-alike species.

62 THE LOGIC OF MIGRATION: A TALE OF TWO TEALS

Cinnamon Teal
Spatula cyanoptera

THE DRAKE CINNAMON and Blue-winged Teals, despite looking nothing alike, are very closely related. Across a broad swath of the western United States, where the two species occur, hybrids are relatively common. Certain aspects of their ecology are similar as well. For example, both of these ducks are complete migrants, or close to it.

"Complete migration" is a fuzzy term. It depends on which book you're reading. Complete migration can refer to the phenomenon whereby all individuals of a species migrate, but it also signifies the situation in which the summer and winter ranges of a migratory species do not overlap. For sure, it can be both of those things.

Most duck species are not complete migrants, and that makes the return of the teal especially sweet for American birders. A drake teal—Cinnamon or Blue-winged—poking about the sparkling waters of a fresh-thawed marsh is a sure sign that spring has sprung. For birders in eastern North America, the Blue-winged Teal is just about the last duck to get back each spring. In the West, though, the Cinnamon Teal is typically the very *first* duck to return!

Latitude likely has something to do with it. Blue-winged Teal migrate considerably farther, on average, than their Cinnamon counterparts. The North American breeding range of the Cinnamon Teal barely touches Canada, but some Blue-wings make it all the way to Alaska; and during the winter months, our Cinnamon Teal withdraw mainly to Mexico, whereas many Blue-wings get as far south as South America. Thus, we predict that Blue-wings should migrate later than Cinnamons (§58) and that they should leapfrog over them (§59).

Wing morphology comes into play here, too. Even though the Cinnamon Teal averages heavier and longer overall than the Blue-winged, it is the Blue-winged that has a greater wingspan. This, too, is something we might have predicted: Longer migration equals longer wings (§61).

The lesson ought to be clear enough: Migration makes sense. But there's still one nagging problem, which we turn to presently.

63 WHY DO BIRDS MIGRATE?

Wilson's Warbler
Cardellina pusilla

Y OU'RE WALKING QUIETLY along a trail in the Guatemalan rain forest, enraptured by a motmot here, a trogon there, humming-birds everywhere. You're supposed to be searching for a Resplendent Quetzal, seen yesterday in the vicinity, but you can't resist the temptation to gawk at *yet another* Crescent-chested Warbler. There are gaudy warblers back home, of course, but this one is over the top: yellow, blue, green, gray, black, and white, with a blood-red slash across the breast. The Crescent-chest descends to eye level, where it is joined by a perfectly prosaic Wilson's Warbler, yellow overall with a black cap, its tail habitually cocked. The species is familiar to almost anybody who has gone looking for warblers in Canada or the continental United States. And that gets you to thinking about something.

The birds seem to have it good here, and the Crescent-chested Warblers sensibly stay put. They are more or less permanent residents. But the Wilson's depart en masse each year for northern climes. Why? The biannual migration is arduous, to say the least, killing a substantial fraction of the population every year. Wouldn't it make more sense to spend the whole year in the rain forest with the resident species?

Difficult question. The rain forest, despite its apparent plenty, probably cannot support breeding populations of the Wilson's Warbler. So the birds get out of Dodge—or Quetzaltenango—and repopulate their sprawling breeding grounds farther north. But that doesn't really answer the question, does it? What force or forces compel Wilson's Warblers to migrate, but Crescent-chested Warblers to be comparatively sedentary? It's in their genes, of course, but that still doesn't answer the question. Why has one species evolved to be *this* way, and another *that* way?

In posing these questions, we've entered the realm of life history theory, which combines theory, observation, and experiment to understand the diversity of biological strategies of birds and other organisms. Life history theory is a relatively young discipline, developed in the latter half of the 20th century. We're still in the question-asking phase, and that's exciting.

64 LIFE HISTORY THEORY: FLAPPY FLIERS FLY AT NIGHT

⋘ ⋘ ⋘ ⋘ ⋘ ⋘ ⋘⟨⟩⟫ ⋙ ⋙ ⋙ ⋙ ⋙ ⋙ ⋙

Yellow-billed Cuckoo
Coccyzus americanus

HE SOUND IS loud and resonant and, more than anything else, weird: a descending gurgle, a self-absorbed chuckle, as if its utterer were just a bit mad. This is the flight call of the Yellow-billed Cuckoo, rarely heard by day but routinely heard by folks who go birding at night. We already know that a great many birds are active at night (§52), but the idea that birds actually *migrate* by night still comes as a surprise to some birders. And we're not talking about a trickle of migrants, engaged in short-distance flights across the township or county.

Our cuckoo may well have been flying for hours, and there's nothing to stop it. The bird will keep flying till daybreak and perhaps beyond. On a good night, you might hear a dozen or more Yellow-billed Cuckoos. But that's nothing compared to all the warblers, sparrows, and thrushes you're hearing—easily thousands, perhaps tens of thousands. Now expand that idea geographically, and you realize that *millions* of birds might migrate over your state or province during the course of a single night.

There's a saying among the ornithologists who study migration: Flappy fliers fly at night. Although many larger birds—hawks, waterfowl, cranes, etc.—typically migrate by day, cuckoos and other small birds—call them "flappy fliers"—do it at night. Why? As is so often the case in life history theory, multiple forces are no doubt acting in concert. First off, it's probably safer: By flying under cover of darkness, small birds avoid the predatory hawks, falcons, and gulls that tend not to be active at night. Second, aerodynamics: The air at night is, on average, less choppy than it is by day. Third, and this may sound a bit odd: Because they can't do other things at night. Hence the fly-all-night, feed-all-day strategy of many migrants.

Next question: How do they do it? For starters, how do they even see where they're going?

65 HOW DO NOCTURNAL MIGRANTS KNOW WHERE TO GO?

Indigo Bunting
Passerina cyanea

ARLY EACH AUTUMN, millions of hatch-year Indigo Buntings migrate from the species' breeding grounds in the United States and southern Canada to their wintering grounds in Middle America and the Caribbean. These birds are only weeks old, yet they somehow find their way across the continent. Not only that, they do so chiefly at night (§64). They've never done it before! They simply get up and go, arriving in Nicaragua or Hispaniola a month or two later. It is as though they were endowed with an inborn, or innate, sense of direction. But that's not quite right.

In the case of the Indigo Bunting, the bird actually *learns* a star chart soon after hatching. Behavioral ecologist Stephen Emlen, in a series of experiments with captive buntings in planetariums, showed in the 20th century that Indigo Buntings learn to recognize the rotation of the night sky around the North Star—and to fly south in the opposite direction. If you trick a captive bunting and rotate the planetarium around the wrong star, the bunting adjusts and migrates relative to this new definition of north. *That. Is. Amazing.*

Flight calls also play a role. The flight call of the Indigo Bunting, like that of the Yellow-billed Cuckoo (§64), is distinctive and easily recognized—not only by humans, but also by other Indigo Buntings. As the birds fly over at night on spring and fall migration, they constantly utter their flight calls as they go. Think of it as a homing beacon, like an airplane pilot's constantly updated flight plan.

The airplane metaphor is apt in another way. Just as pilots may switch from visual flight rules (VFR) to instrument flight rules (IFR) if weather conditions deteriorate, so can many bird species go to a sort of backup navigation system if the night sky is overcast. For sure, clear skies with a gentle tailwind are preferred. But a bird without a star map isn't necessarily flying blind. To learn more, we'll turn now to the extraordinary navigational abilities of a nonmigratory species.

66 FLYING BLIND

⋘ ⋘ ⋘ ⋘ ⋘ ⋘ ⋘◇⟫ ⟫ ⟫ ⟫ ⟫ ⟫ ⟫ ⟫

Rock Pigeon
Columba livia

FIRST, A DEFINITION. The species known to birders and scientists as the Rock Pigeon is simply the familiar city pigeon. Both names work. Pigeons flourish in cities, we all know, but they also occur in the rimrock-and-canyon wildernesses of the American West. Many of them commute daily between the two utterly different habitats, traversing miles of desert or forest, largely undeterred by headwinds and precipitation. But there's one thing Rock Pigeons can't do: They can't, or at least they won't, fly under cover of darkness.

So you might think they navigate by ground-based landmarks they can't see at night. That's presumably the case, but it's not the end of the story. It is possible to impair a pigeon's vision, either with surgery or with special goggles, in such a way that it can still see light but cannot distinguish among objects in the landscape. And if you do that, the bird *will* fly—with astonishing accuracy. Pigeons blindfolded in this manner have been released from spots hundreds of miles from home. They then fly straight back home, not stopping until they are directly above their starting point, whereupon they put on the brakes and flutter downward, coming to rest within their cote!

We're still not sure exactly how they do this, but decades of experiments have shown that pigeons see the environment in ways we cannot. They are able to perceive polarized light, ultraviolet light, and even the Earth's magnetic field. They can also sense infrasound, far too low for humans to perceive, and they may follow their nose via olfactory signals. (Pigeons cannot navigate with sonar, as far as we know, but the cave-dwelling Oilbird of South America actually can.)

Any one of these sensory inputs is probably inadequate for pigeons to navigate blindfolded those many miles. Instead, they likely apply an integrative approach, processing multiple stimuli simultaneously. And although pigeons have received particularly close scrutiny from researchers, it is believed that many other species possess similar navigational capabilities.

67 MIGRANTS POWERED BY HYPERPHAGIA

⋘⋘ ⋘⋘ ⋘⋘ ⋘⋘ ⋘⋘ ⋘⋘ ⋘⟨⟩⟩⟩ ⟫⟫ ⟫⟫ ⟫⟫ ⟫⟫ ⟫⟫ ⟫⟫ ⟫⟫

Ruby-throated Hummingbird
Archilochus colubris

THERE ARE TWO WAYS to get from the Yucatán Peninsula to the central Gulf Coast of the United States. One route is to go around the long way, overland, hugging the coasts of Veracruz and Tamaulipas, and then Texas. Ornithologists call this strategy circum-Gulf migration, and it is favored by several migrants we've already met, including the Tree Swallow (§55), the Orange-crowned Warbler (§58), and the Indigo Bunting (§65). An alternative, and more drastic, solution is to fly straight across the Gulf of Mexico. Swainson's Thrushes (§61) and Yellow-billed Cuckoos (§64) apply this trans-Gulf strategy. So do Ruby-throated Hummingbirds.

From Mérida, the capital city of Yucatán, to New Orleans (*not* the capital of Louisiana), the shortest distance is about 625 miles. That's the equivalent of 24 marathons. Our hummingbird, meanwhile, weighs in at three grams, or, equivalently a tenth of an ounce. *It weighs less than a sheet of paper.*

Marathoners "carbo-load" in preparation for the big race, and Ruby-throated Hummingbirds do something similar. But much more extreme. It's referred to as *hyperphagia*, combining the roots *hyper-* ("a lot") and *-phagia* ("of eating"). The metabolic details are complicated, but the short version is that the birds gorge themselves on nectar (natural or artificial) and arthropods (especially spiders) in the days leading up to the Gulf crossing, converting the food to fat, which they burn off during the nonstop flight.

The fuel efficiency of migrants is staggering. The Blackpoll Warbler, which overflies a substantial chunk of the Atlantic Ocean on its fall migration from Canada to South America, burns fat at a rate of 750,000 miles per gallon. Running out of gas isn't an option, by the way, for a hummingbird or a warbler flying over open water. They can't land for a while and rest. Even if they could, they wouldn't be able to refuel; there aren't hummingbird feeders and aphid-filled hemlocks out in the middle of the Gulf of Mexico. They do it all on a single tank. And that ought to humble even the proudest Prius engineer.

68 FALLOUT!

Sanderling
Calidris alba

I N THE 2011 MOVIE *The Big Year,* one of the protagonists bursts into his boss's office and announces that he won't be coming to work. He breathlessly declares, "There is going to be major fallout in a few hours!"

His boss inquires with a mix of concern and bewilderment: "Nuclear fallout?"

The protagonist, played by Jack Black, sets the record straight: "Bird fallout . . . I'm talking about a major storm hitting the Gulf of Mexico in the middle of migration season; I'm talking about headwinds and downpours and a hundred thousand birds literally dropping from the sky!"

Avian fallouts are dramatic and problematic.

Dramatic: A trio of Sanderlings, uncommon in spring in your county, are scampering across the swim beach at a reservoir near your home. Yesterday afternoon, the beach and reservoir had been devoid of birdlife. The weather was too nice. But a storm came in overnight, grounding migrants on passage. You catch movement out the corner of your eye, and you see another, larger flock of frenetic Sanderlings, at least a dozen. You get on the phone and notify the birding public that a fallout is under way.

Problematic: Fallouts are undeniably dramatic, but they aren't good for birds. A fallout is, at best, a delay. Our swim beach Sanderlings, now numbering 20+ (a new spring record for the county!), don't really want to be there with you. And as soon as the weather clears, they'll be on the move again. These animated sandpipers have quite a ways to go. To say that Sanderlings are Arctic breeders is an understatement; most breed only in the so-called high Arctic of Ellesmere Island and the northern shores of Baffin Island and Alaska.

Fallouts are, to a large extent, predictable. The Jack Black character in *The Big Year* got it right: Headwinds + downpours = birds dropping from the sky. If bad weather is forecast, call in sick. Go birding. Experience the problematic drama of a fallout.

69 "VIS MIG"

Franklin's Gull
Leucophaeus pipixcan

"ENGLAND AND AMERICA are two countries separated by a common language," George Bernard Shaw is said to have quipped. So it is in the realm of birding. An American birder in Britain quickly becomes lost in all the talk of "blockers" and "Sibes," of "dudes" and "robin strokers," of being "gripped off," of "PG Tips," and more—a fair bit of it unpublishable.

Several of the entries in the British birder's lexicon are useful and descriptive, and have caught on in recent years on this side of The Pond. For example, "vis mig," short for v̲i̲sible m̲i̲gration. Rhymes with "fizz pig," and it denotes the act or experience of witnessing migration as it actually happens. Vis mig gets the blood flowing. Sometimes it is startling.

Picture yourself on a fine but breezy morning in late April. The first of the warblers have returned, and the House Wrens and Brown Thrashers are back. Then you hear it: anxious, urgent squealing above the budding trees. You scamper down the trail to a clearing, you look up, and you see them: a string of Franklin's Gulls powering straight north. They are absolutely stunning, with bright pink breasts; their heads are jet black except for white marks above and below the eye. Those eye crescents give the impression of someone staring through an executioner's hood.

Their flight style appears leisurely, even buoyant, but that is deceptive. These birds are going fast! They've got places to go. They're soon out of earshot, and, in a couple minutes, they are gone, beyond the reach of your binoculars. Franklin's Gulls are long-distance migrants; most winter off the west coast of South America, especially near Lima, Peru. They take migration seriously, and you feel blessed to have glimpsed them on the home stretch of their long journey north. Vis mig refers to a material phenomenon, of course, but that's not really the point. Vis mig is an experience.

70 LAYOVER

Least Flycatcher
Empidonax minimus

S
OME BIRDS SEEM disinclined to join in the pageantry of spring migration. The Least Flycatcher, for example. Many individuals of this species migrate under cover of darkness, so vis mig (§69) is out. Don't bother listening for Least Flycatchers amid the chorus of nocturnal migrants (§64–65), either; the species appears to lack a flight call. And although any migratory species can get caught up in a fallout (§68), Least Flycatchers tend not to; they engage in a fairly protracted and broad-front spring migration that blunts the impact of fallout conditions. The Least Flycatcher is an unremarkable yet efficient migrant.

Go out on a typical morning during the peak of their spring migration through the eastern United States, and you will see them in the high single digits. Least Flycatchers don't flock, but neither are they randomly distributed across the landscape. They favor bits of greenery with places to rest, hide, and, most importantly, feed. Studies of "time budgets" for birds on these migratory layovers indicate that feeding occupies the vast bulk of their time during the daytime hours. It's not just that they're hungry. Many of them also have a metabolic need to bop around, as they start to lose energy when they sit still for too long.

Certain stopover sites, referred to as migrant traps, are legendary in birding lore. East of the Rockies, where you are most likely to find migrating Least Flycatchers, these sites include a "Magic Hedge" in Chicago (really, that's its name), the "Ramble" in New York City's Central Park, Mount Auburn Cemetery in Cambridge, Massachusetts; Magee Marsh (near Toledo, Ohio); and Point Pelee (the southernmost point in Canada). But any woodlot or hedgerow, adequately provisioned with newly hatched insects, is sufficient. Such places do not necessarily attract our attention, but they play an essential role in the annual cycle of the no-nonsense Least Flycatcher, the little gray bird that migrates with little fanfare, with or without our notice.

71 CHECK THE WEATHER BEFORE YOU GO OUT!

≪≪ ≪≪ ≪≪ ≪≪ ≪≪ ≪≪ ≪≪ ◇ ≫≫ ≫≫ ≫≫ ≫≫ ≫≫ ≫≫ ≫≫

Broad-winged Hawk
Buteo platypterus

SEVERE WEATHER CAN INDUCE dramatic migration phenomena like fall-outs (§68), but the effects of weather are typically more subtle. Still, if you have a general read on weather conditions—especially with regard to the regional "wind field"—you can get surprisingly good at anticipating migration events in your area. For example, the first push of spring-migrant Broad-winged Hawks up the I-25 corridor of Colorado and Wyoming often coincides with southeasterly winds, ideally on the heels of several days of over-cast and winds out of the north or west. Under such conditions, the birds are almost invariably seen in flight, often quite a ways up, sailing straight north.

Awareness of the tight coupling of April southerlies and Broad-wing flights was achieved relatively recently, through the efforts of dedicated folks at seasonal hawk watches and rank-and-file birders contributing reports to the internet. The key insight was that this is a regional phenomenon, that you need to pay attention to wind conditions a hundred or more miles to the south. That lesson has broad applicability.

Broad-winged Hawks are circum-Gulf migrants (§67), so don't look for them amid the throngs of birds coming in off the Gulf of Mexico. But *do* look for trans-Gulf migrants about 18–24 hours following the occurrence of light northerly winds across the Yucatán Peninsula. You won't experience a fallout, but you will see many incoming migrants nevertheless—and you will do so because you checked the weather 500+ miles away. Other examples abound: everything from overland flights of nighthawks to inshore passages of tubenoses (seabirds usually seen far from shore).

"Everybody talks about the weather," the saying goes, "but nobody does anything about it." That's not really true of birders, though, who rejigger their weekend schedules and even call in sick when the weather forecast favors an April Broad-winged flight—or any of countless other migration phenomena. And it's certainly not true of the birds themselves, for whom wind speed and direction can be a life-or-death matter.

72 RADAR ORNITHOLOGY

Black-and-white Warbler
Mniotilta varia

I**F YOU ARE** a birder over a certain age, you doubtless recall how you used to be able to get a recorded weather forecast by telephone. You would dial the number, hold the receiver up to your ear, and listen to the recording. Today we still use our phones to get the weather, but in ways we couldn't have dreamt of in the 20th century.

It's the middle of the night, and you're up and about for whatever reason. You check your phone, and you see that birds are migrating over your area right now. You grab a light jacket, slip on a pair of sandals, and step outside. You can hear a few thrushes, bell-like and rather low-pitched, but this is mainly a sparrows-and-warblers flight. Their flight calls are generally similar: short, clipped, and high-pitched. But there are differences. One common call has a hard, hissing quality about it; this is the flight call of the Black-and-white Warbler, fairly distinctive for a hearer with sufficient practice.

For 15 or 20 minutes you stand there mesmerized, simply taking it all in. It's not just the river of migrants that amazes you; it's also the fact that you found out about this phenomenon in the first place. Animated radar loops in real time—who knew? Not so long ago, nobody had any idea that you could view bird migration via the U.S. National Weather Service's NEXRAD (<u>next</u>-generation <u>radar</u>) network of Doppler radar stations. That all changed when Clemson University ornithologist Sidney Gauthreaux had the insight in the late 20th century that certain radars can indeed detect birds and other flying animals. And today we get it on our phones! Google your location + BASE REFLECTIVITY, and you're set.

Doppler radar can't distinguish among different species—yet. It might one day be possible to separate large birds like ducks from small birds like Black-and-white Warblers, but distinguishing among the various warblers seems unlikely given current technology. Then again, few if any of us foresaw the day (or night) that we would use our phones to view bird radar.

73 MORNING FLIGHT

American Redstart
Setophaga ruticilla

THE GROUP OF birders has assembled right on time. Pleasantries are exchanged, coffee mugs are topped off, and the field trip leader offers a general encouragement: Winds were light and southerly overnight (§71), and Doppler radar (§72) was lit up with birds. But the first hour of birding is decidedly slow: a few resident species singing on territory, ducks at the duck pond, a couple of roosting raptors, and practically no migrants.

Then the sun hits the treetops, revealing a dazzling adult male American Redstart, a migratory species in the area. An instant later, another redstart pops into view; this one is a second-year male, an odd mix of olive-yellow, dirty black, and dull orange, distinct from the gleaming orange-and-black of the older male. In a moment, the tree is loaded with migrants: a half-dozen warblers of two or three species, a fidgety kinglet, and a methodical vireo. *Where'd they all come from?* It's almost as if they arrived on those first beams of sunlight in the treetops. And that, strange as it may sound, is pretty close to the truth.

In the hour or so after sunrise, American Redstarts and other nocturnal migrants often keep on going. Why? One reason isn't terribly surprising: Especially on cool mornings, insects are inactive; it makes more sense for migrants to push on a bit longer, not putting down till the sun begins to warm the vegetation. Basically, they're waiting for breakfast to cook. Another reason, less intuitive but complementary with the first, has been brought to light by recent advances in the biotelemetry of migrating birds: On cold mornings, passerines actually expend less energy in full-on migratory flight than sitting around waiting for breakfast.

The phenomenon we're talking about is referred to alternately as morning flight or onward migration. For a cutting-edge challenge in bird ID, see if you can visually identify individual birds as they fly over in the dawn's early light. Or just relax: Enjoy your own breakfast, then join the birds for theirs.

74 MIGRATION TOGGLE SWITCH

Rufous Hummingbird
Selasphorus rufus

WHAT GOES UP, must go down. That adage applies well to tennis balls tossed in the air, and you might think it applies to bird migration. In the broadest sense, that's true: The birds that hurry north each spring do indeed journey back south in the autumn. But fall migration isn't just a rewind of spring migration.

The bulk of the spring migration of the Rufous Hummingbird is early and westerly. These glowing orange balls of energy reach California by February, Washington state by March, and southeastern Alaska by May. Yes, Alaska. This species, diminutive even among the hummers, migrates farther relative to its body length than any other bird on Earth (§23). On return to their West Mexican wintering grounds, though, Rufous Hummingbirds take a very different route—through and even well to the east of the southern Rockies. This west-in-the-spring/east-in-the-fall pattern, termed "elliptical migration," is repeated by a great diversity of species: Townsend's Warbler, Cassin's Vireo, American Golden-Plover, White-rumped Sandpiper, and others. Rarer is an east-in-the-spring/west-in-the-fall strategy, performed by the Ovenbird and a few other species.

The duration of migration also differs between spring and fall, with the southbound migration being more protracted in many species than the northward movements in spring. That is a coarse generalization, though, varying among and even within species. Within species: Banding studies have shown that male and female Rufous Hummingbirds differ in how fast they migrate in spring compared with in fall. Other seasonal differences involve diet, energy budgets, and flocking behavior.

The analogy of rewinding the tape doesn't work, but how about the idea of a toggle switch? Going from spring to fall is like hitting the CAPS LOCK key. You're still typing, but the result looks very different. Keep that thought on the back burner. It's going to be a while before we experience fall migration (§§126–141); but when we get there, we're going to see that it offers fresh new insights into bird biology.

PART THREE

NOW WHAT?

June–July

75 NOW WHAT?

Killdeer
Charadrius vociferus

THE MUDFLAT WAS teeming with migrating sandpipers a week ago, but today they are gone. Just yesterday, you saw a White-crowned Sparrow and heard a Swainson's Thrush, both migratory species where you live. They, too, have departed. Spring migration is over. Dejected, you and your birding buddy head back to the bike rack and agree to meet up again in the fall.

Migration withdrawal, it is termed, only half-jokingly. Time to mow the lawn or watch *Law & Order* reruns or whatever else one does in between spring and fall migration. Fortunately, the affliction is short-lived. The birderly disposition is fundamentally sunny, and the onset of migration withdrawal is commonly reversed as fast as you can say "Killdeer!"

The big bird is standing on the mudflat in front of you and your companion, and it's not going anywhere. This plover is one of the handful of shorebirds that will spend the whole summer with you. The Killdeer is a common breeder in your area, and this one probably has a nest nearby. The bird is boldly patterned below; its tail is orange and impressively long; and its oversize eye is perfectly ringed by a thin circle of blood-red bare skin. You take a few steps closer, and the bird does something odd: It crouches down, fans its orange tail, and emits a low, slow trill. You get even closer, and the bird lurches into flight—barely. This is the "broken wing" display of a Killdeer with a nest nearby; the bird is trying to fake you out, to lure you away from its young or its eggs. You could spend the whole summer studying this one fascinating species!

The summer months are, for many birders, a time to intensify their contributions to the science of ornithology. In the lessons that follow, we're going to see that there are more opportunities than ever before for citizen-scientists to get involved, to make a difference, and to have a lot of fun in the process.

76 CONFIRMED!

<<< <<< <<< <<< <<< <<< <<<>>> >>> >>> >>> >>> >>> >>>

Turkey Vulture
Cathartes aura

AWAY FROM OUR big cities, the Turkey Vulture is one of the most widespread and easily spotted birds in the summer months in the Lower 48 and southern Canada. Just look up! In many places, TVs are aloft continually through the warmer hours of the day. On overcast days or early in the morning on sunny days, you might see one or a dozen perched—typically in trees, less commonly on buildings and outcroppings. You get the picture: This is a common bird, easily observed.

Despite its ubiquity, the Turkey Vulture holds a special place in the hearts of birders who participate in state and provincial Breeding Bird Atlas (BBA) projects. A BBA is pretty much what it sounds like: an atlas, or map, showing where birds breed. For most BBAs, the boots on the ground are rank-and-file birders, volunteers who pound the pavement—and the fields and forests—in search of nesting birds. And one of the greatest thrills of atlasing is to confirm breeding by the Turkey Vulture.

Huh? Didn't we just say that the species is utterly commonplace? That's true, but it is also mythically hard to confirm as a breeder. Turkey Vultures place their nests in such venues as caves, cliffs, and deep within hollow logs. Chances are, some enterprising Turkey Vulture has made its nest in a hollow log that rolled into a cave on a cliff face! Unlike most other birds, vultures are rarely caught in the act of carrying prey or other foodstuffs back to a presumptive nest; instead, they regurgitate offal to their young. And they are famously furtive around their nests, timing their comings and goings so as to avoid the prying eyes of BBA volunteers.

Rare indeed is the birder who spends a summer day afield and somehow avoids laying eyes on one, two, or a hundred Turkey Vultures. Rarer still is the birder who can lay claim to having confirmed nesting by the species.

77 A SUMMER PROJECT

⋘ ⋘ ⋘ ⋘ ⋘ ⋘ ⋘ ⋘◇⋙ ⋙ ⋙ ⋙ ⋙ ⋙ ⋙ ⋙

Red-eyed Vireo
Vireo olivaceus

"JUST ANOTHER BORE" is the assessment of your companion. Yes, but you note that it's "CF." The two of you watch together until you realize this is an "ATE" situation.
What on Earth is going on?

Answer: You are participants in your state or province's Breeding Bird Atlas (BBA, §76), and you're trying to confirm nesting by the Red-eyed Vireo, or Red-eye for short. This is the "preacher bird" in colloquial parlance, a slow-moving, canopy-loving, olive-gray birdlet that sings right through the midday hours. The species is abundant in broadleaf forests in the eastern United States and southern Canada, so much so that atlasers have adopted the shorthand BORE—denoting just another bloody ole Red-eye. One of the best ways to confirm nesting is to catch birds in the act of carrying food (CF) to nestlings. But you have to stay with the bird for a while to make sure you're interpreting the behavior correctly; what if the vireo gobbles down the caterpillar for itself, instead of delivering the prey to dependent young? When this happens, the bird ate the evidence (ATE), and breeding has not been confirmed.

One gets the sense that atlasing is a lot of fun. What starts off as a wary agreement to study birds for a couple mornings quickly leads to a summertime of obsession. You find yourself overcome by a peculiar need to confirm breeding by as many species as possible in your atlas block, an area of a few square miles. In due course, you may take on two or three additional blocks. And in extreme cases, you may enlist in a blockbusting effort, rapidly covering as many blocks as possible in the closing years of an atlas project. That's right, BBAs are multiyear undertakings; it is possible to devote a sizable chunk of your birding life to atlasing.

No two ways about it, there is a special satisfaction to be had in the documentation of confirmed breeding—even in common species like the Red-eyed Vireo. But we haven't addressed one key matter: What is the point of the BBA?

78 A MODEST PROPOSAL

Hooded Merganser
Lophodytes cucullatus

THE IDEA IS conceptually straightforward: Create a map showing where Hooded Mergansers breed in New York state. And while you're at it: Show how the species' breeding range in the state has changed over the course of the past couple decades. Identifying the bird isn't the hard part: For most of the year, the adult male Hoodie, with his wild 'do and high-contrast feather patterns, sports just about the most absurdly awesome plumage of any bird on Earth; the female, although not as gaudily attired, is nevertheless one of the most distinctively shaped ducks in North America, or anywhere else, for that matter. No, the hard part is that New York is nearly 50,000 square miles, an impossibly large area for even the most dedicated birder to survey.

But what if you pooled the efforts of *thousands* of birders? Enter the Breeding Bird Atlas (BBA, §§76–77). The BBA is remarkable for being big science conducted by amateurs. The BBA was "crowdsourcing" before crowdsourcing was even a thing.

The Hooded Merganser range map in the New York BBA is highly detailed, with some big patterns overall: the densest concentration in the Adirondacks, none at all on Long Island, the five boroughs, or the counties immediately north of New York City, and scattered occurrences at lower elevations upstate. An accompanying change map shows how the Hooded Merganser's population in the state is anything but stable: expanding in the upstate lowlands, withdrawing a bit from the species' redoubt in the Adirondacks, and completely extirpated from Long Island.

The range maps and change maps in *The Second Atlas of Breeding Birds in New York State* are the heart and soul of a big book that reports a big science project of great interest to pure and applied biologists. And not just New York; most other states and provinces have produced one or two atlases of their own, just as thorough, just as credible, and just as important as New York's. Who said birders only look at birds?

79 HOW MANY BIRDS ARE THERE?

≪≪ ≪≪ ≪≪ ≪≪ ≪≪ ≪≪ ≪≪◇≫ ≫≫ ≫≫ ≫≫ ≫≫ ≫≫ ≫≫

House Wren
Troglodytes aedon

CERTAIN BIRDS—FOR EXAMPLE, rails, creepers, and various grassland and marshland sparrows—seem determined to thwart human efforts at detecting them. The House Wren is not such a bird. A singing House Wren is impossible to ignore; the song is rollicking and effervescent, it runs on and on, and it is amazingly loud for so small a bird. Drive down a country lane with the car window open, and you get the impression that the species is continually within earshot. A question comes to mind: How many are there?

For a first stab at the analysis, consult the House Wren map in a Breeding Bird Atlas (BBA, §§76–78). If you're in the northern two-thirds of the Lower 48 states, you'll see that an awful lot of squares ("blocks") are highlighted in a dark color, indicating that the species was present and confirmed as a breeder when the atlas project itself was in progress. But that's an extremely rudimentary measure of abundance, a simple indication of presence versus absence. BBAs are not intended to estimate abundance. However, a different citizen-science initiative, the North American Breeding Bird Survey (BBS), is designed with that very purpose in mind.

We're going to spend the next couple lessons looking at how BBS data can be used to measure bird populations. But, for now, let's address something more fundamental: How do you conduct a BBS? Briefly, it's a survey of birds seen and heard at half-mile intervals along a 25-mile driving route. You get out of your car, watch and listen (especially the latter!) for three minutes, jot down what you detected, and move along to the next stop.

Hypothetically: You see one House Wren at your first stop, you hear two at the second, you see and hear zero at your third stop, and so forth and so on all the way to the 50th stop (heard two, saw one). You've done your part! The next step in the process: some serious number crunching by the biostatisticians who run the BBS.

80 HOW MANY BIRDS WERE THERE?

$\lll$ $\lll$ $\lll$ $\lll$ $\lll$ $\lll$ $\lll$ $\Diamond$ $\ggg$ $\ggg$ $\ggg$ $\ggg$ $\ggg$ $\ggg$ $\ggg$

Cliff Swallow
Petrochelidon pyrrhonota

Y OU'RE IN THE MIDST of your Breeding Bird Survey (BBS, §79), at the 20th of the 50 data-collection points along a 25-mile driving route. You've been piling on the Yellow Warblers and House Wrens, and now you hear a new one: a twangy note, soft and rolling, given by a bird in flight. You're pretty sure you know this call, but you want to be certain: Yep, it's a Cliff Swallow, heading your way, its "headlights" (a creamy-white patch on the forehead) fixed right on you. You've been doing this BBS route for a decade, but this is your first detection of a Cliff Swallow. You get another at the next stop, and then you hit the jackpot at stop #31: at least a dozen adults entering a culvert, the site of a newly constructed nesting colony. Birders have mused that the species ought to be renamed the Culvert Swallow, and you see why.

The overarching power of the BBS is that each route is repeated year after year after year. That permits analysis of long-term population trends. A Cliff Swallow detection by itself is pitifully insignificant from a scientific perspective. But compare the number of detections this year versus last year, or this decade versus last decade, and you're starting to get somewhere. Now pool the data from thousands of BBS routes, repeated annually, and you have one of the most valuable biological monitoring programs in the history of science.

According to the BBS, the Cliff Swallow has been increasing by around .75 percent per year during the past 50 years. And the House Wren, which we met last time (§79), has also been increasing, although by a modest .25 percent per year. Such trends—upward for Cliff Swallows and House Wrens, but downward for many other species—are of major interest to bird biologists everywhere. And to think: It all starts with birders devoting one morning, admittedly a long morning, per summer to counting birds.

81 A CHALLENGE FOR ORNITHOLOGY: HABITAT BIAS

⋘⋘ ⋘⋘ ⋘⋘ ⋘⋘ ⋘⋘ ⋘⋘ ⋘⟨⟩⋙ ⋙⋙ ⋙⋙ ⋙⋙ ⋙⋙ ⋙⋙ ⋙⋙

Western Kingbird
Tyrannus verticalis

KENN KAUFMAN'S BIRDING MEMOIR, *Kingbird Highway*, takes its name from a bit of bird biology: Kingbirds are the sorts of birds you see along roadsides. *Kingbird Highway* is a book about hitchhiking across America, and Kaufman must have encountered thousands of kingbirds in the course of his travels. Western Kingbirds, in particular, have a thing for the highways and byways of the continent. These lemon-and-gray flycatchers love to perch on fences, wires, billboards, and practically anything else you might see along a road; kingbirds catch flying insects, sometimes scooping them up from right in front of an oncoming semi.

Given that the North American Breeding Bird Survey (BBS, §§79–80) is a car-based and road-based study, it will come as no surprise that the Western Kingbird is well represented in the field notebooks of project volunteers. Indeed, the species is, in a statistical sense, *overrepresented* by the BBS. In contrast, the wood-pewees, forest-loving relatives of the kingbirds that eschew roadsides, are *underrepresented* by the BBS. Fortunately, the survey has been designed in such a manner as to eliminate these biases. The devil is in the details, of course, but the basic principle is straightforward: Any bias—a surfeit of kingbirds, a paucity of wood-pewees—ought to be consistent year after year after year. In the all-important BBS population trend analyses (§80), then, the average annual population change should be unbiased on a species-by-species basis.

What if the habitat along the road changes? The BBS has been running for more than 50 years, during which time roadside woodlands have been cleared (more kingbirds), old pastures have been reclaimed by saplings (fewer kingbirds), and so forth. The wizards at the BBS have ways of incorporating habitat conversion into their analyses, and they have even addressed one of the most vexing of questions in the analysis of long-term datasets: What about changes not in the things observed (kingbirds), but, rather, in the observers themselves?

82 A CHALLENGE FOR ORNITHOLOGY: BIRDER BIAS

≪≪≪ ≪≪≪ ≪≪≪ ≪≪≪ ≪≪≪ ≪≪≪ ≪≪◇≫≫ ≫≫≫ ≫≫≫ ≫≫≫ ≫≫≫ ≫≫≫

Grasshopper Sparrow
Ammodramus savannarum

S OME BIRDERS have been doing their Breeding Bird Survey (BBS, §§79–81) routes for 30, 40, even 50+ years. Habitats along their routes have changed over the decades (§81), and so, in all likelihood, have the birders conducting the surveys. Birders' skills, like athletes', erode with age; the process is slower and less dramatic than in the case of, say, an NFL running back, but still. At the same time, a birder's mental game often improves with age—same as the professional athlete's.

Consider a BBS volunteer just getting started. He drives his route, hearing the high-pitched "primary" song of the Grasshopper Sparrow at six of his 50 stops. He never lays eyes on one of these puffed-out, buffy-breasted birdlets; the BBS is chiefly an aural undertaking. Next year, the volunteer gets the species at the same six stops, plus two more. In due course, he learns the softer, indeterminate secondary song of the species and then the extremely high-pitched flight call. The result: Grasshopper Sparrows at a dozen stops. The number of detections has doubled (from six to 12), but that has nothing to do with the true abundance of the species along his route.

Now jump ahead 30 or 40 years in the time line. Our BBS volunteer's aging ears can still pick out some, but not all, Grasshopper Sparrow primary songs; the secondary songs are harder still, and the ultrasonic flight call of the species is now fully beyond the hearer's ability. He compensates with an enhanced mental game—knowledge of the species' microhabitat preferences (§§18–19), recollection of where he ticked off the bird in previous years (§22), etc. The result is that he's down a bit from his high of a dozen detections, but not by all that much.

BBS analysts have devised ingenious methods for handling so-called within-observer effects (as well as among-observer effects), but a larger point remains: Change happens. It happens to bird populations, it happens to the habitats birds depend on, and it happens to the birders who observe these things.

83 WHITHER THE FIELD NOTEBOOK?

≪≪≪≪≪≪≪≪≪≪≪≪≪≪≪≪≪≪◇≫≫≫≫≫≫≫≫≫≫≫≫≫≫≫

Gadwall
Mareca strepera

THE BIRD EMERGES from hiding and is in plain view: It's a male (drake) Gadwall, gray overall with a black rear end. You stick with the bird; a minute later, it is joined by another, an adult female (hen). They appear to be a pair, and you wonder if they're nesting nearby.

If you were in one of your Breeding Bird Atlas blocks (§§76–78), your sighting of a pair of Gadwalls in suitable habitat would constitute probable breeding. But you're not atlasing. Okay, if you were doing a Breeding Bird Survey (§§79–82), you would note the two Gadwalls on your datasheet and then proceed to your next stop. Neither are you performing a systematic bird survey. And although an early-summer sighting of the species is always a pleasure, your find isn't rare enough to justify issuing the rare bird alert (§149) for your state or province. You're simply out birding at a local freshwater marsh, and you've come upon a pair of Gadwalls. What are you to do about it?

In the old days, say, in the beginning of the 2000s, you would have jotted down the sighting in your field notebook: "2 Gadwalls, ♂ ♀, Oxbow Park, June 6, 2001." Then what? The answer, if we're honest with ourselves, is probably nothing. Or end of story. We wrote things down in our field notebooks, and that was that. Keeping a field notebook is a fine idea. It's good discipline. It makes us better birders. But the typical field notebook from two decades ago is gathering dust. Wouldn't it be wonderful if all those notebook entries could somehow be made available to the entire birding community?

Fast-forward a decade. eBird had launched a few years earlier, and by the early 2010s was in wide use by the birding community. We're going to spend the next few lessons exploring how eBird works, so, for now, just the briefest of overviews: eBird delivers your field notebook entries to the whole wide world.

84 EBIRD: JUST DO IT

≪≪ ≪≪ ≪≪ ≪≪ ≪≪ ≪≪ ≪≪〉〉 〉〉 〉〉 〉〉 〉〉 〉〉 〉〉

Chimney Swift
Chaetura pelagica

ALTHOUGH POPULATIONS OF this "cigar with wings" have declined in recent decades, the species remains fairly common within its breeding range—basically, the eastern three-fifths of the Lower 48 states. Spend a few hours birding in the daytime hours on a summer day, and you are bound to encounter Chimney Swifts: You might see them high above, their wings appearing to beat out of unison (an optical illusion); and you might well hear them, chattering sharply as they zip this way and that. One thing, though, you will almost never, ever, see is a Chimney Swift doing anything other than flying. The vast majority of birders have *never* seen a perched Chimney Swift!

Chimney Swifts, like Gadwalls (§83), are somewhat confounding to the methodologies of both the Breeding Bird Atlas (§§76–78) and the Breeding Bird Survey (§§79–82). They nest in—wait for it—chimneys, and rather few of us ever go looking in chimneys for birds or anything else. Away from the nest, swifts go pretty much wherever they please; the presence of one or even dozens of birds doesn't necessarily signify local breeding. But they're up there, and we sense that our observations must be worth something. So we eBird them.

We've mentioned eBird a number of times now (§§22, 46–48, 83), but we haven't yet seen how it works. No more beating around the bush. Let's upload an eBird checklist. Go to eBird.org, click on "Submit Observations," and enter your location (Holiday Inn–Riverside, Minot, North Dakota) and date (June 14, 2009). All eBird checklists must have a location and date. Next you're prompted with a checklist of the bird species expected for that location and date, and you enter all the birds you saw and heard—including one (1) Chimney Swift. That is a real eBird entry, by the way. See for yourself: *ebird.org/ebird/view/checklist/S5110635.*

Your checklist is online now, available for all the world to see. What comes next is nothing short of astounding.

85 EBIRD: A LIFETIME OF MEMORIES

Common Murre
Uria aalge

IMAGINE IF YOU had a way of dialing up the record of every single encounter you've ever had with the Common Murre: your lifer, decades ago, on sea rocks along the California coast; adults with young, out at sea a ways, when you were on a family vacation to Alaska; a portside flyby on a pelagic trip out of Massachusetts; and many more. Let's be more precise than "many" more; let's say exactly 18 additional sightings, for a grand total of 21 encounters in your life with this elegant relative of the heavyset auks and puffins.

With eBird, this is theoretically possible. All you have to do is enter a checklist after each birding trip. Then go to the "My eBird" tab on the homepage. Click on "Your Life List," then search for or scroll down to "Common Murre," and, voilà, all your sightings pop up. Immediately, you see the basic stats: where, when, and how many. Now click on a particular checklist: Asilomar State Beach, Monterey County, California, June 26, 2007 (*ebird.org/ebird/view/checklist/S2998655*). Your Common Murres (*n* = 10) are there, along with all the other birds you saw, plus whatever additional notes you entered (weather, companions, anything).

Go back for a moment to the beginning of the process: All you have to do is enter all those checklists. Fortunately, eBird makes it easy. If you have the app, eBird knows where you are, when you started your checklist, and when you finished. (It seems inevitable that, sooner or later, eBird records will be subpoenaed in a domestic litigation case!) And even if you submit your checklist from a laptop, after you're done birding, the data entry process goes quickly and smoothly.

One more thing, and this is huge. In addition to having access to all your Common Murre sightings, you can dial up *anybody's* sightings of this black-and-white seabird. And that suggests a role for eBird that goes way beyond the personal satisfaction of reliving a lifetime of pleasant memories.

86 EBIRD: IT TAKES A (GLOBAL) VILLAGE

American Pipit
Anthus rubescens

IT'S TAKEN YOU and your companions half a day to get here—an alpine meadow far above the U.S. Forest Service trailhead where you started your long hike. Everywhere you step, American Pipits put up from the stunted vegetation. The birds are streaky, with big black eyes; they are svelte overall, their straight-edged tails notably long. Many of them flush just a hundred feet or so, but a few launch into breathtaking display flights: The birds fly up almost vertically, singing a pulsing series of *cheep!* and *peep!* notes as they go.

You're in the moment, as they say, inclined to believe that there is something special about this particular juncture in space and time. The biology of the American Pipit suggests a different interpretation, however. The species breeds widely across the Alaskan and Canadian tundra, and its range swings well south into the southern Rockies. After the short summer breeding season, pipits head for lakeshores and coastlines mainly in Mexico and the southern half of the United States. And during migration, singles and small flocks strut across cornfields, pastures, and parklands wherever such habitats occur.

How does your observation, right here and now in the western Wyoming high country, fit into the global distribution of the American Pipit? Answer: Consult eBird (§§83–85). To initiate the investigation, click on the "Explore Data" tab and then "Species Maps." Enter "American Pipit," and you see a map of the Earth with purple pixels. Play around with the settings (date, location, zoom in/out) to refine your analysis. That's all well and good, but the output, on a screen-by-screen basis, is static; you get a single image in space and time. What if there were some way to animate the maps, to watch how the pipits' populations disperse throughout the year?

Go to *tinyurl.com/AmPi-eBird-animated.* If a picture is worth a thousand words, then an animated "Occurrence Map," like this one, is worth a million. It is mesmerizing to watch the pipits' march across the continent. Warning: More than one eBird user has reported the condition of being addicted to these animated range maps!

87 EBORG

⫷⫷ ⫷⫷ ⫷⫷ ⫷⫷ ⫷⫷ ⫷⫷ ⫷⫷◇⫸ ⫸⫸ ⫸⫸ ⫸⫸ ⫸⫸ ⫸⫸ ⫸⫸

Blue Jay
Cyanocitta cristata

A LITTLE WHILE AGO, someone posted to one of the birding e-lists that Google had acquired eBird (§§83–86). It was a match made in heaven: Google would provide better range maps and even software for ID'ing photos of mystery birds, while eBird would hand over valuable user profiles to Google. April Fool's! This never happened. But an awful lot of birders fell for it. It was frankly plausible.

When birders talk about "eBorg," they're only half-joking. On some days, it seems as if we spend more time eBirding than real birding. Perhaps. But there's a converse to the preceding. The urge to eBird gets us into the field more than ever before.

You're on a business trip. That's bad enough. Worse: You're in the North Jersey suburbs of New York City, and it's June. Now don't take this the wrong way: Many birders consider New Jersey to be one of the greatest birding destinations in America. But not the suburbs around New York, and not during the summer doldrums.

You're an eBirder, though, and you have a need—a very real need—to create an eBird checklist for Morris County. Really, you shouldn't. You have a big presentation to prepare for; important people to meet; deadlines to worry about. But you can't help yourself. You walk out into the hotel parking lot, where you are greeted by a simple Blue Jay. You know in your head that it's one of the most ordinary and unremarkable of bird species in suburban habitats like this one. Yet the bird sparkles in the afternoon sun. It hops down from a low perch in an oak, grabs an acorn from the lawn, and flies off. You dutifully eBird the experience of your short time afield *(ebird.org/ ebird/view/checklist/S18927094)*, then head back inside for an evening of business. You've done your part for science, and that's wonderful. That's the whole point of eBird. But you've also done a world of good for your own frame of mind. Being an eBirder is good for the soul.

88 ¡VIVA LA REVOLUCIÓN!

≪≪≪ ≪≪≪ ≪≪≪ ≪≪≪ ≪≪≪ ≪≪≪ ≪≪◇≫≫ ≫≫≫ ≫≫≫ ≫≫≫ ≫≫≫ ≫≫≫

Wilson's Phalarope
Phalaropus tricolor

T HE FEN IS unprepossessing: just a "marsh" (not really) with a few "pine" trees (spruces, actually) jutting out of it. You know from past experience that the birdlife here is sparse. Back in the day, you might have declined the invitation to spend the morning at the site. But not today, not in the age of eBird. You want to get your boots muddy—more like, sopping wet—in this austere but fascinating place.

A female Wilson's Phalarope flies by and you get a photo *(macaulaylibrary .org/asset/61909921)* of this dapper, silver-and-chestnut shorebird. Then she drops down into the fen proper, carpeted with shrubby cinquefoil and shooting stars. Her drab mate awaits her, and you get another photo *(macaulaylibrary .org/asset/61909241)*. Images of phalaropes in flight aren't all that uncommon, but photos documenting the microhabitat favored by mated pairs are rare. As soon as you can get an internet connection, your photos are on eBird, in the cloud, accessible to anyone online. In the comments section, you jot down a few notes. And you provide similar documentation for the other birds of the fen: audio of a Lincoln's Sparrow *(macaulaylibrary.org/asset/61908871)*, photos of a Brewer's Blackbird *(macaulaylibrary.org/asset/61930011)*, and so on and so forth for all the bird species ($n = 14$) in the fen.

This sort of birding wasn't possible at the dawn of the 21st century. Check that. This sort of birding hadn't been conceived of at the time. Searchable online galleries of digital photos were just beginning to come online, and digital repositories for audio were still a few years off. Our records were all over the place: checklists here, photos there, audio (as if) somewhere else.

eBird has changed the practice of birding in a thousand different little ways, but it has also revolutionized the outlook of the birder. All of a sudden, every phalarope in every fen on every eBird checklist contributes to our knowledge of the species. Each time we go birding, we make a difference. We are become a collective.

89 BIRD OBSERVATORIES

≪≪ ≪≪ ≪≪ ≪≪ ≪≪ ≪≪ ≪≪◇≫ ≫≫ ≫≫ ≫≫ ≫≫ ≫≫ ≫≫

American White Pelican
Pelecanus erythrorhynchos

ALL AROUND, YOU hear flapping and splashing; in your peripheral vision, you detect motion and pattern. On any other summer morning, you'd set yourself to the task of compiling a list of the avian species present. But not today. You hand an instrument to the field crew supervisor, deftly extricating an immense white bird from a net.

Your sole focus is on the American White Pelicans packed into their nesting colony on a nearly barren island in the middle of a large lake. The birds' huge beaks are impressive even at a distance; close up, they're positively menacing. You've undergone all the requisite safety training, but working with the birds is nevertheless unnerving.

You're a volunteer with the regional bird observatory, contracted by a government agency to monitor the population health of the handful of pelican colonies in the watershed. In addition to performing a basic population census, you check the pelicans for feather condition, nest parasites, and hatchling weight. Another project volunteer is a veterinarian; she draws small blood samples for further analysis.

Bird observatories—several dozen in the United States and Canada—do work like this, and nearly all of them depend, to a lesser or greater degree, on the contributions of volunteers. Observatories are typically NGOs and almost always collaborative ventures, partnering with agencies, foundations, and even commercial interests. Most are champions of Breeding Bird Atlases (§§76–78), Breeding Bird Surveys (§§79–82), and eBird (§§83–88), but many emphasize specialized research on single species or on suites of ecologically connected species. Science-based conservation is invariably the raison d'être for a bird observatory, and education is usually a major secondary focus.

One of the coolest things about bird observatories is that they offer volunteers the opportunity for direct involvement in research. Sign up for training, learn a bit of pelican biology, and you'll soon be telling your friends that you got to handle a bird with a 10-foot wingspan. How cool is that!

90 BREEDING SYSTEMS: COLONIALITY

Burrowing Owl
Athene cunicularia

"HAPPY FAMILIES ARE all alike," according to Leo Tolstoy, but cultural anthropologists have demonstrated a wide variety of successful strategies for domestic life. In some human cultures, so-called nuclear families, more or less discrete from one another, are the norm. In others, extended families are more prevalent. And some cultures excel at communitarian family life, whereby unrelated or distantly related persons share essential domestic duties.

Birds, like humans, are all over the cultural map when it comes to strategies for domestic life, typically referred to in the scientific literature as breeding systems. Spend a summer morning in a particular sort of habitat, and it seems as though every bird species has its own unique breeding system. (Sorry, Tolstoy.) For example: the wide variety of strategies employed by grassland birds. Many of these species can be a challenge to see at the nest, but one of them, the Burrowing Owl, is gratifyingly easy to observe.

Owls in grasslands? Most owls are indeed forest birds, but a few favor open habitats. And the Burrowing Owl—ovoid overall and knock-kneed, with intense amber eyes—seems to go out of its way to be conspicuous. That may seem anthropomorphic, but it is not. Burrowing Owls nest in tight colonies consisting not only of conspecifics, but also prairie dogs! The rodents excavate holes in which the owls nest (the dogs, not the birds, do the bulk of the burrowing), and the birds are tasked with keeping sentry over the colony. If a coyote or a Ferruginous Hawk gets too close, the Burrowing Owls sound the alarm for the prairie dogs. Some ranchers still call them "howdy owls" for their supposed friendliness.

The arrangement is not optional. Take prairie dogs out of the picture (unfortunately, many ranchers continue to poison them), and the Burrowing Owls close up shop. They can't simply migrate to the nearest forest and make like Barred or Flammulated owls. Many aspects of avian breeding biology are stubbornly hardwired, with sobering consequences for bird conservation.

91 BREEDING SYSTEMS: TERRITORIALITY

Cooper's Hawk
Accipiter cooperii

"A MAN'S HOUSE IS his castle," it is said, an aphorism that applies well to an adult male Cooper's Hawk around the nest. Even more so, it applies to the adult female, bigger and fiercer than her mate. Unlike American White Pelicans (§89) and Burrowing Owls (§90), colonial species that tolerate and indeed depend on other birds in their homes, Cooper's Hawks are fiercely territorial. The opposite of the owl and the pelican, Cooper's Hawks are intolerant and uncooperative. If another Cooper's Hawk, an interloper, ventures too close to the nest, everyone within earshot knows about it! And not just other Cooper's Hawks: other raptor species and even humans. A close relative of the Cooper's Hawk, the rarer and larger Northern Goshawk, is legendary for driving humans away from the nest.

A bird's territory comprises not only the actual nest, but also the surrounding bit of real estate. Among small birds, like warblers and sparrows, the territory may be well under an acre; among the larger raptors, the territory can span hundreds of acres. How are these territories marked out? The long and short of it is that the birds just know, in the same way that most homeowners know where their property ends and their neighbor's begins.

The analogy can be extended further. Just as human neighbors generally obey widely accepted definitions of property limits (fences, handshakes, contracts, etc.), so birds tend to recognize territorial markers that are all but invisible to human eyes. Avian territories are most clearly established by song, as legally binding, so to speak, as the title to a house. Disputes occasionally arise, but, in general, it's not worth it. Good fences make good neighbors, in avian as well as in human affairs.

A final point of analogy. Territorial birds, like human homeowners, recognize the existence of large swaths of real estate that are held in common trust: parks, roads, playgrounds, etc. Biologists refer to the entire ambit of an individual as its home range, where birds come and go as they please—except to steer clear of one another's inviolable territorial boundaries.

92 BREEDING SYSTEMS: "IT'S COMPLICATED"

Bushtit
Psaltriparus minimus

I N "THE CORBOMITE MANEUVER," one of the most famous episodes in the original *Star Trek* series, Captain Kirk and the *Enterprise* crew encounter a gargantuan spaceship piloted by a comically small alien. It's much the same with Bushtits and Bushtit nests. Bushtits are absolutely tiny—little cotton balls with a toothpick for a tail. Yet their nests are ginormous, elaborate, pendulous affairs that one commentator has likened to a basketball player's dirty tube sock hanging from a tree.

A pair of Bushtits may require several weeks to complete the nest, with the dark-eyed male and the yellow-eyed female coming and going constantly during the daylight hours. The casual observer would be excused for imagining that the industrious Bushtits are paragons of traditional family values. Industrious they certainly are, and virtuous they may be, but traditional they are not.

Communes of up to 40 individuals join in the care and keeping of one another's nests and nestlings. Any particular nest is tended by one or more supernumeraries, generally males and generally nonbreeders, who help in all aspects of raising the young. The Bushtit's breeding system is referred to as "cooperative breeding" or "semi-sociality," also exhibited in North America by Acorn Woodpeckers and Florida Scrub-Jays. The three species are unrelated, but the underlying selective pressure is the same: high investment in nests and nest care. Basically, the birds need all the help they can get.

How do the supernumeraries benefit from forgoing reproduction? There are two main explanations. First, they acquire experience for subsequent breeding attempts. Second, if they are closely related to the nestlings (for example, if the supernumeraries are the nestlings' uncles or cousins), they enjoy a genetic advantage from promoting the well-being of their blood relatives. The two explanations are not mutually exclusive, and helpers may benefit from both.

Bushtits at a suet feeder or backyard hawthorn are undeniably sociable, and that's not a value judgment. That is the essence of their behavioral ecology.

93 BABY BIRDS: EARLY BLOOMERS

Gambel's Quail
Callipepla gambelii

W E'RE FAMILIAR WITH the idea of *precociousness* in humans. Mozart was precocious, able to play the piano and violin while a toddler, and beginning to attract attention as a composer while still in his first decade of life. A similar idea applies in the study of avian developmental biology, but the word to describe it is slightly different: "precocial." If we say that a bird species is precocial, we mean that the young develop rapidly. And if we spend any amount of time at all with a family group of Gambel's Quail, we quickly acquire an appreciation for the precocial way of life.

We're walking along a nature trail in an urban park in one of the big cities of the Desert Southwest—Tucson, say, or Las Vegas. It's hot. The air is filled with the strangely commingled aromas of creosote bush and asphalt. At first, we barely notice the quiet commotion just off the trail, the soft clucking and the pitter-patter of little feet. Then a sudden riot of sound and fury: a family group of quail bursting across the trail right in front of us, an adult leading the way, another adult bringing up the rear, and at least a dozen fuzzballs in between.

They're so small, we have to check to make sure they're birds. Yup. Gambel's Quail are able to walk—indeed able to run so fast as to appear like a gray blur—almost immediately upon hatching. Not only that, they can *fly* at this age! Those fleet-footed fuzzballs might be just a day old. They're well on their way to independence, but not quite yet. Mom shows them where to find food, and Dad watches out for predators. The parents swap roles from time to time, though, and sometimes a third adult gets involved—for reasons that aren't well understood.

The precocial developmental strategy reprises the idea of life history theory (§§63–64), with its emphasis on variation among species. So if our Gambel's Quail are early bloomers, there must be late bloomers as well.

94 BABY BIRDS: LATE BLOOMERS

Lark Sparrow
Chondestes grammacus

CERTAIN SPARROWS ARE hard to ID, but not the Lark Sparrow. The adult male in breeding plumage is strikingly patterned on the face with black, buff, and bright rufous. The female is a bit duller, but impressive nonetheless. And even without the bold markings on the face, the Lark Sparrow is distinctive; the species is large overall, its long tail flashes white corners, and a prominent black spot, or stickpin, stands out on the otherwise clear breast.

You've spotted a Lark Sparrow and you stay with it for a bit. The bird plucks a "worm" (a caterpillar) from a sand sagebrush and flies a short distance to a juniper. It's carrying food, so you suspect there's a nest nearby (§77). Sure enough! You quickly note the nest and its tightly bunched occupants, then back off. You don't want to stress the adult any further.

The nestlings are amorphous, unfeathered blobs with huge eyes swollen shut. They could be any species of sparrow. They could be any species of *bird*. Not quite. But Lark Sparrows and a great many other species—well over half of all the birds on Earth—are altricial, meaning the young are born naked, helpless, and looking more or less the same. Contrast this with the precocial strategy of Gambel's Quail (§93).

What sorts of birds are altricial? The more "advanced" birds (§34), farther down the checklist, trend altricial, whereas the more "primitive" birds at the beginning trend precocial. But that is a gross generalization, with plenty of exceptions. As with so many things in birding, and in life in general, it is tempting to say that any particular bird species is this way or that, altricial or precocial. The distinction is a useful one, and a suite of physiological and behavioral characters are indeed associated with one life history strategy or the other. At the same time, it is valuable to see these developmental strategies as more of a sliding scale than absolute opposites.

95 BABY BIRDS: PARASITES

<<< <<< <<< <<< <<< <<< <<< <<◇>> >>> >>> >>> >>> >>> >>>

Brown-headed Cowbird
Molothrus ater

W E HAVE JUST SEEN how much the precocial Gambel's Quail (§93) and the altricial Lark Sparrow (§94) differ in nestling developmental biology. That said, the adults of both species behave much the same: utterly devoted to their young. The needs of day-old quail and day-old sparrows are very different, but both are lavished with equivalent amounts of parental TLC. With the Brown-headed Cowbird, though, it's a whole 'nother ball game.

Cowbirds, in the blackbird family, are brood parasites. The adult female cowbird, muddy gray-brown all over, lays her eggs in other birds' nests, then skedaddles. Neither she nor her mate or mates have anything to do with raising their own young. The adoptive parents do it all, and they do so at a particularly steep price: Some or all of their biological offspring are sacrificed for the cowbird nestling. The cowbird hatches earlier, develops faster, and hogs up its adoptive parents' attention; some cowbird hatchlings go so far as to evict their stepsiblings from the nest.

One might think that female cowbirds are bad parents (deadbeat moms), but that's a problematic biological assessment. By spreading her eggs across the landscape, sometimes in up to 20 different nests, Mom is promoting the welfare of her offspring-to-be. Even if only half the cowbird eggs are accepted by their foster parents, the female cowbird has left an impressive genetic legacy.

Brood parasitism has arisen a number of times in avian evolutionary history, with the cuckoos of Europe and Asia being the most famous example of all. New World cowbirds and Old World cuckoos are obligate brood parasites, meaning there is no other way. That is in contrast to facultative brood parasitism, practiced in North America by cuckoos and some ducks; these birds are opportunistic about it, dumping their eggs in some situations, but raising their own young in others.

Any way you slice it, nestling developmental strategies vary among the birds of North America and beyond. But the overarching biological logic is the same: to fledge as many young as possible.

96 BIRD NESTS: CLASSIC

Pine Siskin
Spinus pinus

FINDING THE NEST of a songbird is a special treat. American woodlands average several nests per acre, but you can walk for miles without ever laying eyes on one. Even the big birds—robins and grackles and magpies and such—are adept at concealing their nests. And those of the smaller species are practically invisible, except to biologists and birders specifically searching for them.

The classic songbird nest is a cup or saucer of twigs, lichens, moss, mud, and spiderwebs. Understatement and subtlety are the guiding principles of their makers—typically, although not always, both parents. These are not soaring cathedrals. They're more like the miniature carvings of ancient China.

The nests of the smaller species—warblers, finches, sparrows, etc.—are exquisite. If you find one, a question leaps to mind: How was this marvelous object created? How does a tiny Pine Siskin, lacking the artisan's lathe, do it? The bird doesn't have opposable thumbs. Why, it doesn't have any hands at all. The answer, to put it in imprecise but basically accurate terms, is that the bird just knows.

Our Pine Siskins have selected a nest site in a Douglas fir. It's near the trunk, about 15 feet up, on a sturdy bough beneath a mat of densely clustered needles. The birds know to start the nest by laying *this* particular twig in *that* particular way. They know that a bit of moss goes *here,* that a strand of spiderweb goes *there.* But this is not the same thing as following the step-by-step instructions for a desk or table from IKEA. The nest-building process is surprisingly analogous to the emerging technology of self-directed machine learning, in which one step advances and influences the next. Think of a computer playing chess, programmed with a relatively small suite of instructions: Probably start with a pawn, maybe a knight; bishop moves like *this,* queen moves like *that;* and so forth and so on, all the way to checkmate. Bird-brained our siskins may be, but they are grand masters.

97 BIRD NESTS: NONTRADITIONAL

Common Nighthawk
Chordeiles minor

"WAS THAT EVEN A BIRD?"

It's almost as if a piece of the rock-and-gravel landscape just lifted up and fluttered off a short distance. The female nighthawk, perfectly camouflaged where she was resting, couldn't have been more than a few paces ahead. She's circling around now, evincing some amount of interest in your next move. You step forward, and then you see it: a pair of slightly ovoid "stones," off-white with darker flecking. They're just lying there; they were just laid there, by the nighthawk, who was incubating until you inadvertently flushed her from the nest.

Pine Siskins (§96) and Common Nighthawks are polar opposites when it comes to nidification, a fancy word for the business of building and maintaining bird nests. And while the siskin's saucer-shaped contrivance is in some sense normative, the *ur*-nest, the nighthawk's home reminds us of the extreme diversity of avian nidification strategies. Plovers and alcids do it the nighthawk way—just a simple scrape, if that, in the sand (plovers) or on a rock outcropping (alcids). Most herons and hawks do it like the siskins and many other songbirds—elaborate habitations of mud and plant matter, equal parts earthenware and tapestry.

At one level, nidification is hardwired. A nighthawk would no more know how to build a siskin nest than you or I. But birds are flexible and resourceful, and many species have adapted to human-modified environments: Chimney Swifts in chimneys, phoebes and dippers under bridges, bluebirds in bird boxes, Ospreys on navigation structures, Purple Martins in "apartments," and more. Nighthawks get in on the action, too, frequently nesting on the flat roofs of buildings in towns and cities. Best of all are roofs with gravel, for all intents and purposes identical to bare ground.

Nighthawks aren't bad parents for their disdain of traditional nidification. Less is more for these cryptic, unobtrusive, no-frills minimalists. They've figured out what works for them, and they do a good job of it.

98 BIRD NESTS: IF YOU BUILD IT, THEY WILL COME

≪≪ ≪≪ ≪≪ ≪≪ ≪≪ ≪≪ ≪≪◇≫ ≫≫ ≫≫ ≫≫ ≫≫ ≫≫ ≫≫ ≫≫

Bufflehead
Bucephala albeola

THERE IS SOMETHING especially compelling about the proverbial— and sometimes literal—hole in the wall. A hole is sturdy, safe, and permanent. Accordingly, nestling survival is significantly higher among cavity nesters than among open cup nesters like Pine Siskins (§96), ground nesters like Common Nighthawks (§97), and most other birds.

There's just one problem. Excavating a hole is hard work. You can do it in a riverbank or on soft ground, the strategy of Bank Swallows, Belted Kingfishers, and, surprisingly, certain seabirds. Even harder—in both senses of the word—is a tree trunk. That's what woodpeckers are famously good at. But a remarkable diversity of nonwoodpeckers also use tree cavities. Woodpeckers and a few other birds are so-called *primary cavity nesters,* in distinction from the secondary cavity nesters that occupy old woodpecker holes.

House Wrens, Tree Swallows, and Eastern Bluebirds are familiar secondary cavity nesters. Less familiar is the Bufflehead—the same birds that winter in tight rafts in the back bays along our coastlines. These miniature ducks are secondary cavity nesters, occupying holes excavated by Northern Flickers and Pileated Woodpeckers.

Woodpeckers aren't the only builders of Bufflehead homes. Humans through the ages have been possessed of an uncontrollable urge to get in on the action. Indigenous Americans attracted Purple Martins by hanging hollowed-out gourds suitable for nesting, and contemporary Americans of all stripes and persuasions delight in building and installing bird boxes. If you live somewhere with Buffleheads in the summer months, give it a whirl and put out a box for these round-bodied, stiff-tailed, black-and-white ducks.

There are no guarantees in this birding life, but installing a bird box is often a high-yield initiative. Why is that? Are there not enough woodpecker holes to go around? And another question: If tree holes—natural or artificial—are so great, why aren't more species secondary cavity nesters? We turn to those interrelated matters presently.

99 RESOURCE LIMITATION: NO ROOM AT THE INN

Ash-throated Flycatcher
Myiarchus cinerascens

B ACK IN THE late 20th century, ecologist Carl Bock and his colleagues conducted a conceptually straightforward yet intriguing experiment. They installed nest boxes—lots and lots of nest boxes—in foothill woodlands in the Desert Southwest. When the field crew went to check on the boxes, they found that practically all of them were occupied. So the researchers put out more boxes, and those too were quickly occupied.

The strong inference was that nest sites are a limiting factor in the ecology of secondary cavity nesters. There simply aren't enough holes to go around. On the long time scale of evolutionary biology, a bird species faces a choice, or to use the term preferred by ecologists, a tradeoff. Invest considerable time and energy in building your own nest (§96); or take a pass on the whole nest-building thing (§97), exposing your eggs and hatchlings to predation and the elements; or bide your time in hopes of chancing upon an unoccupied woodpecker hole (§98).

The Ash-throated Flycatcher, a plucky denizen of dry Western woodlands, elects for the bide-your-time strategy. To be clear, this isn't a choice for any particular flycatcher pair. It's an innate feature of the species' biology. A few other flycatchers—for example, the closely related Great Crested Flycatcher of moist eastern forests—has likewise made the evolutionary choice to nest in holes. It's a high-risk, high-return strategy. High return: Nothing beats the safety and security of a hole. High risk: An Ash-throated Flycatcher that can't find a hole is an Ash-throated Flycatcher that won't produce any young.

The Bock team's results likely apply beyond the ecology of secondary cavity nesters. Think of the Peregrine Falcons that have readily taken to nesting on skyscrapers, suitable substitutes for the cliff faces originally favored by the species. South of the border, the widespread but rare Orange-breasted Falcon has a knack for finding its way to Mayan ruins. Everywhere we look, it's the same: For a great many bird species, the availability of nest sites is a limiting resource.

100 RESOURCE LIMITATION: FLOATERS

Ovenbird
Seiurus aurocapilla

WHILE AWAY A summer morning in a broadleaf forest in the northern United States or southern Canada, and you will find yourself immersed in surround-sound Ovenbirds. In front of you and behind you, left and right, they sing their pulsing song: *teacher! teacher! teacher! teacher!* They don't really say those words (§41), but the mnemonic is hard to get out of our heads. Anyhow, Ovenbirds everywhere.

How many? The Breeding Bird Survey (BBS, §§79–82) provides an initial estimate, along with long-term population trend analyses that are of critical interest to conservation ornithologists. To refine the BBS estimate, we get into the heart of the Ovenbird's breeding habitat, map territories, and extrapolate the results to whole landscapes and beyond. Let's say we find 40 territories in a 100-acre swath of prime real estate (old-growth beech-maple forest). Now let's say we know that there are 10,000 acres of such habitat in a watershed of particular conservation concern. Do the math, and that comes out to 4,000 pairs of Ovenbirds, for 8,000 adults altogether (two adults per territory), under the idealized assumption of full occupancy.

That was simple in the abstract, but an awful lot of behind-the-scenes work, both theoretical and logistical, goes into "40 pairs per 100 acres" and "10,000 acres of suitable habitat." And there's something else. In species like the Ovenbird, there may be a substantial additional population of floaters, mainly males that are unmated and nonvocal. They're there, but impossible to detect by song-based survey methods. Floaters are the ornithological equivalent of dark matter, all around us but essentially undetectable to physicists.

Are floaters important? Do they compete with other Ovenbirds for limited food resources? If a territorial male dies, will a floater move in on the "widowed" female? Even if a floater's influence is ecologically negligible *this* summer, what are its reproductive prospects *next* summer? And what are its ultimate genetic contributions to *Seiurus aurocapilla*? In asking these questions, we have begun to explore the intellectually challenging realm of population dynamics.

101 POPULATION DYNAMICS: THE DUCK FACTORY

≪≪ ≪≪ ≪≪ ≪≪ ≪≪ ≪≪ ≪≪◇≫ ≫≫ ≫≫ ≫≫ ≫≫ ≫≫ ≫≫

Canvasback
Aythya valisineria

T HE REGION IS KNOWN AS prairie pothole country. It doesn't have precise geopolitical or biogeographic boundaries, but it is basically the northern Great Plains of the United States and the southern prairie provinces of Canada. "Prairie" makes sense: This is the land of endless vistas of wheatgrass, bluestem, and sedges. "Pothole" refers to the countless small and occasionally large lakes that dot the region. In Minnesota alone, there are far more than the 10,000 lakes proclaimed on the license plate.

The math is simple: Water + prairie = ducks. Multiply that by the several hundred thousand square miles of south-central Canada and the north-central United States, and you have the potential for immense numbers of Canvasbacks and other waterfowl that depend critically on the region for raising their young. Waterfowl biologists call this landscape the Duck Factory, emphasizing its essential role in productivity.

The idea of productivity, as applied to Canvasbacks and other birds, isn't the same thing as the economist's definition of the term. We're not talking about how efficiently a bird works! Rather, we're much closer to the demographer's idea of fertility. In other words, how many of a hen Canvasback's offspring make it past some critical threshold like fledging. Extrapolate that to a whole population of Canvasbacks (all the breeders in southern Saskatchewan, say), and you have a measure of annual productivity.

What happens in Vegas stays in Vegas, perhaps, but what happens in Saskatchewan does not. The Canvasbacks that delight birders every winter in the Chesapeake Bay watershed (and elsewhere) were produced in Saskatchewan (and elsewhere). Some years these sleek ducks are plentiful, gathering in large rafts in the open water beyond the Phragmites-clogged marshes of the Bay. In other years, they are distressingly scarce. Conditions on the wintering grounds (habitat destruction, water pollution, hunting, etc.) are significant determinants of mortality. But the question of productivity was determined months to years earlier—and hundreds to thousands of miles away.

102 POPULATION DYNAMICS: SOURCE AND SINK

⋘⋘─⋘⋘─⋘⋘─⋘⋘─⋘⋘─⋘⋘─⋘⟨⟩⋙─⋙⋙─⋙⋙─⋙⋙─⋙⋙─⋙⋙─⋙⋙

Blue-gray Gnatcatcher
Polioptila caerulea

THE BIRD'S CALL is thin and peevish: short, nasal, and high-pitched, often doubled or trebled. This sounds like the utterance of a tiny bird, and that is indeed the case. The Blue-gray Gnatcatcher is an avian mite. Take away the long tail and the fairly long bill, and all you have left is a wee ball of bluish feathers. The species occurs across much of the Lower 48 states, with the greatest concentration in the Southeast. In the hollows and river bottoms of Kentucky, say, the bird is almost constantly within earshot on muggy summer mornings.

In the same way that the northern Great Plains can be thought of as the continent's Duck Factory, so might the coal country of the Upper Ohio River Valley be considered a Gnatcatcher Factory. We could extend the idea more broadly, and conjecture that the whole landscape is a factory for migratory songbirds. A June morning in the region's oak-hickory-tuliptree forests is sure to yield a large list of warblers, vireos, flycatchers, and more. They are not necessarily fledging young, however. Or, at least, not nearly as many young as one might think. What's happening?

These birds nest in forests that are heavily fragmented by agriculture, subdivisions, power line rights-of-way, and thousands of miles of roads. Brown-headed Cowbirds, which parasitize other species' nests (§95), flourish in fragmented landscapes. So do nest predators like crows, Blue Jays, blackbirds, raccoons, and opossums. If productivity falls below a certain level, our gnatcatcher finds itself in a population sink. Above that level: a population source.

The riot of birdsong is deceptive. These fragmented forests are unhealthy. If a grackle or another nest predator discovers a gnatcatcher nest, there is no question as to the outcome. And if a cowbird lays an egg in a gnatcatcher nest, the adults desert, dooming both the cowbird egg and their own eggs. The nesting season has gone down the drain.

103 POPULATION DYNAMICS: FECUNDITY

Eurasian Collared-Dove
Streptopelia decaocto

THE INVASION OF the western hemisphere by the Eurasian Collared-Dove is one of the most astonishing vertebrate range expansions in the annals of modern biology. As recently as 1990, the North American range of this Old World species was limited mainly to Florida. Less than 30 years later, collared-doves have overtaken almost the entire continent, pushing well into Alaska and northwestern Canada; southward, they have penetrated to well south of the Tropic of Cancer.

The vast majority of avian introductions die aborning. A much smaller number take hold locally; examples in our area include Eurasian Tree Sparrows around St. Louis, Rosy-faced Lovebirds around Phoenix, and Purple Swamphens in and around the Everglades. Rarest of all are species that spread like wildfire: House Sparrows and European Starlings in the 19th century, House Finches and Cattle Egrets in the 20th century, and now the Eurasian Collared-Dove. What is the secret of their success?

In the case of the collared-dove, we don't know what triggered the rapid expansion around the turn of the 21st century. The birds had been present in the Caribbean and South Florida for at least a quarter century before something set the range expansion into motion. Fascinatingly, the range expansion here has been synchronized with a parallel population explosion across Eurasia.

But this we do know: Once collared-doves are established, they breed like crazy. Even in colder climes, they are double brooded (meaning they nest twice per year) and often triple brooded (three nestings). Their breeding season is virtually continual. Even on snowy afternoons around Christmas in ski towns in the Rockies, you can hear them singing! If rabbits multiply, then collared-doves exponentiate. Their fecundity—essentially the same measure as the demographer's fertility rate for humans—is off the charts.

The story of the Eurasian Collared-Dove prompts a question: Is the species *bad* for other birds like Mourning and White-winged doves? Collared-doves aren't predatory, but might they compete with native species for limited resources? The answer to that question is surprisingly elusive.

104 POPULATION DYNAMICS: FIND YOUR OWN NICHE

<<< <<< <<< <<< <<< <<< <<<◇>>> >>> >>> >>> >>> >>> >>>

Rock Wren
Salpinctes obsoletus

THE SPECIES IS well named: Rock Wrens live among rocks. You can find them bopping around outcroppings above the timberline; they flourish amid talus pilings in the foothills; they abound in the butte-and-mesa country far from the mountains; and they make their homes on volcanic islands off the California coast. You won't find Rock Wrens in the company of Marsh Wrens and Sedge Wrens, and you tend not to find them around Cactus Wrens and House Wrens, either. But what about Canyon Wrens?

To be sure, there is broad overlap between these two wren species of the American West. Rock and Canyon wrens often sing within earshot of one another, and a morning spent in suitable habitat may yield tallies in the low double digits of both. Nevertheless, they differ in various ecological details. The Rock Wren, with its gray-brown plumage, matches the granitic scree and outcroppings that proliferate in the region. The Canyon Wren is more likely to be seen scurrying mouselike up and down canyon walls, where its orange-brown plumage conceals it against the backdrop of sandstone-dominated substrates. Other differences in morphology, diet, and migratory strategy predispose the two wrens to further niche differentiation.

We understand the idea of the niche in human affairs, and a similar concept applies to ecology. A key element of niche differentiation, often referred to in the literature as niche partitioning, is competition and, in particular, the avoidance thereof. Competition-mediated niche differentiation may, in turn, be a major agent of evolutionary change. In this view, common ancestors of today's Rock and Canyon wrens could have been driven by competition to diverge into the distinct species we see today.

Despite the role of competition in powering evolution, it may be relatively insignificant in contemporary ecological time. Remember, niche differentiation tends to promote the avoidance of competition. Nevertheless, the world is not overrun with Rock Wrens. If competition for food, say, or nests (§99) isn't limiting Rock Wren populations, then what is?

105 POPULATION DYNAMICS: RUN FOR YOUR LIFE

⋘ ⋘ ⋘ ⋘ ⋘ ⋘ ⋘◇⋙ ⋙ ⋙ ⋙ ⋙ ⋙ ⋙

European Starling
Sturnus vulgaris

THE BIRD IS belting out its tunes from atop the tallest perch on the highest point of the big department store. The tunes are a jumble of squeals, squeaks, and whirring sounds. The utterances of the European Starling are not exactly musical, but they are oddly arresting, and such connoisseurs of beauty as Mozart and Shakespeare esteemed this tune-smith. As to its singing perch, our starling is standing on the pileum (§27) of a plastic owl. And not just any owl. It's a Great Horned Owl, or, at least, a reasonable facsimile thereof.

The Great Horned Owl is one of the most fearsome avian predators on the continent, but the starling is not easily fooled. Still, this is a teachable moment. If this had been a real Great Horned Owl, our glossy songster would be freaking out. Starlings are wary birds, flushing readily and even avoiding eye contact with humans. (No joke about that latter point; a recent paper demonstrates that European Starlings are averse to human stares.)

Starlings, like almost all birds, spend a fair bit of their lives dealing with predators—often evading their detection, sometimes escaping their clutches, and, on rare occasion, even going after them. So much about avian biology—the existence of alarm calls, cryptic plumages, flocking behavior, and more—reflects the powerful evolutionary force of predation. Predators make a difference. How much? In particular, what are the relative roles of competition (§104) and predation in avian population dynamics? That has been one of the dominant questions in academic ecology for the better part of the past century.

On a day-by-day basis, finding food and avoiding predation are two of the prevailing concerns of most birds. To some extent, birds can do something about competition and predation, both in contemporary ecological time and at the longer time scales on which evolution operates. Now what about the things over which birds have no control?

106 POPULATION DYNAMICS: LUCK OF THE DRAW

≪≪≪ ≪≪≪ ≪≪≪ ≪≪≪ ≪≪≪ ≪≪≪ ≪≪◇≫ ≫≫≫ ≫≫≫ ≫≫≫ ≫≫≫ ≫≫≫ ≫≫≫

Great Blue Heron
Ardea herodias

"**E**VERYBODY TALKS ABOUT the weather, but nobody does anything about it." We've already seen how that statement of mild exasperation applies (or doesn't apply) birders (§71), and now we're going to see that it conveys an important truth about avian population dynamics. We'll do so by spending a summer afternoon at a Great Blue Heron rookery.

Everything's humming along just great at this heron commune high in the treetops along a midsize river. Some of the young have fledged and are beginning to find food on their own, but they still hang around in the vicinity of the rookery. Others will fledge any day now. For months, the parents have done everything they can to maximize their offspring's probability of survival, a complex calculus of finding food, deterring predators, and all the other terms in the equations of population dynamics (§101–105).

Then it happens—a derecho, the term meteorologists give to a widespread outbreak of fast-moving severe thunderstorms. The rookery sustains tremendous damage, with many birds killed outright and nearly all the nests destroyed. And not just this rookery, but a great many of them within the derecho's path, extending across multiple U.S. states and Canadian provinces. In the course of a single afternoon, the whole region's Great Blue Heron population has taken a big hit.

Events like this are abiotic and stochastic. The abiotic part is straightforward: The determining factor, the storm, is not biotic, or, in essence, biological. Rather, it is nonbiological. The stochastic part is trickier, but basically gets at the unpredictable nature of the occurrence; for our purposes, a stochastic process is a random one. And it comes down to this: The poor herons had essentially no control over what happened.

How important are such events in the grand scheme of avian population dynamics? There are two competing schools of thought: (1) fairly important and (2) overwhelmingly important. The idea doesn't sit well with everybody, but randomness and unpredictability are significant determinants of avian diversity.

107 POPULATION DYNAMICS: KEYSTONE SPECIES

Snow Goose
Anser caerulescens

POPULATION DYNAMICS IS a two-way street. We have thus far assessed the factors, both biotic and abiotic (§106), that influence bird populations; now we will reverse the causal arrow and examine how birds themselves affect the rest of the environment. In addition to direct biotic influences, like predation (§105) and competition (§104), bird populations may have indirect impacts with far-reaching implications within and even among whole ecosystems. To see how, let's head to the rarely visited but ecologically critical lowlands around Hudson Bay, home to a large fraction of the world's Snow Goose breeding population.

The species' numbers have exploded in recent years, with negative consequences for the Savannah Sparrows that also breed here. The voracious geese devour the region's grasslands, causing the release of salts into the topsoil, in turn poisoning willows and other shrubs in which Savannah Sparrows nest. The pathway from geese to grass to salt to shrub to sparrow is an example of a trophic cascade, and the species that triggers the cascade—in this case the Snow Goose—may be a keystone species, the term given to an animal whose removal from an ecosystem causes drastic change.

A thought might have occurred to you: Why are Snow Geese populations skyrocketing? The answer is multifaceted, but an important part of it has to do with increased survival away from the breeding grounds. The winter range is shifting northward, likely because of anthropogenic warming and drying of the climate, presenting the geese with an almost limitless bounty of food in the agricultural landscape of the southern Great Plains. So our trophic cascade begins with humans in the southern United States and results in reduced productivity of Savannah Sparrows along the shores of Hudson Bay.

We're on our final approach now to what is perhaps the overarching theme in contemporary ornithology: All bird populations are affected to a lesser or greater extent by human agency. Hold onto that thought. We're going to put it on the back burner for now. But not for much longer.

108 RETHINKING THE BREEDING SEASON: THE PAIR BOND

Common Goldeneye
Bucephala clangula

THE DAY COULD go on forever. Here in the north woods of central Canada, technically the boreal forest, the sun won't set until after 10:30 p.m. We're far from artificial lighting, so the glow of dusk will extend till past midnight. Yet despite the advanced hour, a family group of Common Goldeneyes is making the rounds, wending their way across a still pond. And they'll be at it again in just a few hours. This whole summer could go on forever.

Of course, that's not really true. In a couple months, hard freezes overnight will be the norm, and soon thereafter the inertness of winter at high latitudes in the continent's interior. The goldeneyes will be long gone by then. During their stint away from boreal bogs and marshes, a substantial part of their time budget will be devoted to the matter of survival—in essence, finding food while avoiding predation. But that's not all. Spend time with goldeneyes in winter, and you'll soon discover that they are consummate flirts.

The drake tosses his head back at a seemingly impossible angle, at the same time emitting a rolling growl and a sharp buzz. Invariably, a hen is nearby. The performance is risqué, but the male's objective is not a one-night stand. Depending on when in the winter goldeneyes are flirting, they are either establishing or reinforcing the "pair bond." Come spring, the birds will migrate together for hundreds or thousands of miles to their nesting grounds in the spruce and fir forests of Canada.

The pair bond is as essential to the nesting biology of the goldeneye as prospecting for a tree cavity (probably an old Pileated Woodpecker hole), laying the eggs therein, and feeding the young. Yet it happens halfway across the continent from the nest site. The old currencies of breeding bird biology—the narrow spatial extent of the territory and home range (§91)—are found to be seriously wanting.

109 RETHINKING THE BREEDING SEASON: EMPTYING THE NEST

≪≪≪ ≪≪≪ ≪≪≪ ≪≪≪ ≪≪≪ ≪≪≪ ≪≪◇≫≫ ≫≫ ≫≫ ≫≫ ≫≫ ≫≫ ≫≫

Snowy Egret
Egretta thula

FOR SEVERAL MONTHS, you've been volunteering with a Colony Watch program run by the regional bird observatory (§89). You were there when the Great Blue Herons arrived at the rookery, when there was still snow in the treetops. In the weeks and months ahead, you dutifully recorded your observations of nest construction, incubation, fledging, and other activities. The protocol you're following requires just one more week of data collection, and you wonder what else there is to see at the colony.

How about something totally new? A trio of Snowy Egrets, as far as you know the first of their species ever recorded at or near the Colony Watch site. Where on Earth did they come from? You check your state's Breeding Bird Atlas (§§76–78), and there aren't even any possible breeders within 25 miles. So you consult eBird (§§83–88), and you begin to connect the dots. Snowy Egrets are absent from the region in June, according to eBird, but they begin to appear in early July. That's weird. Even weirder is that they appear to be arriving from points south.

What you're witnessing is the annual and largely predictable "post-breeding dispersal" of Snowy Egrets. The phenomenon is clearly related to full-on migration, but the distinction is a useful one. Post-breeding dispersal typically involves movements of dozens to hundreds of miles, in contrast to the longer distances traversed by spring and fall migrants. Moreover, this dispersal isn't nearly as directional as the fall migration to come. Many individuals head north, away from the congested colonies, but many others disperse in other directions. Young of the year are particularly well-represented in the diaspora, but many adults enlist as well.

So how are we to define the breeding range of the Snowy Egret? Wildlife managers used to place a high premium on the colony itself, and that's understandable. But an emerging view is that the whole idea of the breeding season—in terms of phenology, as well as geography—is way more encompassing than we used to think.

110 RETHINKING THE BREEDING SEASON: SUMMER OR WINTER?

Sooty Shearwater
Ardenna grisea

EVERYWHERE WE GO along the central California coast, we see evidence of breeding bird activity. In an oak-lined neighborhood a few hundred feet from shore, a juvenile California Towhee, barely fledged, is tended by a watchful adult, while an extended family of Acorn Woodpeckers swarms about a granary, the name given to the permanent colony of the species. Practically at tideline, resident White-crowned Sparrows (of the distinctive coastal Nuttall's subspecies) jam food into the mouths of dependent young; and we infer that a juvenile Pigeon Guillemot just beyond the sea rocks must have been hatched locally.

Farther out, a Sooty Shearwater arcs above the waves. Then another. And another. Perhaps a dozen in all. And if we were to board a boat and head out to sea a couple miles, we would see flocks of thousands of these stiff-winged aerialists. Where do they nest? Definitely not in woodpecker granaries, and probably not alongside towhees in shady backyards. But maybe on sea cliffs with the guillemots, or maybe in tideline crevices in the company of White-crowns? No, nope, and no way.

Sooty Shearwaters breed in burrows dug in the earth on islands off the coast of New Zealand! Our calendar may say summer, but the shearwaters are on their wintering grounds. It's a long haul from New Zealand to California, but that's not the half of the story. Instead of flying a straight line (or, more accurately, a great arc) across the Pacific, the shearwaters crisscross the great ocean in a monstrous figure eight. Some birds traverse a mind-bending 40,000 miles per year, greatly exceeding the legendary 25,000-mile annual round-trips of the Arctic Tern.

A White-crowned Sparrow sings sweetly from a clump of manzanita, and we are reminded of the extreme variation in avian life history strategies (§§63–64). Is the shearwater's strategy better than the sparrow's? The question is perhaps outside the bounds of academic evolutionary biology, but it's the sort of question that conservation biologists increasingly must face.

111 IS HUNTING BAD?

≪≪≪ ≪≪≪ ≪≪≪ ≪≪≪ ≪≪≪ ≪≪≪ ≪≪◇≫ ≫≫ ≫≫ ≫≫ ≫≫ ≫≫≫ ≫≫≫ ≫≫≫

American Crow
Corvus brachyrhynchos

*B*AM! BAM! BAM!
   The bird falls quickly into the meadow, and the world's population of American Crows has dropped by one. From a strictly scientific perspective, the elimination of this single crow is negligible. A hunter could kill 10 or, honestly, 10,000, and the species would still garner a "Least Concern" rating from the International Union for Conservation of Nature, which assesses and ranks the endangerment of species around the world. The American Crow, wily and adaptable, is so abundant that hunting is allowed in the summer months in much of North America.

Which raises a question. Why *isn't* the hunting of most birds allowed in the summer months? As is the case with nearly everything having to do with hunting, the answer to that question is freighted with cultural complications, but the short answer is this: Because, in general, hunting in summer is bad for breeding birds. Credit hunters, even if they are acting out of self-interest, for not wanting to deplete populations too severely. That outlook extends even to so-called vermin like the American Crow. If crow populations ever declined to the point that the species were threatened with extinction, hunters would probably be at the forefront of conservation efforts on the species' behalf.

Needless to say, there are ethical and moral dimensions to the matter at hand. We shall turn to those in due course (§§196–197), and in a manner that may take us outside our comfort zones. But not yet. For now, we need to be truthful about something: In terms of its direct effect on the health of bird populations, modern hunting is almost never bad. If anything, habitat protection and restoration for hunting has been decidedly good for certain bird populations.

The hunter retrieves the crow carcass from the meadow, and glances in the direction of a row of white pines. They were planted there decades ago, for the benefit of game and wildlife, by a state conservation agency. Near the top of one of the pines, a crow is tending her nestlings.

112 HABITAT DESTRUCTION

Marsh Wren
Cistothorus palustris

T HE LITTLE MARSH wasn't much, just a couple acres of rushes, cattails, and pickerelweed. Besides, it was sacrificed for a good cause: a much-needed community center. Young men play basketball here now, seniors fill the lanes in the swimming pool, and moms drop off their kids at aftercare. In this partisan age of ours, the new community center is a rarity—something everyone agrees is a benefit to the region's quality of life.

Tell that to the Marsh Wrens who used to live here.

Three years ago, when construction began, the wetland harbored a dozen pairs of these rambunctious birds, their territories carefully mapped out by volunteers with the local bird observatory (§89). Those birds were the life energy of this marsh. Day or night, you could hear them chattering and sputtering in the emergent vegetation. When they weren't busy scolding one another, they were terrorizing the Yellow-headed Blackbirds that also flourished here. (A peculiar feature of life in freshwater marshes is the animus between Marsh Wrens and "bananaheads," with the wrens poking holes in the eggs of the much larger blackbirds.) You could take in the sights and sounds in this place, and you'd be excused for imagining that every wetland harbors Marsh Wrens and Yellow-headed Blackbirds. But that's not the case.

Both species are fussy about where to nest. Some marshes—like the one that was sacrificed for the community center—are filled to capacity with these birds. But many others are oddly devoid of them. The situation is analogous to the Ring-necked Ducks that winter on *this* pond, but not *that* pond (§22). The wrens and blackbirds that thrived here didn't necessarily get up and go elsewhere. Other wetlands in the area may have been unsuitable or undesirable for reasons we humans cannot fully apprehend.

Case studies like this one—Marsh Wrens galore one summer, Marsh Wrens gone the next—have drastic and unambiguous outcomes. But the less dramatic phenomenon of habitat degradation may be just as deleterious to bird populations.

113 HABITAT DEGRADATION

Willow Flycatcher
Empidonax traillii

WEEDS. WASTELANDS. If we're charitable: thickets. Those are the sorts of places favored by this olive-brown flycatcher with the odd song: *fitz-bew!* The weedier and more thicketed, the better. As to wasted, there's the rub. Willow Flycatchers require overgrown thickets, yes, but only those that are more or less undisturbed.

An ideal situation, especially for the several Willow Flycatcher subspecies of western North America, is a tangle of low-stature vegetation along a creek or river. It's okay for a few honest-to-goodness trees—box elders and maybe a cottonwood or two—to be present, but the dominant woody vegetation will be lower-stature stuff like tamarisk, red osier dogwood, and, most of all, willow. The Willow Flycatcher is well-named. So far, so good.

Enter cattle. Literally. Cows enter, flycatchers exit. The effect isn't dramatic, in the same manner as paving over a marsh (§112) or shooting a bird outright (§111). But the end result is just as devastating. Bulldozer herbivores like cows seriously degrade the riparian vegetation essential to western Willow Flycatchers. Cows trample through the weeds and thickets, eliminating valuable nesting habitat; they cut paths to waterways, draining wet meadows in the process; and they are so massive that they compact the soil, severely limiting regrowth of willows and other streamside vegetation. And cows aren't the full extent of the Willow Flycatcher's woes. Every manner of water management in the West—dams, dredging, diversion, and more—has the same ultimate effect on habitat quality.

Habitat degradation can sometimes be reversed to bring back the riparian corridors required by Willow Flycatchers. Replanting willows works. Restoring river meander works. And removing cattle works. The effects may be dramatic, with apparent full recovery—at least from the Willow Flycatcher's viewpoint—being achieved within just a few years of a mitigation effort. But keep in mind the converse to the preceding: It doesn't take much—just a herd of cattle will do—to decimate the local breeding population of these endearing brown birds with the sneezy song.

114 HABITAT FRAGMENTATION

Scarlet Tanager
Piranga olivacea

EVERYTHING IN THE old forest checks out. The tall trees reach to the sky; a butterfly flits through a clearing; a river (well, a stream) runs through it. Interpretive signage at the trailhead explains that the grove is being protected for migratory birds. In other words: Keep your dogs on the leash; no bikes off the trail; take only memories, leave only footprints.

A red bird blazes across the path, and you wonder if this is it. Nope, it's just a cardinal, a generalist species that flourishes in suburbs and even big cities. Next, you catch a glimpse of crimson in an opening in the canopy. Could this be it? No, not this bird, either. This one is a House Finch, another habitat generalist. The red bird you're looking for, the Scarlet Tanager, is nowhere to be found.

Why is that? The tanager is a forest bird, and you're walking through the woods in a specially designated "forest bird sanctuary." You come upon a high mesh fence, an "exclosure," designed to keep destructive white-tailed deer from browsing the understory vegetation. Even though habitat restoration efforts work wonders in certain instances (§113), this particular forest seems stubbornly resistant to rehabilitation.

The problem is that the forest is too small. The Scarlet Tanager is an area-sensitive species, requiring tracts above a certain minimum size. This isn't just about territory size and home range (§91), for our modest bird sanctuary is surely big enough for multiple tanager territories. Rather, this is about ecosystem function, or, in the case of forest fragments, dysfunction. A forest is more than just a bunch of trees; it is an ecosystem, greater than the sum of its physical, chemical, and, of course, biological parts, operating across large spatial scales. Take out some function or process *here*, and it affects some other function or process way over *there*. A forest fragment without Scarlet Tanagers isn't really a forest; it's just a bunch of trees.

115 HABITAT REDUX

≪≪ ≪≪ ≪≪ ≪≪ ≪≪ ≪≪ ≪≪◇≫ ≫≫ ≫≫ ≫≫ ≫≫ ≫≫ ≫≫

Purple Martin
Progne subis

FOR SEVERAL WEEKS NOW, there has been a decided predictability about the birdlife at the neighborhood park in this big East Coast city. And so it is this morning. The same Laughing Gulls are putzing around the ball fields, the same starlings squeal and sputter from the utility wires, and the same Double-crested Cormorant is perched atop a navigation structure a ways out. Robins are still tending their young, and the family group of Tufted Titmice are still cruising around. You're about to head in for a morning of chores when you hear it: a halting mix of pleasing gurgles and rougher notes. Purple Martins, your FOS and indeed FOY (§56).

"Where have you been all my life?" Or, at least, all this year? A perfectly good martin apartment, put up eons ago by some well-meaning park naturalist, was unoccupied once again this past summer. Why don't Purple Martins nest here anymore?

A large part of the answer may have to do with insufficient food supply. Populations of martins and other aerial insectivores—swallows, swifts, nighthawks, etc.—have declined precipitously in recent years, the result of a dwindling food base. These birds depend on aerial plankton, the sea of small insects and ballooning spiders that used to fill the skies. Their habitat is still there, of course; you can't exactly get rid of open sky. But it's being degraded, just as surely as cattle degrade Willow Flycatcher habitat (§113) and fragmentation degrades Scarlet Tanager habitat (§114). Thinking about habitat requires thinking outside the box.

A martin zooms in close, and a different question—the converse of the one posed a moment ago—occurs to you. What are the birds doing here *right now*? Corollaries: Where did they come from, and where are they going? It's the dead of summer, the doldrums. Is this post-breeding dispersal (§109)? Or something quite different? Those are reasonable questions. And, as we'll soon see, the answers are surprising.

PART FOUR

INFLECTION POINT

August—September

116 INFLECTION POINT

Bullock's Oriole
Icterus bullockii

Y OUR FOY (§56) BULLOCK'S ORIOLE, several months ago, was refulgent, freakishly brilliant on a misty spring morning. The pair you monitored earlier this summer were energetic and obliging, easily studied and impossible not to admire. Bullock's Orioles have a way of getting to you. But the bird you're looking at this morning—is it an adult female or a hatch-year male?—occasions some amount of head-scratching. What is it doing? Why is it even here?

The yellow-and-gray bird has just flown into a yucca. This isn't oriole habitat at all! You pick your way through the scrub for a closer look, but the bird has other ideas. It gives a couple of scratchy call notes, then flies directly away, bounding across the desert landscape and out of sight. The bird couldn't have been breeding in that habitat. Was it an early fall migrant?

Long story short: That Bullock's Oriole was a molt migrant, a term unfamiliar even to many experienced birders. We're going to explore the idea of molt migration in some detail (§§117–118), but first we're going to linger at that flowering yucca in the desert. We've arrived at a sort of conceptual turning point in the birding year.

For a bit more than half the year now, we've been building out our knowledge of bird biology. And for the rest of the year, we're going to deconstruct that knowledge. Don't worry! This isn't some retreat to ignorance. Deconstruction isn't the same thing as destruction. Our approach shall be to unpack the things we already know, or, perhaps more realistically, the things we *think* we know.

In most places in North America, the birds in the second half of the year are roughly the same as the birds in the first half. The two halves of the year differ appreciably in their phenomena, however—an idea we've already broached (§74). In the pages that follow, we're going to extend that thinking further: Bird study in the year's second half challenges and delights us with a revised and richer philosophical outlook on things.

117 THE FIVE SEASONS

Chipping Sparrow
Spizella passerina

THE IDEA OF THE FOUR SEASONS is entrenched dogma for most of us in the temperate latitudes of the northern hemisphere. The spring–summer–fall–winter paradigm is so natural to us that we unthinkingly apply it in all walks of life: quarterly meetings, quarterly taxes, quarterly periodicals, and more. Same with ornithology: spring migration, followed by the summer breeding season, then fall migration, then the nonbreeding season in winter. Lather, rinse, repeat. Bird clubs, bird festivals, bird journals, and more—they all structure their annual cycles around this tetracyclic scheme.

Someone forgot to tell the Chipping Sparrows that breed in the southern Rockies.

On warm nights in July and August, you can hear these little birds—diminutive even among the sparrows—flying straight east across the High Plains beyond Denver, Cheyenne, and Santa Fe. They're done with the breeding season. And their fall migration won't commence until, well, fall. Like the Bullock's Oriole tarrying at a yucca (§116), our Chipping Sparrows are molt migrants. After the short breeding season in the mountains, they migrate at night to molting grounds on the plains. The summer molt may be prolonged, with some individuals spending more time molting than breeding.

Molt is an essential step in the life history of Chipping Sparrows. They have to molt. If they don't, they will die. Hence, the pentacyclic annual cycle of the Chipping Sparrow: northward migration → breeding → molt → southbound migration → cold-weather survival. Or perhaps a simpler, ternary arrangement: breeding → molt → survival. At the same time that Chipping Sparrows are migrating east to molt, Sooty Shearwaters (§110) are massing on their wintering grounds off our coasts. Perhaps their annual cycle is binary: breeding → ocean wandering. In the tropics, meanwhile, a bipartite distinction between the annual dry and wet seasons is the driving force in the annual cycle of hundreds, if not thousands, of bird species.

The annual cycle is real. But its quarterly divisions are a tidy human construct.

118 MOLT MIGRATION

Short-billed Dowitcher
Limnodromus griseus

THE BIRD'S NAME IS, on the face of it, ridiculous. The Short-billed Dowitcher's bill is well over twice the length of the head; it's practically the length of the body. If you put this bird's bill on a pigeon, warbler, or gull, we'd be talking about the Long-billed Pigeon, Long-billed Warbler, or Long-billed Gull, respectively. The thing is, there's already a Long-billed Dowitcher, whose bill is ever so slightly longer, on average, than the bird called the Short-billed Dowitcher. In the same way, Yao Ming (seven feet six) was a short basketball player—compared with Manute Bol (seven feet seven).

Despite their great similarities in plumage and morphology, the two dowitchers differ appreciably in various aspects of their ecology. Three more or less discrete subspecies of the Short-billed breed farther south than the Long-billed; Short-bills in winter are pretty much restricted to the coasts, whereas Long-bills are widespread inland across the Southern states. Their fall migration strategies differ, too.

Short-billed Dowitchers wrap up their breeding season early, with southbound migrants showing up on mid-latitude mudflats by the Fourth of July. Short-bills take their sweet ole time heading south, but Long-bills are even more dilatory. That's because the Long-billed Dowitcher, unlike the Short-billed, is a molt migrant. Bullock's Orioles (§116) and Chipping Sparrows breeding in the Rockies (§117) likewise are molt migrants. Baltimore Orioles, however, are not molt migrants; neither are Chipping Sparrows that breed in eastern North America.

Some birds are molt migrants, some aren't. Short-billed Dowitchers fall in the latter category; they don't normally begin their molt until they arrive on the wintering grounds. This has consequences for field ID! If you see a dowitcher on migration and it's molting, then it is most likely not a Short-bill.

We've sort of gotten ahead of ourselves. We haven't really said what molt is. Clearly, it has something to do with feathers and, more specifically, with their growth and replacement. But we want to know more than that, don't we?

119 WHAT IS MOLT ANYWAY?

Bobolink
Dolichonyx oryzivorus

MALE BOBOLINKS IN SPRING and early summer are snazzy, as if they were blackjack dealers on a riverboat casino. But when they're headed south in late summer and early autumn, they're utterly different, clad in bright earth tones like hippies. Over the course of their annual visit to North America, Bobolinks seemingly transmogrify from one creature into another, and, in fact, some European colonial natural historians thought the spring and fall birds were different species. What are we to make of this?

Male Bobolinks have two complete molts every year. At some point during the summer, the male discards his black-and-white breeding garb, exchanging it for the brown-and-gold plumage he'll sport on the nonbreeding grounds in South America. Next spring, it goes the other way: Fall/winter plumage drops, spring/summer plumage grows in. The female's molt strategy is the same; although her spring/summer plumage is strikingly different from her mate's, she too undergoes two complete molts annually.

Everything about the male Bobolink's molt strategy makes good conceptual sense. Imagine a blackjack dealer with a secret life as a hippie. He wears one wardrobe at work, a completely different one at play. The early colonial naturalists—those who realized that the two Bobolinks are just the one—were intrigued by its apparent annual mood swings: industrious in the spring and early summer, supposedly indolent in the late summer and early autumn.

The male Bobolink's easily understood molt strategy—two different plumages, corresponding to two discrete complete molts—is extremely rare. Only one other species in our area, the Franklin's Gull (§69), does it this way. Why? Partly because of the tremendous distances these migrate; consider also the effects of increased solar exposure, arising from the fact that these two species favor open habitats during the course of *two* summers each year. Feathers wear down from sunlight and migration, and the birds need fresh new feather coats for the arduous journeys north and south. Then again, other species migrate as far as, or even farther than, Bobolinks and Franklin's Gulls. How do they do it?

120 THE "BASICS" OF MOLT

Eastern Wood-Pewee
Contopus virens

LIKE THE BOBOLINK (§119), the Eastern Wood-Pewee is a complete, long-distance migrant. The wood-pewee's trans-hemispheric travels aren't quite as impressive as the Bobolink's, with the birds making it "only" as far south as Bolivia. Nevertheless, they fly far, with at least some individuals covering greater distances in a year than certain Bobolinks. The wood-pewee's molt strategy (§119) is rather unlike the Bobolink's, however.

Instead of molting twice annually, the plainly attired Eastern Wood-Pewee molts only once. This single molt commences in the austral spring, after the bird has arrived on its South American wintering grounds in October. Sometime in the austral summer, the bird grows in its new coat of feathers. The bird is ready for its arduous flight northward again.

Birds *have* to molt (§117). Feathers wear down, and birds without feathers are walking (not flying) dead. With few exceptions, birds undergo at least one complete annual molt. Think of molt as a routine renovation of a bird's essential survival tools.

For birds breeding in the northern hemisphere, molt typically happens in the second half of the year, especially in late summer and autumn. We refer to this complete annual molt in fall as the prebasic molt. The end result of this prebasic molt is a bird's basic plumage, a fresh new coat of feathers.

To repeat in technical terms now, our wood-pewee undergoes its prebasic molt shortly after arriving in South America. It migrates north in its new basic plumage, which it will retain throughout the breeding season. Then it migrates south in worn basic plumage. The cycle from one basic plumage to the next is called, efficiently if unimaginatively, a plumage cycle. Adult wood-pewees cycle from one basic plumage to another, whereas adult Bobolinks sport two plumages in each plumage cycle: the basic plumage acquired in our fall, followed by an alternate plumage acquired in our spring.

Okay, that was a somewhat terminological discussion. The key concept is that (almost) all birds (almost) always have at least one (generally) complete annual molt, the prebasic molt, every year.

121 TWO FOR THE PRICE OF ONE

<<< <<< <<< <<< <<< <<< <<<◇>>> >>> >>> >>> >>> >>> >>>

House Sparrow
Passer domesticus

B IRDERS JOKINGLY REFER TO these sociable birds as "Black-throated Browns." It's an allusion to all the wood-warblers that go by the name "Black-throated"—there are Black-throated Blue, Black-throated Gray, and Black-throated Green warblers. It's also an acknowledgment that this common doorstep species is uncommonly beautiful. The adult House Sparrow in spring and summer is complexly patterned in Quaker gray and chestnut above; below, the throat and breast are strikingly black. In fall and winter, however, the male's markings are much subtler, with just a few black flecks on the throat and breast.

Think back now to the molt strategies of the Bobolink (§119) and the Eastern Wood-Pewee (§120). Which of those two strategies—two distinct plumages per year (Bobolink) as opposed to just one (wood-pewee)—do you suppose applies to the House Sparrow? Expectations and appearances to the contrary, the House Sparrow does it the wood-pewee way, with only one molt per year. How does that work?

Like pretty much all North American birds, the adult male House Sparrow undergoes a complete prebasic molt (§120) in the late summer and autumn. The resulting basic plumage (§120) is drab. Or perhaps we should say, it *appears* drab, for it is concealing a wonderful surprise. Not even a millimeter beneath the dull beige feather tips are the colorful chestnuts, grays, and blacks that we see in spring and summer. Paradoxically, the fresh basic plumage appears dull; then, with a further paradoxical flourish, that fresh plumage wears down to the striking "Black-throated Brown" plumage of the breeding season.

The male House Sparrow's molt strategy is ingenious. The bird acquires its breeding-season garb not through a time-consuming and energetically costly prealternate molt (§120), but, rather, via passive feather wear. The bird's feathers are going to wear down anyhow, so why not make the most of that fact of avian life? It boils down to this: The House Sparrow has one plumage (and one corresponding molt) per annual plumage cycle.

122 A FALSE DICHOTOMY

Ring-billed Gull
Larus delawarensis

T HE PLACE IS FOUL, reeking of cow manure and dead carp. You're at an old fishing pond where the water's been drawn down for a few weeks now. The birds: a dozen European Starlings lined up on the rickety pier; a couple American Crows squabbling over some item of offal; Franklin's Gulls loafing on a mudflat; and a lone Ring-billed Gull resting in what shallow water remains.

Never one to turn down the opportunity to ponder avian plumages, you get to wondering about the diversity of molt strategies (§§119–121) exhibited by the birds gathered here. The Franklin's Gulls, in the earliest stages of their long journey south, have two complete molts (and two corresponding plumages) per year; they're like Bobolinks (§119). The crows are like wood-pewees (§120); they molt only once a year, transitioning from one look-alike plumage to the next. And the starlings do it the House Sparrow way (§121); they have only one molt a year, but their basic plumage, newly acquired in late summer, wears down through the winter months to reveal a very different look the following spring.

What about the Ring-billed Gull?

The simplest answer is that Ring-billed Gulls, like Bobolinks and Franklin's Gulls, have two molts per year. But the spring molt (or prealternate molt, §§120–121) in the Ring-billed Gull is incomplete. The species has a complete annual molt (the prebasic molt, §§120–121) starting right now, in late summer; then it molts some, but not all, of its basic plumage in the early spring. We say it has a partial prealternate molt. (And, like essentially all the birds in our area, a complete prebasic molt.) The best we can say is this: Ring-billed Gulls are like Franklin's Gulls, sort of.

Can we step back for a moment? Birds exhibit diverse molt strategies, and it can seem confusing. Molt confounds our basic instinct to view the world in an either/or fashion. But an overarching organizing principle is coming into view: Molt and the avian annual cycle are inextricably linked with one another.

123 AN INCONVENIENT TRUTH

⫷⫷⫷ ⫷⫷⫷ ⫷⫷⫷ ⫷⫷⫷ ⫷⫷⫷ ⫷⫷⫷ ⫷⫷⟨⟩⫸⫸ ⫸⫸⫸ ⫸⫸⫸ ⫸⫸⫸ ⫸⫸⫸ ⫸⫸⫸

Semipalmated Plover
Charadrius semipalmatus

BY AUGUST, THE "FALL" migration of shorebirds is briskly under way. Some species are molt migrants (§§117–118); others are not. Some pack into dense flocks; others do not. Some will continue on to southern South America; others are nearly at their journey's end. Question: Where does the Semipalmated Plover fit in?

Answer: All over the place. Migrants occur pretty much anywhere there are mudflats and sandbars. Look for these pert plovers up and down our coastlines, and don't count them out inland: Singles, small flocks, and occasional large flocks refuel at rivers, reservoirs, seasonal playas, even flooded pastures. Tracking studies show that "Semis" vary somewhat in the duration of their sojourns, but most don't tarry long. They've got places to go.

Some winter no farther south than the mid-latitude coastlines of the U.S., but others make it halfway down the coasts of Chile and Argentina. In between, in places like Suriname, Colombia, and Mississippi, practically any wetland may harbor wintering Semipalmated Plovers, muddy brown above, white below with a black breast band that varies greatly in extent. Sizable numbers traverse thousands of miles of open ocean to Hawaii and the Azores.

This has consequences for molt. Molt guru Peter Pyle has described southern hemisphere and northern hemisphere molt strategies, and the Semipalmated exhibits both of them. Thus, different molt schedules for birds wintering along the Río de la Plata (35° south) as opposed to those at the Sea of Cortés (30° north). The details don't matter, but a larger result is coming into view: Although all birds must molt (§§117, 120), they enjoy considerable flexibility in how they do it. Birds can suspend or accelerate their molts as their energy budgets allow; they can initiate or forgo molt migration if conditions warrant; and they may tweak the seasonal timing of molt if they wind up in Uruguay instead of Mexico.

It is perfectly acceptable to say that such-and-such a plover is a Semipalmated, end of story. But it is also worthwhile to try to discern the fascinating life history stories that are encoded in a bird's molts and plumages.

124 JUVENILIA

Baltimore Oriole
Icterus galbula

ATHENA SPRANG FULL GROWN from the head of Zeus, according to myth, and in a full coat of armor. In the same manner, our discussion thus far of molts and plumages (§§116–123), of a bird's "armor," may have given the impression that one need study only adults—and adult males at that. As it turns out, everything we've said about adult males basically applies to adult females. Males and females of the Baltimore Oriole look very different as adults, but their molt strategies are the same overall: Both sexes have a complete molt after breeding (technically, the prebasic molt) and a partial molt before breeding (the prealternate molt). There is some variation among individuals (for example, in the extent of the prealternate molt), of course, but it averages out between the sexes. What we've said about adult males (and females) does *not*, however, apply to younger birds.

Before we proceed, a bit of terminology. Peruse the ornithological literature, and you'll see various words to describe birds that aren't yet adults: "immature," "subadult," "juvenile," and the odd word "juvenal." Unfortunately, there is some inconsistency in how these terms are applied, so we'll go with the simpler and conceptually powerful idea of the annual plumage cycle (§120). Fortunately, that idea *does* apply quite nicely to the molts and plumages of *all* birds.

It's a sunny morning in August, and a troupe of Baltimore Orioles, garbed in burnt orange and dusky black, clambers through the treetops. A second-year male (hatched the year before) has almost finished the complete prebasic molt, a full-on adult (hatched two or more years ago) is beginning his complete prebasic molt, and a couple hatch-year male (young of the year) will soon begin a special molt, the preformative molt, unique to young birds. Is that three different strategies? Perhaps. But even as we alternately admire and despair at all the diversity in our little flock of orioles, we affirm the lesson of the Ring-billed Gull (§122): The annual plumage cycle is a key constraint on the physiology and ecology of all birds in North America.

125 "MOLT IS MESSY"

≪≪ ≪≪ ≪≪ ≪≪ ≪≪ ≪≪ ≪≪◇≫ ≫≫ ≫≫ ≫≫ ≫≫ ≫≫ ≫≫

Wood Duck
Aix sponsa

D UCKS IN AUGUST ARE A MESS. Most species are in a so-called eclipse plumage at this time of year, as a result of which many individuals are flightless. This eclipse plumage—drab and disheveled-looking—is held for just a short while, and with good reason: Flightlessness is a decidedly maladaptive trait! The birds need to get back to the business of flying. But to reprise an old lesson (§§117, 120, 123), ducks *have* to molt. So they wear their eclipse plumage briefly, then reacquire feathers that enable them to fly. That plumage is given the name "nuptial," for the splendor of the male.

Can these quaintly named "eclipse" and "nuptial" plumages be fit into the modern paradigm of basic and alternate plumages (§§120–122)? The answer is gratifyingly in the affirmative. It has recently been demonstrated that nuptial and eclipse plumages correspond to the basic and alternate plumages, respectively. On the one hand, that result is counterintuitive: Basic plumages tend to be dull and alternate plumages bright. On the other hand, this scenario comports perfectly with the northern hemisphere plumage cycle, resetting each year (with the prebasic molt) in late summer and fall.

"Molt is messy," the iconoclastic ornithologist Steve Howell (§36) says archly. What he means is that it only looks that way, what with all those partially formed incoming feathers replacing a previous generation of worn and broken feathers. But molt is also ordered and logical and eminently sensible. There are a thousand and one details (more, actually), needless to say, and you can read all about them in Howell's *Molt in North American Birds* (2010). For a million and one details (only a slight exaggeration), consult Peter Pyle's two-volume *Identification Guide to North American Birds* (1997, 2008). Don't sweat the details. Instead, focus on the central interrelated and unifying principles: The molt cycle is annual; discrete molts result in and correspond to discrete plumages; and all birds have to molt.

Molt makes sense.

126 ZUGUNRUHE

Yellow Warbler
Setophaga petechia

THE YELLOW BIRD WITH THE beady black eye casts a quick look your way, then flies off straight across the lagoon. You can hear its flight call: *zzzt*, weak but abrupt, like an electric spark. Come to think of it, you've been hearing that sound the whole afternoon; but it hadn't really sunk in till just now. This is the easily overlooked flight call of the Yellow Warbler, distinct from the call note, an emphatic, clacking *chip!* (Warblers' call notes are often called chip notes, a moniker that seems especially fitting in the case of the Yellow's honest-to-goodness *chip!*)

Yellow Warblers give their flight calls at any time of the year, but there seems to be a decided uptick in the behavior starting around midsummer. How come? It probably has something to do with "zugunruhe."

One of the most wondrous things about bird lovers is that they unself-consciously speak aloud words like "zugunruhe." The word is German, of course, but it's also as English as sauerkraut or kindergarten. It means "migratory restlessness" (from *zug*, "tugging" or "drawing toward," and *unruhe*, "anxiousness"), and it denotes the fidgetiness exhibited by birds getting ready for migration. The phenomenon has been well established with studies of birds in laboratory settings, but zugunruhe (German capital *Z* not necessary; this is a full-on English word, recall) transcends the physiological state of individual birds. You go out on a breezy afternoon in late July or early August, and you just feel it: a collective nervous energy, avian anxiety, zugunruhe.

ZZZT! Another Yellow Warbler, and you don't even bother to look up. The flight call, that little spark, is definitive. The sound proclaims the identity of the bird, but it also gives definition to something grander than *Setophaga petechia*. Those millipascals of sound energy excite something in your brain, and a chain reaction goes off. This is a "Proustian moment," a cavalcade of impressions and experiences, the human experience of zugunruhe.

127 HOW THE SANDPIPER GOT HIS SPOTS

⋘ ⋘ ⋘ ⋘ ⋘ ⋘ ⋘◇⋙ ⋙ ⋙ ⋙ ⋙ ⋙ ⋙

Spotted Sandpiper
Actitis macularius

AT LEAST A THOUSAND SANDPIPERS are strewn out across the lakebed ahead. Where to start? How about the easy one?—the one with the odd shape, funky gait, and huge black spots on the undercarriage. It's the well-named Spotted Sandpiper, one of the simplest shorebird IDs.

Our "Spottie" is joined by another, also oddly shaped and given to weird jerky motions. Even before it landed, we knew what it was; Spotted Sandpipers in flight appear stiff, their wings bowed downward, alternating between short glides and flicking wingbeats. A quick look at this second sandpiper, and . . . wait a minute! It has no spots! The bird is a juvenile—and an object lesson in the field identification of shorebirds on fall migration.

Especially in the earlier stages of the southward migration of North American sandpipers, most individuals can be classified as either juveniles (hatched this year) or adults (hatched one or more years ago). Adults tend to appear earlier and to appear rather worn; juveniles, by contrast, tend to show up a bit later and to look spiffier. That means twice the number of plumages and, if we take a dim view of the matter, twice the perplexity to ponder out on the mudflats. But let's look on the bright side: These plumage differences are the key that unlocks some of the most fiendish of ID conundrums: "peeps" (§19), dowitchers (§118), and more. Consult a field guide for all the inviting details.

Rudyard Kipling, he of the notorious *Just So Stories*, wondered how the leopard got its spots. In the case of *Actitis macularius*, we know that the adult got its spots via the prealternate molt (§122), a phenomenon unrecognized in Kipling's time. Now let's not go too hard on the old chap; you may not have noticed it, but we didn't mention molt, not once at all, in all our lessons on taxonomy, birdsong, spring migration, and the breeding season (§§26–115)! Well, we won't get away with it for the rest of the year.

128 WITH A LITTLE HELP FROM MY FRIENDS

⋘⋘ ⋘⋘ ⋘⋘ ⋘⋘ ⋘⋘ ⋘⋘ ⋘⋘◇⋙ ⋙⋙ ⋙⋙ ⋙⋙ ⋙⋙ ⋙⋙ ⋙⋙

Forster's Tern
Sterna forsteri

"L ook! Out in middle of the lake, beyond the buoy, coming in from the left—the silvery bird with the pointy wings and long tail. Forster's Tern! Make that two! HY leading, AHY trailing."

Translation: HY denotes h̲atch y̲ear, the birder's designation for a bird hatched the current calendar year; AHY signifies a̲fter h̲atch y̲ear, a bird hatched any year prior. The distinction is important for field ID: In many species, the biggest difference in appearance is between HYs and AHYs.

During spring migration (§§55–74), we didn't distinguish between HYs and AHYs for the simple reason that there were none of the former; every bird migrating north through our area was hatched the year before. During fall migration, on the other hand, HYs are legion. Once again, we are reminded that it's a mistake to think of fall migration as a rewind of the spring migration tape (§74).

Our AHY Forster's Tern might be ca. 400 days old. Or it might be 4,000 days old. In any event, it's got some experience. The bird has at least two migrations under its belt (last fall's and this spring's). Our HY, though, might have fledged only 40 days earlier. Yet here it is already on migration!

Until the late 20th century, instinct was believed to be of overwhelming importance in getting HY birds from here to there. The idea was that birds, like bacteria and trees, just "know" what to do. No longer. In recent decades, there has been a revolution in our understanding of avian cognition and culture. We'll come to that a bit later (§§184–185), but for now let's take a closer look at the terns.

After a moment's observation, we discern that the HY is a tagalong. The AHY is probably its parent and almost assuredly a sort of life coach. The HY is a physiological marvel, already capable of migrating hundreds or even thousands of miles. But it gets by with a little help from its friends. Which, when you think about it, is even more impressive.

129 OUT OF THE FRYING PAN

Red-breasted Nuthatch
Sitta canadensis

THE TIMING OF MIGRATION is, to a certain extent, predictable. Tree Swallows and Fox Sparrows migrate early in spring, Mourning Warblers and Alder Flycatchers late. In fall, Common Nighthawks are long gone before Northern Shrikes are on the move. But other birds enjoy some flexibility in when or even whether to migrate at all. The Red-breasted Nuthatch falls into this latter category.

Go birding in August in the Midwest, and your chances of finding one of these birdlets—part pugilist, part pixie—range from "rather improbable" to "fairly likely." If things are hunky-dory in the pine forests where they nest, many Red-breasted Nuthatches will stay put. But if things aren't to their liking, they bail. When birders say, "It's shaping up to be a good fall for nuthatches," what they really mean is that things have been rough on the home front—and that they are about to get worse. Nuthatches and other pinewoods specialists appear to be able to anticipate a poor harvest of the conifer seeds on which they depend so heavily during the long winter.

All things considered, they'd rather hang tight. Migration is always risky, especially when you're not sure where you're going and what you'll find once you're there. But these large-scale decampments are a part of the species' natural history: For as long as there have been forest fires and regional droughts, Red-breasted Nuthatches have responded accordingly. Fluctuation in the food supply is a fact of life for these feisty forest dwellers. Wholesale alteration of their habitat, however, is not.

Drought, fire, and other natural disasters (for example, insect outbreaks) have intensified in recent years in pine forests in North America and elsewhere, with anthropogenic climate change the prime suspect. For now, things are okay. Red-breasted Nuthatches seem to be rolling with the punches. But there are serious concerns about the long-term viability of North American conifer forests. If "it's shaping up to be a good fall for nuthatches," things may be looking bleak—for all of us.

130 INTO THE FIRE

<<< <<< <<< <<< <<< <<< <<<<>>> >>> >>> >>> >>> >>> >>>

Northern Rough-winged Swallow
Stelgidopteryx serripennis

THERE'S A SAYING, "One swallow does not a summer make." It's a fine proverb in its original formulation, a caution about the human psyche. But it's a bit less effective as a biological metaphor. The thing is, swallows are all about summer. Away from our coasts and southern border, the twittering of swallows is proof positive that spring has sprung. Swallows are as emblematic of summer as the crack of the bat and hot dogs on the grill. And most of them are gone well before the first frosts of autumn.

The Northern Rough-winged Swallow—small bird, big name—fits the bill. Or, perhaps we should say, *used to* fit the bill. Earlier this century, birders discovered these dinky brown birds overwintering at a sewage treatment plant in Philadelphia. And not just two or three. Dozens most years, some years the number swelling to more than a hundred.

Birders are still in shock. Swallows are supposed to "fly south for the winter." Especially the Northern Rough-wing, an obligate aerial insectivore (§115) and complete long-distance migrant (§62). In the case of the Red-breasted Nuthatch (§129), we asked: What could make them leave their breeding grounds? In the case of the Northern Rough-winged Swallow, it's the other way around: What could make them stay? Same answer for both: food. Even in the dead of winter, that wastewater plant in Philly is swarming with midges. And swallows feast on midges. It's that simple.

These "sewerage swallows" are compelling. They are doughty and adaptable, and we admire them for their resourcefulness. We can't help but sense, though, that something is amiss, that this is no environmental feel-good story. There is something dystopian about swallows picking bugs off heated chlorine tanks and hot sludge ponds in the dead of winter. And there are many other stories like this one. A wide array of species, including several swallows, have adjusted in recent years to human-modified landscapes by delaying or even forgoing their fall migrations.

131 CANARY IN A COAL MINE?

Gray Flycatcher
Empidonax wrightii

*E*MPIDONAX FLYCATCHERS—empids, for short—give birders fits. They're actually not all that bad in summer, when they sort out by habitat and sing distinctive songs. But on migration, they're undeniably hard to ID. That's especially the case in fall, when field ID is complicated by variation among HYs and AHYs (§128), plus matters regarding the onset of the prebasic molt (§120) that are as yet unsolved mysteries. Pull up an eBird checklist for anywhere in August or September, and you're apt to find an entry for Empid sp. (Sp., pronounced SPUH, is the birder's shorthand for "species unidentified.")

All that said, there is one empid that is relatively easy to ID, even on fall migration. The Gray Flycatcher is notably long-billed and long-tailed, and its low-contrast and soft plumage imparts a distinctive appearance. Most of all, the bird's frequent tail dipping—an exaggeratedly slow downward flick of the tail—separates the Gray from other empids. Grays are so distinctive that even birds out of range may be confidently ID'd. Speaking of which . . .

Of late, birders on the High Plains east of the Rockies have been reporting (and credibly documenting) migrant Gray Flycatchers in places they're "not supposed to be." By itself, the phenomenon might be dismissed as "just one of those things." But it seems to fit into a bigger picture. For one thing, Bushtits and Black-chinned Hummingbirds are doing something similar; like the Gray Flycatcher, those two species are expanding their ranges northward and eastward from arid habitats to the southwest. Also intriguing is a climate change forecast by the National Audubon Society, predicting a major shift north and especially east in the nonbreeding range of the Gray.

To be clear, we're talking about preliminary evidence, an easily overlooked bird, and the complexities of climate change. It's still possible that this is just one of those things. Or it could be the start of something big. One thing's for sure: Avian migratory strategies adapt rapidly in the face of human modifications to the environment (§§129–130). The Gray Flycatcher bears watching.

132 AMERICA'S FLIGHTLESS BIRD

⋘⋘ ⋘⋘ ⋘⋘ ⋘⋘ ⋘⋘ ⋘⋘ ⋘⋘⟨⟩⟫ ⟫⟫ ⟫⟫ ⟫⟫ ⟫⟫ ⟫⟫ ⟫⟫ ⟫⟫

Eared Grebe
Podiceps nigricollis

IN SPEAKING AND WRITING about spring migration, birders are given to exalted language: The phenomenon is lavishly choreographed, full of pomp and circumstance, all pageantry and extravagance, "The Greatest Show on Earth" (§55). Fall migration is different, a time to ponder zugunruhe (§126), molts and plumages (§§127–128), and the strained relationships between birds and humans (§§129–131). You might be able to guess what's coming next. Yes, there is always an exception to the rule.

The fall migration of the Eared Grebe has got to be one of the most astonishing biological phenomena on the planet. After nesting, the birds initiate a dramatic molt migration (§§116–118) to hypersaline lakes in the Great Basin. We're talking about places substantially saltier than the ocean. There they pig out, engaging in hyperphagia (§67) so extreme that their bodies cannot handle it; the grebes metamorphose into avian garbage bags, unable to fly. Then, through a physiological transformation known as hypertrophy, they reacquire the muscle mass and function necessary for flight, and migrate on to coastal winter areas. Are you starting to notice the recurrence of a particular prefix?— *hyper*saline, *hyper*phagia, *hyper*trophy. Everything about the Eared Grebe's annual cycle is crazily intense. It gets crazier. These alternating bouts of volancy (the ability to fly) and flightlessness occur throughout the entire annual cycle, up to five such bouts per year! As a result, many adults are flightless for more than half the year—yet also capable of sustained migration over hundreds of miles of inhospitable desert in western North America.

The secret of their success is food availability, in particular the brine shrimp that reach staggering densities in such favored staging grounds as the Great Salt Lake, Mono Lake, and the Sea of Cortés. These places are under heavy and increasing pressure from humans, though, and their continued viability for the Eared Grebe is uncertain. We return now to the unavoidable truth that the story of migration is inextricably linked with the story of human impacts on the environment.

133 LIGHTS OUT!

Great Crested Flycatcher
Myiarchus crinitus

THE PROCESS HAS BEEN UNDER WAY for two-plus months, but it's gotten noticeable only recently: The nights are getting longer. Not only that, the process is accelerating. Changes in day length are fastest at the equinoxes, slowest at the solstices. There's not as much time as there used to be for evening softball, and our morning commutes commence in semi-darkness now. The birds notice it, too.

One of the multiple triggers for the initiation of bird migration is photoperiod, and by early September most species have begun the journey south. Some migrate by day, but the majority fly by night. We know that in part by going out on cool nights in late summer and hearing the flight calls, anxious and urgent, of nocturnal migrants: thrushes, tanagers, grosbeaks, and more. But other birds are stubbornly silent on nocturnal migration. The Great Crested Flycatcher, for example. So how do we know they're up there? Radar echoes (§72) can't ID the birds by species, and the evidence from observations of morning flights (§73) is somewhat circumstantial. What if there were some way to capture silent nocturnal migrants?

There is, unfortunately.

It is estimated that more than 100 million birds, most of them songbirds on nocturnal migration, are killed annually by collisions with cell phone towers, navigation structures, and especially tall buildings. Walk around the downtown streets of an American metropolis on a September dawn, and you will find dead birds underfoot with distressing frequency. In this way, ornithologists Walter Taylor and Bruce Anderson, in their 1970s-era studies of birds killed overnight by collisions with communication towers in Florida, were able to demonstrate that Great Crested Flycatchers migrate at night.

Can we do anything about it? "Lights out!" initiatives—they're as simple as they sound—are the best way forward. Birds are disoriented in the bright lights of city centers, with many striking buildings and dying on impact. Toronto and Chicago pioneered lifesaving measures for the birds migrating through their airspace, and other cities have followed suit. Where there's a will, there's a way.

134 CATS INDOORS!

Warbling Vireo
Vireo gilvus

"MITZI WOULD NEVER DO SUCH A THING! She can't even catch her own tail!"

Yet there she is, calmly pacing the back patio with her latest catch, a little gray bird that's not quite dead. Mitzi releases her death grip and the bird falls to the stonework. The moribund creature flutters weakly, then Mitzi pounces again. She seems to be enjoying herself. Her prey item is a Warbling Vireo, a small songbird of the treetops. Mitzi may not be able to catch her own tail, but the vireo—wary, cryptic, arboreal—was easily subdued.

Cats are many things, but they are perhaps most of all amazing killing machines. They are naturals, supremely gifted at killing. Fish swim, snakes slither, cats kill. Even an overweight declawed house cat with a big ole bell around her neck will, given the chance, figure out a way to maim every manner of songbird and small mammal.

The number of birds killed annually by cats boggles the mind. A conservative estimate is one *billion* in the United States, very roughly 10 for every cat in the country. That figure may exceed the number of collisions with structures (§133) by a factor of 10. And as with the hazard of building strikes, we want to know: What can we do about it?

Easy. Keep your cat indoors. Encourage your neighbors to do likewise. It's the humane thing to do, and not just for the birds' sake. Indoor cats live longer, healthier lives. Organizations like the American Bird Conservancy provide fact sheets and other resources that make the case for "Cats indoors!" campaigns in language that is clear, compelling, and compassionate.

Bird conservation is, in many respects, complex. You can't just snap your fingers and turn off all the lights in a major American metropolis (§133). Even so, "Lights out!" initiatives in those cities have been successful. Keeping cats indoors, however, is as simple as, well, closing the door. We said it before, we'll say it again: Where there's a will, there's a way.

135 THE PERILS OF PORTABLE TOILETS

<<< <<< <<< <<< <<< <<< <<<>>> >>> >>> >>> >>> >>> >>>

Red-headed Woodpecker
Melanerpes erythrocephalus

Y OU KNEW YOUR DRYER VENT was clogged, but you weren't expecting *this:* a full-on adult Red-headed Woodpecker!

"Um, how long do you spose the bird's been in there?"

The technician reminds you that it's been 10 years since you cleaned your dryer vent. Could the bird really be that old? Consider that bird skins, properly curated, last hundreds of years. Now a dryer vent isn't the same as the climate-controlled steel cabinets of a modern museum collection, but the woodpecker is basically in good shape. You pick it up and are amazed by its lightness; an adult Red-headed Woodpecker weighs under three ounces when alive, substantially less as a carcass. You hand the bird back to the technician and demand to know, "How'd it get in there?"

She explains that woodpeckers and other birds get caught up in pipes and vents, shutters and siding, gutters and other spaces, all the time. Even mine shafts and Porta Potties. Porta Potties? Come again?

Birds of many species are drawn to cavities like moths to a flame. During the breeding season, they're prospecting for nest sites (§§98–99), but migrants and winterers are likewise unable to resist apertures of all sorts. There's got to be food in there, and shelter from the cold, and a place to hide from predators. That's all true, but, unfortunately, there's often no good way back out.

The ventilation pipes of vault toilets promise warmth and insects—and they're death traps. So the Teton Raptor Center's Poo-Poo Project (no kidding) has installed more than 10,000 bird-proof screens over outdoor toilets in all 50 U.S. states. The screens have zero effect on proper sanitation and other Porta Potty functions, but they are 100 percent effective at preventing entry by birds. A related effort is under way to prevent rare rosy-finches from gaining access to the piping associated with mines and old mining claims. This isn't rocket science, and all that's required is a bit of wire mesh. The result: thousands, probably millions, of birds' lives saved.

136 THE DARK SIDE OF GREEN ENERGY?

Eastern Kingbird
Tyrannus tyrannus

ONE OF THE REASONS birds migrate by night is that it's safer (§64). Or maybe it's more accurate to say that it *used to be* safer—for, as we have seen, the proliferation of brightly lit buildings and cell phone towers presents a major new hazard for night fliers (§133). Diurnal migrants face challenges that nocturnal migrants do not, but at least they can see what's in front of them. Now suppose the obstacles ahead are in motion.

The Eastern Kingbird—a snazzy, belligerent flycatcher—migrates mainly by day, yet carcasses of the species are frequently reported around a certain type of infrastructure: large-array wind farms. The massive blades, exceeding a hundred feet in length, spin at close to 200 mph at their tips. They're going too fast for kingbirds and other species to get out of the way. Even powerful fliers like Golden Eagles frequently collide with the rotating blades. And the risk is unabated after nightfall, with bats believed to be especially prone to collisions.

Isn't "green energy"—wind, solar, and so forth—supposed to be good? Green energy is clean energy. It's renewable. It doesn't pollute. Those things are true, but all energy "costs" something. That's one of the immutable laws of physics, and it's also an inescapable truth about biological conservation. And so we circle back to the question that has dominated our thinking in recent lessons (§§133–135): Can anything be done on behalf of the kingbirds and other birds that live and die around wind farms?

Two answers, one straightforward, the other less so. Straightforward: where wind farms are sited. By participating in public hearings and providing expert counsel, birders have contributed importantly to decisions to build wind farms away from local hot spots where birds concentrate for feeding and migration. Less straightforward: kicking the can down the road. The ultimate challenge for biological conservation isn't *how* energy is extracted, it's how *much*. Instead of installing solar panels (requiring lead, arsenic, cadmium, and other toxins) on your roof, consider living more simply—and efficiently.

137 WE'LL LEAVE THE LIGHT ON

Northern Waterthrush
Parkesia noveboracensis

WHAT ARE SOME OF THE bad things that could happen to a Northern Waterthrush migrating through West Virginia? How about getting shot (§111)? We wince at the thought, but waterthrushes are protected, sportsmen know it, and hunting has zero impact on the species. Okay, how about having its habitat bulldozed (§112)? That's another cringe-worthy outcome, but much of the waterthrush's habitat in West Virginia is protected or at least left alone. Other hazards: flying into a building (§133), falling prey to a cat (§134), getting trapped in a portable toilet (§135), and colliding with a wind turbine (§136). Here's another: leaving the light on in your motel room in Arkansas.

In Arkansas? What's Arkansas got to do with it?

To be fair, we could be talking about any U.S. state in the sprawling lower Mississippi River drainage. Electricity in the region is generated in no small part by coal-burning power plants, which spew mercury (and other toxins) into the atmosphere. A generally northeasterly airflow carries the mercury to the Appalachians, where it is bioaccumulated in the food chain. A grimly fascinating step in the process involves the conversion by bacteria of inorganic mercury into methylmercury, which is toxic to waterthrushes and other warblers. In other words: Charge your smartphone in Arkansas (or wherever), kill a Northern Waterthrush several hundred miles downstream.

Let's back up a step. We birders are inclined to storm the barricades when we witness outright habitat destruction—the sight of a front-end loader, say, pushing fill into the bog that sheltered and sustained waterthrushes last fall. That's understandable. And commendable. Wind farms and city skylines elicit similar responses. Even the neighbor's cat on the back fence or the blaze orange of an approaching turkey hunter can trigger bird protection impulses in many of us. Our hearts are in the right place. But our priorities are perhaps misaligned with the most pressing concerns for biological conservation in the 21st century.

138 THE UPSIDE OF HUMAN-MODIFIED LANDSCAPES?

⋘ ⋘ ⋘ ⋘ ⋘ ⋘ ⋘◇⋙ ⋙ ⋙ ⋙ ⋙ ⋙ ⋙

Canada Goose
Branta canadensis

ALDO LEOPOLD AND ROGER TORY PETERSON, two of the most celebrated American nature writers of the last century, were overcome with feelings of heartfelt delight whenever their thoughts turned to *Branta canadensis,* the Canada Goose. For both men, the goose was an emblem of wilderness. "One swallow does not make a summer," wrote Leopold, "but one skein of geese, cleaving the murk of a March thaw, *is* the spring." Peterson: "Few men have souls so dead that they will not bother to look up when they hear the barking of wild geese."

Fast-forward to the present age. The Canada Goose has become a full-on nuisance—legally, aesthetically, biologically. US Airways flight 1549 was famously brought down by Canada Geese earlier this century. In many places, the barking of "wild" geese is heard round the clock; and skeins of geese come and go every day of the year. What has happened?

The species has evolved, both genetically and culturally. Without so much as a whiff of anthropomorphism, we can say that Canada Geese have figured out how to flourish in human-dominated landscapes. Populations that formerly bred on Arctic sea cliffs now nest on high-rise office buildings; flocks that used to search widely for succulent marsh grasses now concentrate at golf courses and corporate headquarters; and subspecies that once exposed themselves to the perils of migration have simply quit migrating altogether. Search YouTube for Canada Geese, and you'll more likely get videos of birds attacking office workers *(tinyurl.com/goose-attacks-man)* than cleaving the murk of a March thaw.

Because Canada Geese flourish in the largest human population centers, we notice them. But other goose species are increasing, with dire consequences for whole ecosystems we rarely visit (§107). Other waterfowl, too: from Black-bellied Whistling-Ducks in agro-ecosystems along the Gulf Coast to Trumpeter Swans in the Midwest and Northeast. How many bird species overall are known or suspected to be increasing in response to human modifications to the environment? You might be surprised.

139 WHAT GOES DOWN, MUST COME UP?

Brown Pelican
Pelecanus occidentalis

S TROLL ALONG THE WHITE SAND BEACHES of the central Gulf Coast, and you're likely to take in one of the most mesmerizing of avian spectacles: Brown Pelicans fishing just offshore. Small to medium flocks sail by, single file, in gentle undulations, their wingtips barely clearing the water's surface. Suddenly they pull up, then fall like missiles into the sea.

Now picture yourself at that same beach 30–35 years ago. Seeing just a single pelican would have been notable; the spectacle of flock upon flock would have been inconceivable. We almost lost the Brown Pelican.

The culprit was the bioaccumulation of pesticides, including DDT, in the marine food chain. Fortunately, DDT and other poisons were banned during the presidency of Richard M. Nixon, a time of major advances for the cause of environmentalism in the United States and elsewhere. Brown Pelican populations responded in a big way, and the species was soon delisted, no longer requiring protection under the Endangered Species Act.

Recent surges in numbers of the Canada Goose (§138) and Brown Pelican are in some sense typical. Although it is understandable to focus on the many anthropogenic causes of avian population *decline* (§§111–115, 129–137), it is likewise imperative that we acknowledge recent and ongoing population *increases* in a great many bird species. In a study of the approximately 250 bird species known to breed in Nevada at the turn of the 21st century, researchers found that approximately 100 had declined in the latter half of the 20th century, but that an equal number had increased. Only 50-ish (ca. 20 percent) had populations that were generally stable.

To be fair, many of these changes—especially the population increases—were reversals of population declines from earlier in the last century. Nevada's own pelican, the American White (§89), is one such species: down for several decades, then back up in subsequent decades. But let's not lose sight of the big picture: Bird populations are dynamic, perhaps more so at the present time than ever before.

140 DEAL WITH THE DEVIL

⋘ ⋘ ⋘ ⋘ ⋘ ⋘ ⋘ ⟨⟩ ⋙ ⋙ ⋙ ⋙ ⋙ ⋙ ⋙

Lesser Scaup
Aythya affinis

LAKE ERIE IMPROBABLY CAUGHT FIRE 50 years ago. Alright, not the whole lake. Not really the lake at all, but, rather, just the mouth of the Cuyahoga River in Cleveland, so fouled with oil and sludge that the surface erupted into flames. Nevertheless, it was a time of reckoning for Americans, an important episode in the early history of the modern environmental movement.

The river is cleaned up now, and Lake Erie—famously declared to be ecologically dead—has roared back to life. Thanks to the Clean Water Act of 1972, the Clean Air Act of 1970, and other environmental safeguards, it seems unlikely that Lake Erie will ever catch fire again. But a new threat, unforeseen at the dawn of the environmental era, imperils the ecological integrity of the region.

Zebra mussels, native to Europe and accidentally introduced to Lake St. Clair in 1988, quickly established themselves in the Great Lakes and today dominate the entire ecosystem. We humans regard mussels as tasty foodstuffs, and so do aquatic birds like the Lesser Scaup, a sharp-looking diving duck whose head glistens purple if the light is just right. Zebra mussels are especially prolific around the shoreline infrastructure (think piers, pipes, jetties), and word got out to the scaups. Their numbers have increased in winter as well as on migration, and waterfowl biologists believe that their migratory range (in crude terms, their "flyway") has shifted in response to this novel food resource. Unfortunately, they're eating junk food.

Zebra mussels are filter feeders, indiscriminately scarfing down any waterborne material big enough to pass through their siphons. That includes toxic selenium, which the mussels bioaccumulate. So even though Lesser Scaup numbers have increased in recent years on the Great Lakes, their overall population is down. Selenium poisoning, affecting various aspects of the species' reproductive biology, is believed to be a chief reason for the decline. The zebra mussels are an ecological Trojan horse, at once irresistible to the Lesser Scaup and a likely cause of sustained population losses.

141 PAVED WITH GOOD INTENTIONS

Northern Shoveler
Spatula clypeata

TWO YEARS AGO, THE MARSH by the freeway was loaded with shovelers, so named for their spatulate bills. The peak count was 200, a new high for the county. All day long, they fed constantly on the crustaceans, insect larvae, and plant matter there. It was quite a sight! And sound! Foraging flocks of shovelers are unique: They bunch up literally shoulder to shoulder, forming a "canopy" where food is concentrated near the water's surface. The whole time, they call softly—a peculiar, mechanical, disyllabic *shook, shook,* repeated steadily.

Last year at the marsh, the maximum count was down to 50—disappointing, but still a regional high count. And this year, just one, a lone male. He flew in one day shortly after the fall equinox, paddled about the shallow waters for a couple hours, then moved on. What happened? What's wrong with the marsh?

Our freeway marsh is an artificial wetland. It was until recently considered useless, a wide expanse of weeds. Kids rode their bikes on the social trails there, a homeless encampment attracted occasional notice, and that was about it. The site seemed perfect for "ecological mitigation."

Several miles away, a natural wetland had been drained for badly needed infrastructure reform: an elaborate spaghetti bowl of highway interchanges. To offset the loss, the useless expanse of weeds was designated a mitigation site, intended to compensate for the 10 acres of wetland lost to highway construction. Dikes were built, canals dug; an observation tower was installed; and, in due course, the bike trails and homeless encampment were flooded.

For the first few years, the wetland mitigation site was hailed as an environmental success story. The new marsh hummed with chorus frogs and swamp katydids and those hundreds of shovelers. Then the whole thing just died. Sadly, that's how it is with most created wetlands. Building a swamp or a marsh is a fiendishly difficult proposition, requiring adaptive management—constant monitoring and tweaking. Most projects aren't conceived, let alone funded, that way. And most mitigation projects, however well intentioned, end in failure.

PART FIVE

WHAT WE KNOW

October—November

142 WHAT WE KNOW

Vesper Sparrow
Pooecetes gramineus

THE BIRD IS a molting mess, but we know what it is. "Vesper Sparrow," someone in the group states matter-of-factly.

The leader nods in agreement, noting that it's an AHY (§128), and taps the entry into the eBird app on her phone. Question: How do we know it's a Vesper Sparrow? Why isn't this a Song Sparrow or a Savannah Sparrow? Both are streaked brown and nondescript overall like the bird in front of us. How do we even know it's a sparrow? Why isn't this a female House Finch or female Red-winged Blackbird—streaky brown birds easily mistaken for sparrows?

The bird flushes, flashing white tail edges ("outer rectrices," to be technical about it). That mark instantly eliminates Song and Savannah sparrows, House Finch and Red-winged Blackbird, and a host of other ID contenders. The bird then alights on a fence post, ruffles its feathers, and reveals a rufous patch on the shoulders (technically, the lesser coverts). This can only be a Vesper Sparrow.

But we knew it was a Vesper Sparrow *before* we saw the lesser coverts and outer rectrices. Again: How did we know? One answer is that we applied all the methods of field ID we've already learned. We assessed the bird's color (§6), pattern (§7), size (§8), and shape (§9)—and we did so automatically and integratively (§10). Date (§23) and location (§21) entered into the picture, as did a broader appreciation of the species' S&D (§25). Knowledge of vocalizations (§§38–54) and molt (§§116–125) likewise informed our judgment.

That's all well and good, but it begs the question. How did we learn all that stuff in the first place? What is the source of our knowledge about Vesper Sparrows? Or, to frame the question in the same manner that the philosophers do: How do we know what we know? The question has been lurking behind practically every lesson thus far. Next up: some provisional answers. And, if we're not careful, additional questions!

143 THE GOOD BOOK

Hairy Woodpecker
Dryobates villosus

EVERYBODY KNOWS WHAT a woodpecker is. Show somebody a wood-pecker—in the wild, at the zoo, or in a photo—and that person will more than likely call it a woodpecker. Whether it's a Darjeeling Woodpecker (found in the Himalayas) or one of our widespread American species, we know a woodpecker when we see it. But which kind? All of a sudden, we've gone from common knowledge to inside baseball.

A medium-size, stiff-tailed, black-and-white woodpecker is hitching its way up the linden tree in the backyard. Through process of elimination, we quickly determine that it is a Hairy Woodpecker. Does this ring a bell? We went through the Hairy-versus-Downy exercise in one of our earliest lessons (§10), but we skirted the question of authority. This is a Hairy Woodpecker, yes, but: Says who?

Not all that long ago, the answer would have been: Because it's in the book. A particular sort of book—smallish, illustrated, with the words "guide" and "birds" in the title. There was a time when every den in every American home held copies of books by Erma Bombeck and Dr. Spock, when books called "field guides" lay on the windowsill of every kitchen. Such books were more than adequate for separating the look-alike Hairy and Downy woodpeckers.

They still are. Even though sales of titles by Bombeck and Spock have declined sharply in this century, interest in field guides still runs strong. What about apps? What about eBird? What about social media? Aren't those things cutting into the market share? The short answer is no. But change is in the air. The print field guide has evolved somewhat in the past several decades, and major changes likely lie directly ahead. The bird books of the future may well not be "field guides" in the modern sense at all. But we're not there yet. We birders are gluttons for knowledge, and we depend on bird books as never before.

For now.

144 THE BIRDER'S LIBRARY

⋘ ⋘ ⋘ ⋘ ⋘ ⋘ ⋘◇⋙ ⋙ ⋙ ⋙ ⋙ ⋙ ⋙

Olive-sided Flycatcher
Contopus cooperi

"THIS *IS* AN OLIVE-SIDED, isn't it?"

The big-headed flycatcher is perched at the tip of a dead branch, the way the species is supposed to. It's got the vest, the smudgy dark breast with a paler stripe running up the middle. And you can see cottony tufts poking out from the wings, another field mark of the Olive-sided Flycatcher.

"But I thought they would be gone by now. Can I borrow your field guide, just to make sure?"

The illustration in *Nat Geo* is a perfect match for the bird in the field. The text confirms that the species habitually perches "on high dead branches, including in migration." It also mentions the species' short tail, something you'd overlooked but now see plainly on the bird in real life.

A couple hours later, when you're doing up your eBird checklist for the morning, an earlier suspicion is confirmed. Your Olive-sided Flycatcher trips the automatic filter: "This bird is rare for this date & location," requiring additional details. No prob. You got photos. Still, you're curious about something . . .

You reach behind to the bookcase, and pull down your state's S&D (§25) volume. It informs you that most Olive-sided Flycatchers are gone by mid-September. Do they breed nearby? The map in your state's BBA (§76) shows that they are uncommon in the high country. What subspecies was the bird you saw this morning? Volume I of Pyle's *Identification Guide* (§125) is clear that it could only have been the nominate subspecies *cooperi*. Where is the species most likely to be found on migration? Your state's birdfinding (one word, like birdwatching) guide has that covered.

You're on a roll now. You consult another one of your field guides. One isn't enough. Many birders own three or four field guides. Some own dozens. There are always exceptions to the rule. Not all birders use binoculars (§§174–175), but most do. And not all birders own bird books. But most do.

145 DETAILS . . . DETAILS . . .

Lazuli Bunting
Passerina amoena

OULD IT BE? You live hundreds of miles east of the normal breeding range of the Lazuli Bunting, but this bird is likely a migrant. You have plenty of photos, and this cinnamon-brown visitor to your Midwestern feeder matches the images in your field guide (§143). You've consulted the S&D book for your state (§144), too, and it's not inconceivable that this bird is what you think it is. The problem is that the molts and plumages of the Lazuli Bunting are, in a word, complex.

You're reasonably confident that the bird is not an Indigo Bunting, closely related to the Lazuli. Breeding males look utterly different, but females and HYs (§128) are similar, HY females especially so. Still, you've done your homework—and the photos are tack-sharp. This is not an Indigo Bunting.

Could it be a hybrid, the offspring of two different species?

No fair! Females and HYs are tough. HY females are really tough. But an HY female *hybrid?* What possible recourse do you have? Even the esoteric Pyle Guide (§125) is mum on the matter of such birds. Which do happen, by the way: Lazuli and Indigo buntings routinely hybridize where their breeding ranges overlap, and HY females, although surely overlooked in the field, must just as surely be out there.

Fortunately, you have access to back issues of *Birding* magazine and other print periodicals that emphasize cutting-edge topics in bird ID. A recent article on buntings in fall and winter seals the deal. This bird falls squarely within the expected range of plumage variation for Lazuli Buntings on fall migration.

A key function of birding periodicals is to deliver timely and specialized content—to go beyond the level of detail in field guides and specialty books. But these journals deliver something else, delectable and perhaps expected: community spirit. Most are published by associations of bird lovers, professional or amateur, with mission statements that are all about sharing and learning together.

146 OLD MEDIA, NEW MEDIA

Dickcissel
Spiza americana

REMEMBER EIGHT-TRACK CASSETTES? They were all the rage in the 1970s, but as obsolete by the mid-1980s as clay tablets and papyrus. Remember compact discs (CDs)? Sure, many of us have a few old CDs lying around. We used them to install desktop computers, listen to music, and store digital photos. No more. Today we upload photos to Flickr and download music from Spotify. And a laptop with a CD drive is about as rare these days as an eight-track player.

We snigger today at CDs, but one CD played a transformative role in modern birding history. This was *Flight Calls of Migratory Birds: Eastern North American Land Birds,* released in 2002 by William R. Evans and Michael O'Brien. Until *Flight Calls* launched, the field ID of nocturnal migrants was a largely insoluble problem. It was a classic Catch-22 (§39): We couldn't see the birds, and we didn't know their flight calls.

Flight Calls delivered not only high-quality recordings but also spectrograms (§§44–47), statistical analysis, and similar species. The birding community hailed the Evans and O'Brien CD as a Rosetta Stone for flight calls. Just pop the CD into your desktop computer, and compare with the real sounds you were hearing in the night sky.

Ahem. Nobody pops CDs into their computers anymore. You might as well ask for *Flight Calls* on eight-track or papyrus. The CD is out of print, but Evans and O'Brien recently put *Flight Calls* online *(tinyurl.com/Flight-Calls-CD)*. Pro tip: Start with a distinctive flight call, like that of the Dickcissel *(tinyurl.com/ FC-Dick)*, a warmly colored relative of the cardinals and buntings. The Dickcissel's flight call is undeniably flatulent, "a low, dry, very buzzy *djjjt,*" according to *Flight Calls*. In recent years, records of vagrant Dickcissels on nocturnal migration have been verified with sound recordings of their flight calls!

Flight Calls broke the code of nocturnal migration. But it was pioneering in a grander way: *Flight Calls* was an early herald of new approaches to birding and nature study in the digital era.

147 THE LEGACY OF BIRDCHAT

Greater Roadrunner
Geococcyx californianus

THE LAYOVER THROUGH Dallas is on the long side, and that gets you to thinking about something: Might there be time to sneak out of the airport, espy a Greater Roadrunner, and get back in time for the next leg of your journey? Today we consult eBird or any of a host of other digital resources for the latest intel on roadrunners near Dallas–Fort Worth International Airport. But let's turn back the clock a quarter century, when the world wide web was a brave new world.

First things first. This is pre-9/11, so getting in and out of the airport, even a big one like DFW, is a piece of cake. Second, eBird isn't yet even a gleam in the eye of the IT staff at the Cornell Lab of Ornithology. You have potential access to roadrunners, but you don't know where precisely to look for one of these fabled, oversize, terrestrial cuckoos. (Roadrunners don't say *beep beep*, by the way; they coo lovingly.) What to do? Answer: Send an "RFI" (request for information) to BirdChat.

BirdChat was, and still is, the flagship of the National Birding Hotline Cooperative, which launched in the era of telecopying and dial-up. And although most of us have junked our old fax machines and 9600 baud modems, many of us still do consult BirdChat on occasion. BirdChat holds a special place in our birderly hearts. It always will.

Birders of Gen X and older well remember their first encounter with BirdChat in the early 1990s. We were astounded by its effectiveness. Bird-Chat was a conceptual breakthrough. You could put something out there ("Can someone help me find a roadrunner near the airport?") and reasonably expect the desired response ("Meet me at passenger pickup, I know a good spot at nearby Valley Ranch, I'll have you back in 90 minutes").

BirdChat delivers a tiny fraction of the firepower of Facebook or eBird, and it's easy to dismiss it as a living fossil in this age of petabyte-scale crowd-sourcing. But BirdChat showed us the way. BirdChat established the conceptual model that defines modern birding.

148 BIRDING LISTSERV(E)(R)S

≪≪≪ ≪≪≪ ≪≪≪ ≪≪≪ ≪≪≪ ≪≪◁▷≫ ≫≫≫ ≫≫≫ ≫≫≫ ≫≫≫ ≫≫≫ ≫≫

Great Egret
Ardea alba

WELL! THAT'S A Great Egret!—slender and sinewy, its bill a golden dagger, the black feet almost glistening as if coated with tar, every feather completely white. This is a fine bird for your part of the province, north of the normal range of the species. But it wasn't entirely unexpected.

In the couple of days leading up to your discovery, the provincial listserv was abuzz with chatter about the recent drawdown of a nearby reservoir. Ducks were massing there, shorebirds were still hanging on, and, maybe, somebody chimed in, a "rare ardeid" (the technical name given to herons and egrets) might put in an appearance. The discovery is all yours; you get the credit for this local first. But the insight to go check out the reservoir came from the listserv.

A listserv is a bit like one of the old rideshare boards on college campuses in the late 20th century. The typical birding listserv is geographically oriented (Saskatchewan, Alaska–Juneau and Southeast, California–Shasta County), although some are thematic (advanced ID, nocturnal flight calls, swallows), and BirdChat (§147) is anything goes.

BirdChat, undead but beloved, is relatively inactive, but other birding lists—especially at the state and provincial level—remain lively. Traffic is down slightly in this age of eBird and Facebook, but not by much. The regional listserv is a digital agora for the birding community. Most, although not all, are housed at Birding News *(birding.aba.org)*, a listserv aggregator hosted by the American Birding Association. Browse at Birding News (it's free), or subscribe (also free) to the lists that you consult regularly.

Finally, a nomenclatorial point. Is it lowercase listserv or all-caps LISTSERV? Or is it listserve (with an extra "e") or even listserver? Birders will be debating that one for as long as there is debate about bird names (§35). In the meantime, go post that Great Egret to your provincial listserv(e)(r). Folks need to hear about it!

149 RARE BIRD ALERTS

Rose-breasted Grosbeak
Pheucticus ludovicianus

THE HANDSOME BIRD is precisely at the location of the eBird stick-pin. Its finder created a "personal hot spot" showing the exact tree in which she'd discovered the Rose-breasted Grosbeak. The eBird rare bird alert went out right away, and you're on site within the hour.

You figured you'd missed the species for the year. Rose-breasted Grosbeaks are uncommon but still to be found in the spring in your state, with a few straggling into midsummer. Fall sightings are rare. But with so many folks out birding on this fine weekend in late September, it wasn't out of the question that someone would come across one. You got it for your year list! Woohoo!

The rare bird alert (RBA) has been with us for a while. By the early 1980s, most states and provinces had RBAs. This was before the smartphone era. Why, this was before the internet, period. How is it possible that there were RBAs so long ago? Believe it or not, they were promulgated by telephones, the kinds with rotary dials, hulking receivers, and coily cables. And answering machines. A volunteer would recite an RBA transcript into the cassette-enabled contraption, and birders could call in and listen to the recorded message.

RBAs were updated weekly.

Like BirdChat (§147) and the *Flight Calls* CD (§146), telephone RBAs were revolutionary. And like BirdChat and CDs, telephone RBAs today seem positively antediluvian. Updated *weekly*? Are you serious? We moderns have come to expect RBAs while the bird is still under observation.

The proliferation of real-time RBAs has been met with some amount of angst in the birding community. Is this really the way we were meant to bird, chasing one rarity after another? Consider that, way back in the benighted era of rotary phones, there were telephone trees for the (relatively) rapid dissemination of news about rarities. It's probably best to view the eBird RBA as the consummation of an ancient longing by the birding community.

150 LET ME GOOGLE THAT FOR YOU

Barn Swallow
Hirundo rustica

NORMALLY SKITTISH, the neighborhood Barn Swallows are uncharacteristically cooperative this morning. Maybe the cooler weather has something to do with it. In any event, these long-distance migrants will be gone any day now, so you delight in the opportunity for photographic study of the flock of two dozen, lined up practically shoulder to shoulder on the utility wire straight ahead. You angle for the perfect capture: diffuse light, plain-gray cloud cover as a backdrop, a really nice depiction of plumage differences in a flock of Barn Swallows.

This is going to be a five-star upload to eBird, easily 100 "likes" at Facebook Birders, maybe even a "Featured Photo" for your state ornithological journal: "Variation in rectrix length in *Hirundo rustica*: A photo study." (Rectrix = birderspeak for tail feather.) You get to wondering about something: Why do their tails vary so? Sure, age and sex have much to do with it; so do the interrelated matters of molt and seasonality. But you retain an old, fading memory—was it at a bird club lecture? in a college textbook?—that aerodynamics and sexual selection are an important part of the story. You want to include that in your write-up for the state journal.

In the old days, you would have gone to the library (remember?) and asked the gently beleaguered librarian to look it up in the card catalog (remember?)—Dewey Decimal or Library of Congress, you could never keep them straight. Today it's all online. Just Google it. Or get a friend to. There's a delicious spoof out there, lmgtfy.com, short for Let me Google that for you.

Seriously, the amount of info about birds online is mind-boggling. Search the string BARN + SWALLOW + TAIL + SEXUAL + SELECTION, and Google returns more than half a million hits. Getting proficient with the internet requires some discipline and judiciousness, but so it is with navigating the shelves at the public library. The internet is here to stay, and we might as well apply this new resource to the study and appreciation of birds.

151 JOIN THE CLUB

⋘ ⋘ ⋘ ⋘ ⋘ ⋘ ⋘ ⟨◇⟩ ⋙ ⋙ ⋙ ⋙ ⋙ ⋙ ⋙

Green Heron
Butorides virescens

"THE GREEN HERONS are still at the wastewater retention pond."
You already know that. You saw it on the listserv (§148), and you'd gotten the eBird alert (§149). This is old news. But the current reporting—by a real live human being standing up at his seat a few rows ahead of you—is different. You smile at his genuine pleasure in reliving the experience of watching the herons bait fish with feathers.

"The bird club's outing on Saturday will stop by the retention pond," the man notes, adding, "and I'll put out chairs for folks who want to linger with the herons."

Sold! You hadn't been terribly enthusiastic to start with about the prospect of a weekend of chores and catching up. The man's infectious enthusiasm is your final undoing. You'll clean out the cellar and fix the busted garage door some other weekend.

Local bird clubs have been around for as long as there've been birders, and they're still going strong. Telephone trees (§149) and CDs of bird calls (§146) are no more, with BirdChat (§147) and other listservs (§148) perhaps on their way out as well. But local bird clubs are, if anything, enjoying a renaissance as we barrel ahead toward the middle years of the 21st century.

Could it be as simple as the eternal human need for companionship, for face time, in modern parlance? We'll return to that point, but let us first note that bird clubs are about more than the opportunity to socialize. Most offer monthly meetings, weekly or semi-weekly field trips, and a more or less regular newsletter. Dues are negligible, typically in the $10–25 range. And many are valuably engaged in citizen-science efforts.

The Saturday morning field trip was delightful. You saw the herons, chestnut and slate-blue ("Green" is a misnomer), with bright yellow legs. You got sharp photos; you enlisted in a club-sponsored bird survey; and you were good-naturedly strong-armed into re-upping for another year. The best thing of all?—the mirth and jollity, the learning and discovery, the shared awe and wonder. Bird clubs, yay!

152 BIRD FESTIVALS

<<< <<< <<< <<< <<< <<< <<<>>> >>> >>> >>> >>> >>> >>>

Golden Eagle
Aquila chrysaetos

A T "OH DARK THIRTY," the tour bus pulls out of the motel parking lot. You find your way to an aisle seat near the back, next to a perfect stranger. Across the aisle: another perfect stranger. The bus merges onto the main highway out of town, and the driver dims the interior lights. The first stop is an hour away, so time to catch up on some well-deserved shut-eye? Not with this crew! Your innominate and invisible companions demand answers to these and other questions:

Where are you from? Have you ever been here before? What species do you most want to see? You also know Ron? No way! Remember the time he . . .

That's how it is with birders, hail-fellow-well-met. Even perfect strangers on a bus to—*Where are we going again?*

Nobody knows for certain. You and the 30+ other folks on the bus have enlisted in the Raptor Circuit field trip, one of several dozen offerings of the bird festival. The online brochure guaranteed a half-dozen species of raptors, with another four or five likely. So you clicked PURCHASE, and here you are. Except no one really knows where "here" is.

The bus is on a broad dirt road now, crawling eastward. It's getting light. A couple more minutes of bumpy washboard, and the bus comes to a stop. Evidently, it's time to start birding.

Golden Eagle! Full-on adult! It's going to land on that pole!

Sure enough. The leaders—two cheery 20-somethings—are on their A game. They instantly get their scopes on the bird, then get the participants queued up at the scopes, all the while providing expert commentary on eagle biology, conservation, and field ID.

The rest of the Raptor Circuit proceeds in much the same fashion. So does the whole four-day bird festival, a gala of field trips and workshops, of vendors and demos, of birds and people. Bird festivals are the most fun you can have with your pants on. Go for it!

153 ORNITHOLOGICAL SOCIETY MEETINGS

≪≪ ≪≪ ≪≪ ≪≪ ≪≪ ≪≪ ≪≪◇≫ ≫≫ ≫≫ ≫≫ ≫≫ ≫≫ ≫≫

American Avocet
Recurvirostra americana

T HE TWO BIRDS are strikingly black and white. A few months ago, they would have been black, white, and Creamsicle orange. But they've molted into their pied basic plumage (§120), which they'll hold for the rest of the fall and well into the new year. Even though they're identical in plumage, these two avocets differ in morphology.

One of them has a sharply upturned bill, which she swooshes through the shallow water as if sweeping the steps. Her companion has a straighter bill, which he jabs at the water's surface as though he were picking up trash with one of those mechanical reach extenders.

She? He? Is this unjustified anthropomorphism?

A day earlier, you would have been excused for thinking so. But then you attended the afternoon scientific paper session at your state's ornithological society meeting, a multiday offering of workshops and meetings, of networking and partnering, of learning and teaching. One of the "papers" (funny name, they're actually oral presentations) in the science session was on sex-related variation in foraging strategies, with a special focus on the American Avocet.

You hadn't known any of that stuff. Chances are, only a handful of the folks in attendance knew it. Most of the other presentations were just as stimulating and revelatory. And you're no dummy; you've been around the birding block more than a few times. The presenters were mostly advanced undergrads and graduate students—knowledgeable, well-prepared, and nervous as all get out. A few were establishment types—older, easygoing, avuncular. University and agency professionals were well-represented, but so were dedicated and highly competent amateurs.

State and provincial ornithological society meetings are hosted by—surprise of surprises—state and provincial ornithological societies. Membership is open to all. Dues are very reasonable, especially if you are a student. And all have websites, although some are rather plain. Google ORNITHOLOGICAL + SOCIETY + your state or province, and let the fun—and learning—begin.

154 BIRD RECORDS COMMITTEES

⋘ ⋘ ⋘ ⋘ ⋘ ⋘ ⋘ ⟨⟩ ⋙ ⋙ ⋙ ⋙ ⋙ ⋙ ⋙

Western Wood-Pewee
Contopus sordidulus

IS IT OR ISN'T IT? The range map says Eastern, but several folks in the group are enamored of the idea that this might be a rare Western. The broad-based bill is dark below, and the wing bars are of decidedly uneven thickness—consistent with the conjecture that this bird is a Western Wood-Pewee. The bird is inarguably dark and dusky, and someone wryly notes that *sordidulus* translates roughly as "dirty little bugger." That's not a bad description of the bird at hand.

The bird vocalizes, giving a short whistle of the sort that might be given by either wood-pewee species on migration. Nevertheless, you obtain an audio recording with your smartphone—just in case it might prove useful. You and your companions get photos, too, hundreds of them. After a quarter hour of field study, the group moves on.

"Well, whaddya say?"

"Honestly," the field trip organizer ventures, "I'm thinking it was a Western. That's my call. Of course, the BRC will get the final say in the matter."

BRC stands for <u>b</u>ird <u>r</u>ecords <u>c</u>ommittee, seven or eight folks tasked with evaluating notable records of avian occurrence—typically at the state or provincial level. They're often referred to informally as "rarities committees" or "rare bird committees," for the understandable reason that their deliberations focus primarily on rare birds.

BRCs are staffed by volunteers and usually, although not always, sponsored and supervised by state and provincial ornithological societies (§153). They vote to accept or reject individual records—basically, the sum total of all the documentation pertaining to the occurrence of a rare bird. The bird itself is not a record. In the case of our presumptive Western Wood-Pewee, the record is defined as the body of evidence—your smartphone recording, the hundreds of photos, and, valuably, anybody's field notes and sketches—supporting the ID.

Was it or wasn't it? Look for the committee's report in the next volume of your state or provincial ornithological society's journal.

155 THINGS BIRDERS DO: LISTING

Ruffed Grouse
Bonasa umbellus

THE BIRD EXPLODES from the forest floor, causing you to jump back and gasp loudly. Flushing grouse have a way of doing that to birders. You judge that it put back down just 100 feet away, but you've lost the bird in the dense woods. Should you go after it? Nah. What's the point? The ID is certain. You got the bird, species #155 for the year. A couple years ago, a Ruffed Grouse in this same forest preserve was your "lifer," your first encounter with the species; that bird was #163 on your life list, an enumeration of all the birds you've seen.

You know that stuff without having to consult a ledger or other accounting of your birding history. When you went out this autumn morning, cool and sunny, you knew your list was at 154. For sure, a large part of your intention was to spend time in the autumn woods, ablaze now in yellows and oranges. But another was to get a year bird. You hadn't added to your year list in 19 days. Many birders have that sort of trivia at their fingertips.

Not all birders are "listers." A few are quite defiant on that point. But most are—because keeping a list is, in essence, a reflection on and celebration of who you are and what you've accomplished as a birder. Many birders are, honestly, pretty haphazard about listing; they keep a life list and that's about it. Others go all-out: They keep county lists, state lists, year lists, even total tick lists. (Add up all your county lists, and you have your total tick list for a particular state or province.)

Is listing bad? Some people say so. But most birders go back to the idea that the listing impulse is rooted in a spirit of reflection about nature. A couple years ago, recall, you chanced upon a very special bird, #163, on a lovely autumn morning like this one. It was, it still is, it forever shall be, a part of who you are and what you're all about.

156 THINGS BIRDERS DO: CHASING

Loggerhead Shrike
Lanius ludovicianus

"IHOPE YOU HAD a NICE WEEKEND?"

"Yes, indeed," you assure your roommate. "Alex and his boyfriend and I successfully chased the Loggerhead Shrike over in Wright County."

You can tell from the expression on your roommate's face that you'd better explain yourself. The shrike, or "butcher bird," is a predatory songbird—hook-beaked and long-tailed with a bandit's mask. As to "chasing," that refers to the act of traveling to "get" a specific bird—not a species, but an actual individual. The object of the chase is a "stakeout," a "good" bird, a rarity, at a more or less fixed point in space. If the bird cannot be pursued—for the welfare of the bird, perhaps, or because it is on private property—then it is not "chaseable."

Is chasing bad? The birding community is ambivalent on this one. Arguments against chasing: (1) The more birders who chase, the greater the collective carbon footprint of the birding community; (2) the potential for harassing the bird, especially by the actions of overzealous photographers; (3) the pointlessness, some would say, of it all.

There are reasoned and principled counterpoints to the preceding: (1) the awareness and appreciation that result from chasing, not only by the chasers themselves but also by local communities and the media; (2) the strong tendency of birders to self-police in all matters involving ethical behavior in the field; (3) the birderly esprit de corps that pervades the whole experience of the chase.

You and your friends saw the shrike, but that's almost beside the point. You got to stand in front of the camera and explain to a TV reporter that shrikes benefit from restrictions on spraying pesticides. Alex celebrated the shrike by re-upping his membership in the state ornithological society. And the three of you renewed old friendships during the couple of hours that you spent watching the shrike and the other birds in the general vicinity.

Was the weekend chase for the Wright County shrike in some sense pointless? If that's the case, then so is playing the sax, tending a garden, or visiting with friends.

157 THINGS BIRDERS DO: BIG DAYS

Ruddy Duck
Oxyura jamaicensis

THIS PINT-SIZE DUCK is a marvel. The male in breeding plumage is oddly proportioned, calling to mind a rubber ducky, and improbably colored. His plumage is bright and sanguine overall; the cheek is gleaming white; and the broad bill looks like it was dipped in a can of blue paint. This is worthy of a kindergartner with a new box of crayons. The birds on the breeding grounds are given to bacchanalian outbursts of belching and bubbling, huffing and hissing, and what is euphemistically referred to as forced copulation. The species is highly unusual in many other aspects of its natural history: nestling biology, molt schedule, egg morphology, and more.

That's all an afterthought today. All you need right now is to see a Ruddy Duck. You and your birding buddies are winding down a Big Day, and you still don't have the species for your list. But you know where to look. While scouting for your Big Day earlier in the week, one of your teammates discovered a small flock roosting in the corner of a small suburban reservoir flanked with cattails. So you make the short detour to the "rez," drive up to the water's edge, see the ducks, and continue on to your next stakeout (§156). You don't even get out of the vehicle.

The Big Day—those capital letters signifying the mock solemnity of the undertaking—is a birderly tradition dating back to the late 19th century. It makes no pretense to field ornithology or conservation science; the sole objective is to find as many species as possible during 24 hours. That said, many Big Days are major fund-raisers, called Bird-a-Thons, for conservation initiatives large and small; and Big Day birders have an uncanny knack for discovering major rarities in the heat of the action. But that misses the point. The Big Day is good, clean fun. People who enjoy doing Big Days are the same sorts of people who delight in running a 10K, climbing a mountain, or advancing to the state finals. It's all good.

158 THINGS BIRDERS DO: BIG YEARS

<<< <<< <<< <<< <<< <<< <<< >>> >>> >>> >>> >>> >>> >>>

Barn Owl
Tyto alba

THE BIRD SITS watchfully in a rock crevice, simultaneously impish and wraithlike. Its plumage—pale beige below, more orangey above—appears soft, like a plush toy. The creature's eyes, wide open, are completely dark, sad and worldly. You can scarcely believe your good fortune at chancing upon this Barn Owl, a valuable and unexpected "tick" for your county Big Year. You and the owl are the only sentient beings at the base of the butte in these lonely badlands, and you decide to linger with the bird. The Barn Owl, sentient? Anybody who's ever entered a staring contest with a Barn Owl would say so. And as we shall see a little later on (§§185–186), the avian brain, and even the avian soul and spirit, are considerably more advanced than we ever knew.

The Big Year—capital B, capital Y—has obvious parallels with the Big Day (§157), but today you're struck by certain differences between the two competitions. The Big Days you've done were frenetic affairs, with no time to stop and smell the roses—or savor the Ruddy Ducks (§157). They were intensely communitarian; for 24 hours, you are in the constant company of other humans. On Big Days, you laugh together, you share together. You eat—well, you snack—together. On the extremest Big Days, you even pee together.

Your Big Year, in contrast, has been a largely solitary, at times a downright lonely, affair. Sure, you're in touch with other birders practically daily. But your Big Year, like almost all such efforts, is a solo undertaking. You'll be at it again tomorrow, searching one of the county's wetlands for a couple of migratory sparrows that eluded you in the spring. Chances are, you'll be the only birder out there.

Everyone who's ever done a Big Year reports that the experience is, more than anything else, an occasion for introspection. Several of the most celebrated birding memoirs ever written are accounts of Big Years. Do a Big Year, and you're practically guaranteed to discover new things about birds—and about yourself.

159 THINGS BIRDERS DO: PATCHWORK

Common Yellowthroat
Geothlypis trichas

THE RUSTLING IN the vegetation could be anything: a wren, a rail, a "good" sparrow, maybe not even a bird at all. Then you hear it, rough and scraping, the sound of two stones being rubbed together. You have a strong hunch now, but you want to see the creature. So you start "pishing"—*pish pish pish pish pish*—and the bird pops up. Yep, it's a Common Yellowthroat, a tad tardy for your area.

You let loose another volley of pishing, and the yellowthroat flies directly at you, returning the favor with its own utterance of avian epithets, those rough and scraping notes that caught your attention a moment ago. The bird weighs just a few grams, posing not even the slightest threat to your well-being, but instinct gets the better of you. Shielding your eyes, you duck out of the way. The yellowthroat alights on a stem of purple loosestrife, and you give it a close look: The bird is a first-fall female, an immature, technically in formative plumage. You're struck by the long tail, which the yellowthroat flips about expressively, wrenlike. The tail contrasts with the bird's short wings, reflecting the relatively short distance traversed by yellowthroats on migration (§61). Something else: The bird has long legs and a sturdy bill, adaptations for its relatively terrestrial lifestyle.

You're immersed right now in "patchwork." Patchwork? Like "pishing," it's one of those words that has meaning for the birder that differs somewhat from what you might expect. Many birders delight in working their local "patches," a park or preserve close to home. The local patch might be a locally or even regionally famous birding hot spot, but, more often than not, it's just a bit of field or forest conveniently close to home. Repeated coverage—weekly or even daily—is common.

There are no rules for patchwork, but one theme is consistent. The "patchworker"—there's another entry in the birder's lexicon for you—revels in the learning and discovery to be attained through detailed study of familiar birds in a familiar setting.

160 THINGS BIRDERS DO: TRAVEL

Great-tailed Grackle
Quiscalus mexicanus

THE WIDE BOULEVARD is lined with universally acclaimed icons of contemporary commercial culture: fast-food restaurants and car dealerships; an Apple store here, a fitness center there; and a Walmart, of course. There's a stretch of town a mile from home that looks just like this. But this could also be a strip mall in South Texas, say, some 2,000 miles from home.

You ease your airport rental to a stop at the sprawling intersection, and you play a little game with yourself. What objects or phenomena within sight would serve as proof positive that you are, in point of fact, far from home? The proliferation of big cars with Texas license plates is suggestive. Then the kicker. You hear it before you see it. Even with the windows rolled up, the caterwauling is audible. The matter is settled: You're definitely not back home in New England. There are no Great-tailed Grackles there.

Most people do not travel several thousand miles just to see *Quiscalus mexicanus,* a Texas-size blackbird with a penchant for feedlots and strip malls. To be honest about it, neither have you. Your goal is to get out of town and down to The Valley, the broad floodplain of the Rio Grande, home to chachalacas, pauraques, kiskadees, and other exotically named tropical birds.

The traffic signals turn green, and you clear the intersection. The grackle is soon out of earshot, but not yet out of mind. In a moment of reflection, you pause to consider how odd it is that you even know the name of this bird. Most people, including those who have lived in Texas their whole lives, do not.

This is Anytown, U.S.A. Except it is not. That grackle, bossy and obnoxious, is for you a totem, precious and powerful. The bird is no doubt still braying by the roadside, still proclaiming that this world of ours is full of wonder and beauty, still exhorting us to go out and drink it all in.

161 ON THE ORIGINS OF KNOWLEDGE: BIRD BANDING

⋘ ⋘ ⋘ ⋘ ⋘ ⋘ ⋘◇⋙ ⋙ ⋙ ⋙ ⋙ ⋙ ⋙

Gray Catbird
Dumetella carolinensis

THE TRIM GRAY BIRD drops onto the trail, and your companion remarks that it must be the millionth Gray Catbird of the morning. That's an exaggeration, but the species certainly is common in the palmetto-and-pine woodland the two of you have been exploring for several hours. You've seen 10 or 20 catbirds and heard easily 50+. Another catbird drops down on the trail and . . .

"Oh! Look! It's wearing a band!"

Sure enough. Around the bird's leg (technically, its tarsus) is a ring of silver, not unlike a wedding band. But with a difference: The inscription is on the *out*side, for all the world to see.

"Get a photo!"

Good idea. There's a lot of info on that band—a phone number, the name of a government agency, and an alphanumeric identifier. For the first time in your life, you find yourself determinedly photographing the tarsus of a catbird!

You get back home, blow up your photos, and see that you are to report the sighting to the U.S. Fish & Wildlife Service (FWS). Then what? Your observation becomes a little piece of the puzzle of avian S&D (§25), the science of understanding how birds are distributed in space and time. Perhaps your catbird was captured and banded at this very location five years ago; or maybe it was banded just weeks ago yet hundreds of miles to the north. Either result sheds some light on catbird S&D. Now multiply that by the hundreds of thousands of catbirds in the FWS database, and you have a richly detailed picture of the comings and goings of *Dumetella carolinensis*.

A huge challenge for ornithological studies based on bird banding is the abysmally low recapture rate. Depending on the species and the situation, one in a hundred would be a decidedly good ROI. The vast majority of banded birds are never captured again—literally in a net or indirectly as when you pointed your camera at that trailside catbird. Fortunately, a host of emerging technologies are equipped to do what banding studies cannot.

162 ON THE ORIGINS OF KNOWLEDGE: STABLE ISOTOPES

Northern Flicker
Colaptes auratus

IT'S BEEN A typical fall morning at the Southeast Atlantic coastal plain banding station. The crew has netted a smattering of migratory warblers and kinglets, along with several trap-happy Gray Catbirds captured here repeatedly during the past couple months (§161). Then the prize catch of the morning—not a rare species per se, but an unusual individual.

The bird is a Northern Flicker, a woodpecker that comes in two basic varieties: red-shafted and yellow-shafted. Where their ranges overlap in the western Great Plains, hybrids (also known as intergrades), showing characteristics of both, are frequent. The bird in the banding station net suggests hybrid origin, but the station director ventures an alternative hypothesis. She points out the abrupt break between the red and yellow flight feathers of the wing, different from the blended look of most hybrids. This bird is a chimera.

"They're different generations of feathers," she explains, adding, "We need a sample for stable isotope analysis."

Birds' feathers carry a chemical signature of their place of origin. Capture a bird, pluck a feather, match its "stable isotope signature" to a continental map of the distribution of hydrogen isotopes in the environment, and you know where the bird was when it grew in its feathers. The capture-recapture requirement of banding studies (§161) is obviated.

The banding station director conjectures that this is a yellow-shafted Northern Flicker who ate the red berries of exotic shrubs and absorbed the plant pigment into its feathers. Stable isotope analysis can corroborate that hypothesis by showing that the red feathers derive from a region with a high density of red berries.

Flickers get around. This one ate intensely red berries while growing in one patch of feathers, not-so-red berries while growing in other feathers. A question remains. How did the flicker get from here to there, or, rather, from there to over there to *way* over there to here? Stable isotope analysis isn't designed for that sort of analysis. But another technology is.

163 ON THE ORIGINS OF KNOWLEDGE: REMOTE SENSING

⋘ ⋘ ⋘ ⋘ ⋘ ⋘ ⋘ ⟨⟩ ⋙ ⋙ ⋙ ⋙ ⋙ ⋙ ⋙

Common Merganser
Mergus merganser

T HE CURRENT IS STRONG, but the small flock of big ducks are paddling upstream, making steady progress. The birds are uniform in appearance, with one exception: A brown-headed female-type (any bird but a male in breeding plumage) has a wire sticking out of its back.

That bird, a hatch-year (first-autumn) Common Merganser, was fitted with a satellite transmitter a month ago. Scientists captured and anesthetized the bird, a veterinarian surgically implanted the lightweight transmitter, and the bird was released. The reason: to understand the meanderings of mergansers, with a particular eye toward conserving the waterfowl habitat. We've long appreciated that ducks and other birds depend on habitats way beyond their immediate nest sites, that even the expansive concept of home range is insufficient for encompassing all the needs of an individual or population (§108). With the advent of new technologies like satellite telemetry, ornithologists have made dramatic progress toward quantifying remarkable peregrinations, even of birds like sage-grouse that we thought were largely sedentary.

Satellite telemetry isn't the only show in town. Tiny geolocators have shed light on the dispersal capabilities of small birds like the Black Swift, a species whose winter range was unknown until recently. Autonomous recording units "listen" to and quantify the phenomenon of nocturnal migration by Dickcissels and other species. Biotelemetry has been applied to studies of the metabolism of Swainson's Thrushes on active migration. And such technologies have consequences for outreach and education; think of the live "nest cams" that stream to popular websites like the Cornell Lab's. All of the preceding are examples of remote sensing, the term given to any technology for seeing a bird (or any other object) without actually being there.

An eagle flies by, spooking the mergansers. They put into flight, their wings flashing white and gray, gone in an instant beyond a bend in the river. How far did they go? Someone in a remote sensing lab hundreds of miles distant knows the exact answer to that question.

164 ON THE ORIGINS OF KNOWLEDGE: SCIENTIFIC COLLECTING

⋘ ⋘ ⋘ ⋘ ⋘ ⋘ ⋘ ⟨⟩ ⋙ ⋙ ⋙ ⋙ ⋙ ⋙ ⋙ ⋙

Virginia Rail
Rallus limicola

THE BIRD MUST have died very recently—earlier this still early morning or overnight. It's just lying there in the middle of the road. You pull over, hop out, and retrieve the carcass of a Virginia Rail, roadkill no doubt. The specimen is in perfect condition, an ironic thing to say about any creature that just met a violent end.

Live rails tend to be poorly glimpsed blobs of black and brown slinking about muddy marshes, but this bird glistens golden-bronze in the October sunrise. You admire it for a minute, caressing its feathers with just a twinge of self-consciousness. Then duty calls. You retrieve a gallon-size ziplock freezer bag from the trunk and carefully place the rail therein. Next stop: the Ornithology Department in your city's natural history museum. The preparator—you're on a first-name basis with him—gratefully accepts the donation and notes various details of your contribution to the museum's collection.

The importance of museum collections cannot be overstated. With regard to their scientific value, many people would say that they are the single most important resource to the modern ornithologist. Yes, the *modern* ornithologist; museums are as relevant to basic science in the 21st century as they were centuries ago. With regard to their conservation value, they are nearly as important. Museum collections are *the* record of global bird diversity, the baseline for every bird conservation initiative at the present time.

There's just one problem. Everything in a museum is dead. Like the rail you just relinquished to the preparator. Your rail is a *salvage* specimen, found dead. But the vast majority of objects in the museum's collections are not. They were shot by collectors, scientists with guns.

In case it didn't get through the first time: Museums are monumentally important to scientific research *and* biological conservation. But a question lingers for many in the broader birding community: Is it really okay to kill animals for science? We'll defer the question for now—but not for much longer (§§197–198).

165 ON THE ORIGINS OF KNOWLEDGE: DIGITAL PHOTOS

<<< <<< <<< <<< <<< <<< <<<><>>> >>> >>> >>> >>> >>> >>>

Laughing Gull
Leucophaeus atricilla

A MONTH AGO, the beachside parking lot was seriously infested with Laughing Gulls. Today there is just the one. Many gulls are hardy, wintering at high latitudes even well inland. But not Laughing Gulls, nearly all of whom withdraw in the colder months to our southern shores and points south. Some persist well into the autumn, though, and a few make it right through the winter. This bird, the one still hanging on in the parking lot with all the Herring Gulls, seems to be a candidate for establishing winter residency.

An insight occurs to you. You pitch a few French fries in the direction of the gull flock with the expected result: *Finding Nemo* meets *The Birds*. You get a few photos of the Laughing Gull, then move along. What kind of an insight was *that*?

Your plan is to repeat your "research" tomorrow, and the next day, and the next . . . for as long as the Laughing Gull remains. In this way, you will create a library of digital photos as the bird's plumage changes—through both wear and molt (§§116–125)—in the months ahead.

Until recently, molt studies were a matter for museum research (§164). But there's a fundamental problem with a specimen: It's a snapshot, an instant in time. You can't compare a dead bird with the *same* dead bird two weeks or two months later. But you *can* do exactly that with a photographic study. You can compare an actual, nonmetaphorical snapshot with another, and another, and another . . . A recent study of rare Harlequin Ducks overwintering at the Great Salt Lake provided just that opportunity, with birders photo-chronicling the complex and little-studied molts of the species over the course of many months.

For decades, birders have fantasized about a device like a *Star Trek* tricorder: Just point it at a bird, and get a readout on its molts and plumages and more. Digital photography has gotten us closer to that outcome than we ever imagined.

166 HOW WE LEARN: SCREEN TIME

≪≪ ≪≪ ≪≪ ≪≪ ≪≪ ≪≪ ≪≪◇≫ ≫≫ ≫≫ ≫≫ ≫≫ ≫≫ ≫≫

Northern Harrier
Circus hudsonius

CERTAIN HAWKS ARE challenging to identify: forest hawks in the genus *Accipiter,* habitat generalists in the genus *Buteo,* and in various plumages even the two eagles (Bald and Golden). The Northern Harrier, however, is a slam dunk. In shape and behavior alone, the species stands out; if a slim, long-tailed, stiff-winged raptor is hunting just above ground level, there's a good chance it's a harrier. Add in the species' distinctive plumage—including a facial disk characteristic of owls—and the harrier is unique among North American hawks. Factor in sex-related (§11) and age-related (§12) variation among harriers, though, and the situation becomes somewhat complicated.

According to conventional wisdom, adult harriers are easily sexed: Females are brown and streaky, males silvery with black wingtips. The latter are evocatively known as "gray ghosts." But there's a hitch. Raptor ID expert Jerry Liguori recently demonstrated that many female-like adult harriers are in fact males. "It's complicated" (§92).

A female-like harrier has been hanging out in the fallow farm fields by your house the past several days, and you've succeeded in getting good photos of the wary creature. You want to learn more about your bird. You have facility with the various modes of delivery of knowledge about birds (§§143–154), you're acquainted with the ways in which birders apply knowledge (§§155–160), and you have a basic grasp of how such knowledge comes to be in the first place (§§161–165). One matter remains: the knowledge milieu. In what social setting or settings do we generate, disseminate, and apply knowledge about birds?

Online social media is an easy and obvious starting point. You post photos of your harrier to the Advanced Bird ID group on Facebook; you solicit additional input from the ID Frontiers listserv; you blog about the bird. Discussion quickly ensues. Birders in your home state chime in, of course, but so do raptor experts overseas. In no time at all, consensus is achieved. The question is settled. Second-year male harrier.

But you're not convinced the online community got it right.

167 HOW WE LEARN: FACE TIME

Savannah Sparrow
Passerculus sandwichensis

IT'S TEMPTING TO DISS social media. Depending on which self-proclaimed authority you consult, Facebook is either poisoning children's minds or destroying adult relationships—or, more likely, both. On top of that, much of what's posted to social media is "fake news." You can't believe anything you read about climate science and public opinion, the critics caution, and even the comparatively peaceful realm of nature study is threatened with social media Armageddon.

A few days ago, you posted photos of what you considered to be an interesting Savannah Sparrow—clearly darker and longer-billed than the individuals typical of your location well inland. You were deliberately cautious in your wording ("possible," "potential," "presumptive"), but folks evidently read right past that. A social media Dumpster fire quickly flared up. Several days later, it's still simmering. The online back-and-forth has been entertaining at times, but you also feel a pang of remorse about your bit role in the flame war that ensued. So you do something radical. You actually pick up the phone and call one of the incendiaries in the matter. The two of you agree to go birding together.

"Steve," we'll call him, is erudite. No surprise there. He *is* an expert, after all. He's also charming, which you hadn't anticipated. But it makes sense; what came across as merely clever online translates into downright likable in real life. It gets better. This Steve is patient and kindly, genuinely interested in sharing his knowledge with you—while at the same time learning from you.

Let's not throw the baby out with the bathwater. You met Steve on the web. As a result of online interactions with him, you wound up delving into the evolution of plumage and morphological variation in the Savannah Sparrow. And you wouldn't be standing here right now, in front of a real live sparrow and in the company of an actual human being, were it not for social media.

168 HOW WE LEARN: ME TIME

≪≪ ≪≪ ≪≪ ≪≪ ≪≪ ≪≪ ≪≪◯≫ ≫≫ ≫≫ ≫≫ ≫≫ ≫≫ ≫≫

Northern Mockingbird
Mimus polyglottos

I N THIS ALWAYS-ONLINE and hyperconnected world of ours, we value time off the grid as never before. "Me time" is good for our well-being, but that's not the point we're going to develop here. Time spent by oneself has the potential to contribute significantly to our understanding of birds and nature.

You're halfway down the front steps when you're hit with a micro-insight. You do a one-eighty, return to the house, reach into your pocket, and extract your smartphone. With a ritual gesture, you place the contraption on the countertop by the door. You'll eBird your time afield at some later point; if you find a rarity, the birding community will just have to wait to hear about it. *Now* you're ready for an hour of patchwork (§159).

A mockingbird greets you at your patch. This silver-and-white bird is familiar, but it's doing something that strikes you as peculiar. Your "mocker" is singing steadily, and you wonder why. It's early November. Does the species defend winter feeding territories? Answer: Yes. Is the bird male or female? Answer: Winter singing by female mockingbirds is little-studied. Call that a semi-answer. Do mockingbirds update their repertoires so as to reflect the seasonal comings and goings of the species they imitate? Answer: Unknown. Call that a nonanswer—and that's exciting.

Next step in the learning process: Share with the birding community and consult experts, both online (§166) and in person (§167). Who knows where this will lead, what collaborations might arise, what new knowledge could come of it? Or maybe it's nothing, a random blip of electrical activity in the right temporal lobe of your brain. In any event, consider where it came from. Newton (apple whacks him on the head) and Archimedes (naked in the bathtub) achieved their seminal insights whilst engaged in me time. So it is when we engage the natural world away from the consensus-driven knowledge milieu of social media and the inevitable groupthink of traditional learning communities.

169 THE PRIME DIRECTIVE: FIELD ID

Pied-billed Grebe
Podilymbus podiceps

WHAT ARE SOME of the things birders know about the Pied-billed Grebe? Here's one: The Pied-billed, like other grebes, will routinely pluck one of its own feathers and ingest it, apparently as a digestive aid. Here's another: This dumpy brown bird has a remarkable way of submerging. A Pied-billed Grebe will rapidly compress its body feathers, squeezing out air and increasing the bird's density; then, like a tiny submarine, the bird sinks unobtrusively below the water's surface. Other things birders know about *Podilymbus podiceps:* The species builds a floating nest, it migrates chiefly at night, it sings a loud song.

We need to take a step backward. Several steps backward. Before we knew all about the physiology of grebe digestion and submersion, before we knew anything of the species' nidification (§97), migrations, and vocalizations, *we knew it was a grebe.* Or maybe we didn't even know that much. But we knew it was a *something,* that it was *this* species, or *that* one. And we were confident that, given a good look, we could say *which* something, which species, it was.

The Pied-billed Grebe in fall and winter is drab, practically featureless. The bird is just a brown clump of feathers (minus the handful it's eaten); even the namesake pied bill becomes uniform and nearly colorless by mid-autumn. It's not immediately obvious why it's a grebe at all. Why couldn't it be a duck or an alcid?

We know. We just know. And if we don't, we know that we are to know. Call it the Prime Directive, or perhaps the Hippocratic Oath, of birding: the conviction that a bird can, and ought to be, identified in the field. First, field ID; then, as time allows, physiology and such.

What if the preceding scenario is substantially wrong? What if a few—or perhaps a great many—birds cannot be ID'd in the field? Even more heretically, what if it doesn't matter?

PART SIX

WHAT WE DON'T KNOW

December

170 WHAT WE DON'T KNOW

"Western" Flycatcher
Empidonax difficilis

"**W**HATEVER THIS IS, it's a good bird!"

The group of birders has spotted an *Empidonax* flycatcher. Five species of empids (§131) breed in the state, but it's November. So the possibility of a vagrant from western North America must be admitted. Indeed that is the case. This empid is awash in olive-yellow, its eye-ring pinched behind the eye. The eye-ring is distinctively shaped like a teardrop.

"Folks, we've got a 'Western' Flycatcher," the bird's discoverer excitedly declares, adding precisely, "just the third state record." When she says the bird's name, she signifies with air quotes that it is somehow problematic. This is a "Western" Flycatcher, not a Western Flycatcher.

Not long ago, there actually was a no-quotes Western Flycatcher. Then the species was split into two (§30), giving us the Cordilleran Flycatcher and the Pacific-slope Flycatcher. The two species differ in where they breed ("Cordie" in the interior West, "Pack Slope" from the Sierra-Cascades axis westward) and in certain vocalizations (disyllabic "position note" in Cordilleran, slurred into a single syllable in Pacific-slope). And that's it. Away from the breeding grounds, silent Cordilleran and Pacific-slope flycatchers are *impossible to identify in the field*.

It doesn't matter how many photos you get. The position notes of vagrants are unreliable, so it probably doesn't matter if you get sound recordings, either. Hence, "Western" Flycatcher, denoting that we cannot know. The scientific name of the erstwhile Western Flycatcher was *E. difficilis*, as if to prophesy the difficulties of the present age.

Finding a vagrant "Western" Flycatcher is undeniably exciting. "Whatever it is," the bird is notable—a rarity, a "good" bird. But it's more than that. When we ponder the "Western" Flycatcher, we are forced to confront the tension—it's a healthy tension—between what we know and what we don't know. The lesson of the "Western" Flycatcher is that birding and nature study are less about the attainment of existing knowledge than about the quest for new knowledge.

171 "GOOD BIRDERS DON'T WEAR WHITE"

Tundra Swan
Cygnus columbianus

EVERY FEATHER ON the big bird is white as snow: all the flight feathers, every feather on its ample underbelly, each one of the thousands of feathers on its preposterously long neck. Why is that? Is whiteness an adaptive trait, allowing Tundra Swans to blend in against the snowy and icy environments in which they often occur? Could whiteness instead be maladaptive, causing the birds to stand out in other sorts of environments? Or maybe those *adaptationist* interpretations are instances of barking up the wrong tree, a possibility we'll turn to before too long (§§181–182). Another hypothesis: Perhaps white feathers, lacking complex melanin molecules, are less expensive, metabolically speaking (§183). Yet another: Maybe Tundra Swans simply like white feathers. That scenario is less exotic and less anthropomorphic than you might think (§184).

We're distracted from our cygnine cerebrations by the appearance of a birder across the way. Her down jacket is all white, prompting us to reflect on the maxim that "good birders don't wear white." There's actually a book by that title, a book so successful that it has a sequel: *Good Birders Still Don't Wear White*. Don't be fooled by the title. It's tongue-in-cheek, an exhortation to question authority, to think outside the box. But it's also based on a real incident, wherein a pair of rare Eared Quetzals went berserk whenever they saw birders attired in white.

Quetzals don't like white. Case closed. But most birds on this Earth aren't quetzals. Birds see color in ways we do not. What humans perceive as muted and understated—think of the hunter's camo—may stick out like a sore hallux (the avian thumb). And what quetzals perceive as offensive might delight a Tundra Swan, or, more likely, elicit no particular reaction at all.

Birding, like any other human pursuit, is characterized by a certain amount of conventional wisdom. And birding, like other human pursuits, is most rewarding when we challenge the conventional wisdom.

172 SLACKERS

⋘ ⋘ ⋘ ⋘ ⋘ ⋘ ⋘ ⟨◇⟩ ⋙ ⋙ ⋙ ⋙ ⋙ ⋙ ⋙

Black-crowned Night-Heron
Nycticorax nycticorax

A T WHAT TIME of day do you suppose night-herons are most active? Take a wild guess. That's right, they're most active at night. Walk around a seaside dock at midnight, and you're likely to encounter a Black-crowned Night-Heron. You might espy one in the lights of the marina, but you're more likely to hear the species. Its call, given by the bird in flight, is explosive, a low-frequency hoot, rising slightly: *Quaw!*

During the daylight hours, night-herons roost in woody vegetation at the water's edge. Don't look for them out in the open, where cormorants and kingfishers pose. Instead, they favor hidden perches, typically well within a tree or tall shrub. Your best bet for satisfying study in the daytime is in the late afternoon, when the birds are starting to stir, beginning to turn their thoughts to a night of hunting for frogs and crayfish.

In other words, you don't have to go out at first light to see night-herons. If anything, they seem particularly inert during the morning hours. Yet birders are strongly conditioned to go birding in the morning. The traditional field trip commences at "oh dark thirty," the idea being that birds are more active at dawn. That's true of some birds some of the time. But it doesn't apply to night-herons and many other birds. Neither does it apply to most humans.

Well-meaning birders have given much thought to the problem of outreach—how to make birding more fun and accessible. Here's a simple yet radical thought: Ditch the conventional wisdom about blisteringly early field trips. Are you involved in field trip planning for a bird club or a birding festival? Then consider scheduling so-called slacker trips, convening after breakfast or even after lunch. You'll almost certainly succeed in attracting folks who are not cheered by the prospect of rising before dawn. You might miss one or two species, but, really, that's about it. Besides, you'll find yourself in the company of fellow slackers—cheery and enthusiastic, well-rested and properly breakfasted, just like yourself.

173 THE KIDS ARE ALRIGHT

Willet
Tringa semipalmata

THE MAN APPEARS to be by himself, standing at the edge of the tidal pool. Check that. The man is standing *in* the tidal pool, ankle deep in cold brine. His gaze is fixed on a flock of medium-large sandpipers. The birds are Willets, but the man is endeavoring to divine *which sort* of Willet. At this time of year, most are Prairie, or Western, Willets; those birds breed well inland but winter along our southern coasts. Saltmarsh, or Eastern, Willets are possible too; they are common breeders here in the warmer months, but most are gone by now.

The man isn't at a famous seashore or wildlife refuge. He's a patchworker (§159), determinedly working the same stretch of back bay that he visits day after day. All appearances are that he's engaged in some salutary and solitary me time (§168). But that's not quite correct. The man turns around, revealing the presence of another human being, his infant child, studying the Willets from a BabyBjörn.

Birding has its false prohibitions: You can't wear white (§171), you can't sleep in (§172), etc. Add to that list: You can't go birding with young children. That's ludicrous! They are fantastic companions, arguably superior to any adult: amiable and devoted, eager and hardy, and, more than anything else, engaged and in the present moment.

The infant raises her little arm, a nonverbal signification that something is afoot. She's onto something. The Willets are fidgeting about, getting ready to take flight. The man readies his camera, hoping for a dramatic photo of *inornata,* the Western subspecies, on the wing.

It's easy to say that the man is paying it forward, preparing his infant daughter to be a biologist or environmental lawyer. Honestly, that's not why he's out there in the rising tide. That's not why *she's* out there. They're out there together, delighting in the experience of the crisp November day, marveling at birds and nature *right now.*

174 BARE-NAKED BIRDING: SEE BETTER

Golden-crowned Kinglet
Regulus satrapa

ALL THE BIRDS in the flock are small and active, but this one is exceptional: tinier than the titmice and nuthatches, fussier than the chickadees. It's a kinglet, olive-gray all over, the two choices in North America being Ruby-crowned and Golden-crowned. The kinglet is hovering, actually hovering, in front of a clump of hemlock needles. The bird is a blur, its field marks impossible to make out. No matter, you're reasonably confident that it's a Golden-crowned, more spasmodic and more inclined to hover than the Ruby-crowned.

The bird snatches a tiny invertebrate—was it a springtail, perhaps, or a thrips?—from the hemlock needles and pauses for a moment on the snag of a streamside buckthorn. It has an olive-yellow wing bar—a contrasting stripe across the feather tract known as the secondary coverts. This is different from the white wing bar of the Ruby-crowned. The face is boldly marked: A black stripe, technically a transocular line, cuts through the eye; the eyebrow, or supercilium, is white; and a yellow patch on the crown is ringed in black. Definitely Golden-crowned. The kinglet erects its crown, revealing blaze orange feathers. This is a male.

All that detail, and the bird is scarcely four inches along. Modern optics are amazing.

Ahem. You discerned all that detail with the naked eye. You've deliberately left your binoculars behind. You've set out this afternoon to do a bit of *bare-naked birding*, a practice whose name appears to have originated with activist and provocateur Ted Eubanks.

Birders have long known that behavioral and ecological cues play a huge role in field ID. On the kinglet, these include the hovering flight, the penchant for hemlocks, and distinctive vocalizations. You don't need binoculars for that stuff. Neither do you need them for supercilia, transocular lines, and secondary coverts. Be patient. Be still. The birds will draw near, and you will see them as never before. Practice bare-naked birding, and you will discover anew that your eyes are more amazing than the best binoculars.

175 BARE-NAKED BIRDING: SEE FARTHER

Swamp Sparrow
Melospiza georgiana

THE FIELD TRIP LEADER hears the call note, a bright *chip*, noting that it's "short-duration, mid-frequency." The bird flushes, dark overall but with brighter rufous on the wings. It puts down beyond the old pump house, and the leader gushes about the radiant beauty of this HY Swamp Sparrow.

The trip participants didn't hear the call note. They didn't spot the bird in flight. And during the two or three seconds the first-winter Swamp Sparrow was visible in the teasels, folks were struggling with the stubborn focus knobs on their inexpensive binoculars.

The playing field isn't level. The leader huddles with the group and divulges her Plan B. Put down your binoculars, she advises. We're going to stand quietly over there, with the sun behind us. The bird will pop up again, she promises. Swamp Sparrows respond well to pishing. Just look at the bird.

It works. The bird reemerges and just stays put, unafraid of the motionless birders. One of the participants remarks that the bird has a white throat. Another comments on the fine streaking on the back. Yet another sums up the whole experience: Beautiful!

Needless to say, binoculars have their place and purpose. A Swamp Sparrow 500 feet away requires study with binoculars. But binoculars can be a crutch. They induce tunnel vision—literally. And they vary massively in quality. The field trip leader with the $3,000 Leica bins sees differently from participants with $75 throwaways from the big-box store.

Consider participating in or organizing a bare-naked birding field trip. Start late (§172). Bring the kids (§173). Wear white (§171). Lighten the load, and leave the bins behind. The camaraderie alone will be worth the proverbial price of admission. And you know what? You'll see more: more species, more individuals, more field marks, more feathers. You won't *really* see farther. Open your eyes. Look at the world, bright and beautiful. You'll see farther than ever before.

176 JEKYLL AND HYDE

⫷⫷⫷ ⫷⫷⫷ ⫷⫷⫷ ⫷⫷⫷ ⫷⫷⫷ ⫷⫷⫷ ⫷⫷◇⫸⫸ ⫸⫸⫸ ⫸⫸⫸ ⫸⫸⫸ ⫸⫸⫸ ⫸⫸⫸ ⫸⫸⫸

Yellow-breasted Chat
Icteria virens

THE LONG-TAILED BIRD watches motionless from a tangle of bitter-sweet and bayberry. You're pretty sure you know what it is, but you require better viewing. And if it's what you think it is, you'll have to *see* it. The species is utterly silent at this time of year.

The bird hops to a break in the dense foliage and obligingly perches in profile. You can see its bright white "spectacles" and namesake yellow breast. This is *Icteria virens,* rarely reported but easily overlooked in Atlantic Coast thickets in late fall.

To someone who knows the Yellow-breasted Chat on its breeding grounds, the preceding must seem odd. Chats on the breeding grounds are the loudest birds in town. They sing all day long. They sing all *night* long. Their songs are bizarre and surreal, an odd mix of flutelike whistles and laser tag outbursts, simultaneously sad and clownish, equal parts deranged and endearing.

Can the chat in November, sullen and skulking, really be the same species as its ebullient counterpart on moonlit nights in mid-June? And what sort of a species is it anyhow? The former question is rhetorical, needless to say. But what of the second question?

Basically, we don't know what the Yellow-breasted Chat is. For the longest time, it was placed in the wood-warbler family Parulidae. But that was a provisional arrangement, a placeholder. Currently it is in its own family, Icteriidae, thought to be related to the blackbirds. But we're not totally clear on that, either. So you'll see phylogenies in which the chat's placement is termed *incertae sedis,* Latin for "position uncertain."

The chat is a definite something, though, and that gives us great comfort. It is either *this* or *that,* an aberrant warbler or a quasi-blackbird, or perhaps something else altogether. We don't yet fully know, but we are confident it is *one thing or another.* Now what if that assumption were all wrong? We're going to spend the next several lessons examining that exotic possibility.

177 SCHRÖDINGER'S HAWK

Red-shouldered Hawk
Buteo lineatus

THIS ELEGANT BUZZARD comes in two distinct flavors: in the Pacific coast states, a subspecies called *elegans;* and in the East, a group of subspecies referred to as *lineatus*. The former sport a few broad white stripes on their black tails; their bright rusty breasts lack streaking. The latter have more but thinner white stripes on their tails; their streaked breasts are washed in paler rufous. The two buzzards' ranges are wholly disjunct, separated by well over a thousand miles. Thus, there is zero gene flow between *elegans* and *lineatus*. So why are they mere subspecies?

Many other East-West pairs, accorded full-species standing, appear to be more weakly differentiated than the two Red-shouldered Hawks. Think of the two wood-pewees (Eastern and Western) and the two meadowlarks (again, Eastern and Western). Other examples: eastern Glossy and western White-faced ibises; interior Nelson's and coastal Seaside sparrows; and the notorious Cordilleran and Pacific-slope flycatchers.

The general consensus is that the two Red-shouldered Hawks aren't there yet. Speciation is under way. Millennia from now, *elegans* and *lineatus* may be sufficiently distinct to be considered separate species: the California Buzzard, let's say, and the Swamp Buzzard. But when exactly? At what point in the speciation process is the bifurcation fully established?

Evolution doesn't work that way. Evolution is ongoing, continual, always unfolding. It's not as if one species suddenly splits in two: Red-shouldered Hawk on December 31, 4019; California and Swamp buzzards on January 1, 4020. Rather, there's a period during which the bird is simultaneously one species and two species. This duality echoes quantum mechanics, with its electrons that are simultaneously here and there, with objects that are both waves and particles—Schrödinger's memorable, if imaginary, cats that are both dead and alive. Birders joke that birds in taxonomic limbo are likewise Schrödingerian.

Physicists have come to accept such dualities. Have birders?

178 PARADIGM SHIFT

≪≪≪ ≪≪≪ ≪≪≪ ≪≪≪ ≪≪≪ ≪≪≪ ≪≪◇≫≫ ≫≫≫ ≫≫≫ ≫≫≫ ≫≫≫ ≫≫≫ ≫≫≫

Red Crossbill
Loxia curvirostra

SPLITTING (§30) IS all the rage today. The bird formerly known as the Sage Sparrow was split in 2013 into the Sagebrush and Bell's sparrows. The stand-alone Whip-poor-will became the Eastern and Mexican whip-poor-wills in 2010. And then there are the multiway splits: The Scrub Jay was split in three in 1995, and one of the resulting species was further split in 2016.

In all these cases, the splits are fundamentally geographic. You might even christen it the Fundamental Law of Avian Speciation, whereby spatially discrete populations differentiate and evolve into new species. Reproductively isolated species frequently co-occur, but valid subspecies are almost invariably defined according to their breeding ranges: Subspecies *A* here, Subspecies *B* there, Subspecies *C* over there, and so on. Geographic variation is the touchstone of avian diversity, and spatially differentiated subspecies are the powerhouse of avian speciation.

Unless we're talking about the Red Crossbill.

Red Crossbills in North America comprise at least nine "types" that appear in certain essential respects to behave as separate species. Practically identical in plumage, they nevertheless differ in vocalizations, bill morphology, and feeding ecology. And they stick to the flock: Type 2s consort with other Type 2s, Type 5s with other Type 5s, etc. Red Crossbills exhibit assortative mating, pairing with their own, correct type. Are the different types indeed good species? Or are they just subspecies?

Here's the wildest thing. They aren't—they can't be—good subspecies. Red Crossbill types are not geographically differentiated. Speciation in the Red Crossbill complex is proceeding in the absence of properly defined subspecies. The Red Crossbill has somehow broken through the subspecies paradigm.

If the Red-shouldered Hawk is Schrödinger's hawk (§177), simultaneously one species and two, then the Red Crossbill conjures up the incompatibility of the equations of relativity and quantum mechanics. Like gravitational lensing and quantum entanglement, speciation in the Red Crossbill is an indubitably real phenomenon. But there's something wrong with the "math."

179 FUZZY MATH

Yellow-bellied Sapsucker
Sphyrapicus varius

THIS WOODPECKER HAS a great name. "Yellow-bellied Sapsucker" was a burn, or roast, long before burns and roasts were even a thing. But it is the bird's scientific name that really gets at what this woodpecker is all about. First, *Sphyra-*, deriving from the Greek word for "hammer." All woodpeckers hammer into trees, but the sapsuckers take it to an extreme, undaunted by the live hardwoods that thwart many other woodpeckers. Next, *-picus,* meaning "woodpecker." And *varius* signifies what you might have expected: The Yellow-bellied Sapsucker exhibits great variation in plumage. Male and female, old and young, summer and winter—they're all different.

Until 1985, the name Yellow-bellied Sapsucker was given to what ornithologists currently treat as a complex of three species: the Red-breasted Sapsucker of the Pacific slope, the Red-naped Sapsucker of the interior West, and the Yellow-bellied Sapsucker of eastern and Canadian forests. That's the essence of *varius* as it applies to this bird.

Most Yellow-bellied Sapsuckers can be told from most Red-naped Sapsuckers, which in turn can be separated from most Red-breasted Sapsuckers. Within the Red-breasted Sapsucker, northern and southern populations are further differentiable. So far, so good. Now for the tricky part.

Sapsucker ranges overlap: Yellow-bellied with Red-naped, Yellow-bellied with Red-breasted, Red-naped with Red-breasted, and northern Red-breasted with southern Red-breasted. Yes, a Yellow-bellied Sapsucker is instantly distinguishable from a southern Red-breasted Sapsucker. But plumage characters grade from Yellow-bellied to Red-breasted like this: Yellow-bellied → Red-naped → southern Red-breasted → northern Red-breasted.

Such an arrangement is termed a "Ring Species" complex. The two ends of the ring—in this case Yellow-bellied and northern Red-breasted Sapsuckers—behave like good species, genetically distinct and reproductively isolated from one another. Yet genes flow across the ring, according to the pathway set out above. One species or multiple species? Ring species are yet another example of the shortcomings of an either/or approach to bird taxonomy.

180 TWO FOR THE PRICE OF THREE

Nashville Warbler
Oreothlypis ruficapilla

A FEW NASHVILLE WARBLERS make their way to southern California every winter. The seasonal average is around 25 reports, although that figure varies from year to year. Hold on a sec: *Nashville* Warblers in sunny SoCal? So they breed in Tennessee and winter in San Diego? Nope, nothing of the kind. Birders gleefully note that wood-warblers are, on the whole, atrociously named: Cape May and Connecticut warblers are rare in Cape May and Connecticut, respectively; Palm and Magnolia warblers breed in conifers; Worm-eating Warblers don't eat worms; and what the heck is a prothonotary anyhow? But check this out: The Nashville Warblers that winter in small numbers along the California coast used to be called Calaveras Warblers. And that *is* a good name.

In a manner recalling the Red-shouldered Hawk (§177), the Nashville Warbler comprises two geographically discrete populations, *ridgwayi* of western North America and nominate *ruficapilla* in the East. (On a technical note, the so-called "nominate" subspecies is the one with the same name as the full species.) Western *ridgwayi* was originally described as a separate species, named for Calaveras County, California, home to Mark Twain's "Celebrated Jumping Frog." It is longer-tailed than *ruficapilla*, with a brighter rump. It habitually twitches its tail, unlike *ruficapilla*, it sings a looser song, and it utters a sharper "chip note." In all these respects, it is more similar to another species, the Virginia's Warbler, than to its congener, *ruficapilla*.

Once upon a time, Virginia's, "Calaveras," and *ruficapilla* Nashville warblers were the same species. How did their ancestor evolve into three? Was there an initial split between Virginia's and *ridgwayi-ruficapilla*, followed by a subsequent split of the latter into "Calaveras" and eastern Nashville? That is the implication of current taxonomy. Or did *ruficapilla* first split from Virginia's *ridgwayi*, as implied by the suite of morphological and behavioral traits shared by the latter two taxa?

We don't know. But this we do know: Three distinctive populations, currently classified as two species, occur in our area.

181 ADAPTATION

Brown Creeper
Certhia americana

THIS IS ONE of the most widely distributed forest bird species on the continent, breeding from central Alaska to Nicaragua, from coastal California to the headlands of Canada's Atlantic provinces. You can probably guess what's next: The bird exhibits extensive geographic variation, so much so that ornithologists have invoked a "Brown Creeper complex," comprising multiple species (§§177–180). Sure enough. There have been rumblings in recent years about possible splits along both East-West and North-South axes. But we're going to go in a different direction for the next few lessons. We're going to look at the characteristics and qualities that we humans ascribe to *this* bird or *that* bird. What is the je ne sais quoi of *Certhia americana?*

Laying eyes on a Brown Creeper recalls the experience of surveying the art in *Where's Waldo?* You know Waldo is there—but where? And you know the creeper is there. You've heard its feeble calls. You can stare straight at a Brown Creeper, in real life or in a photo, and look right past it. The bird's upperparts are patterned like bark. The bird itself is flattened. As the creeper forages on a trunk or bough, it hugs the bark as tightly as possible; even its tail is pressed stiffly to the tree. It doesn't poke or peck at its food, in the attention-getting manner of a woodpecker or a nuthatch; the creeper's bill, thin and decurved, is designed for working the furrows with little notice. And its throat is gleaming white, reflecting light onto prey items—spiders and small insects—that the creeper can see but that you cannot.

The Brown Creeper is many things: a species, or perhaps a complex of species; a collection of objects, a population; in the present formulation, a marvel of adaptation, exquisitely suited to its environment, the essence of perfection. These and other constructs are ontological, ways of ascribing a state of being or essence to something. They are conceptually powerful. But are they real?

182 ADAPTATIONISM

Black Vulture
Coragyps atratus

E VEN AMONG VULTURES, this species is notably gross and gnarly. Black Vultures are aggressive and obnoxious, more so than the relatively peaceable Turkey Vultures with whom they consort. Their powers of olfaction are poor, so they frequently raid carrion previously discovered by Turkey Vultures; Black Vultures scavenge on what others have scavenged! They have a special proclivity for garbage dumps, charnel pits, and dog food. Their call is a horrific hiss, loud and long. The species' scientific name, *atratus,* derives from a Latin word denoting a person clothed in black. The Black Vulture is the goth of the bird world.

Perhaps the most vulturine thing of all about the Black Vulture is its unfeathered head, a trait it shares with the Turkey Vulture. Surely, an adaptation for mucking around rotting corpses, yes? Charles Darwin, whose *Origin of Species* is frequently interpreted as a manifesto for the power of adaptation, has this to say about the matter:

> The naked skin on the head of a vulture is generally considered as a direct adaptation for wallowing in putridity; and so it may be, or it may possibly be due to the direct action of putrid matter; but we should be very cautious in drawing any such inference, when we see that the skin on the head of the clean-feeding male turkey is likewise naked.

Darwin is alerting us to the danger of what Stephen Jay Gould, writing more than a century later, would term "adaptationism," the conviction that every trait of an organism has been molded by natural selection to match the environment. To be sure, adaptation is central to Darwin's theory. But Darwin realized—and Gould subsequently reiterated—that many traits do not necessarily reflect current adaptive pressures. They may well be maladaptive. In any event, they just are. The analogy isn't perfect, but think of wisdom teeth, male nipples, and the appendix.

In the meantime, what about Darwin's "clean-feeding male turkey"?

183 MEMES: THE EVOLUTION OF CULTURE

⋘⋘ ⋘⋘ ⋘⋘ ⋘⋘ ⋘⋘ ⋘⋘ ⋘⟨⟩⋙ ⋙⋙ ⋙⋙ ⋙⋙ ⋙⋙ ⋙⋙ ⋙⋙

Wild Turkey
Meleagris gallopavo

T HE PLUMAGES AND morphology of the Brown Creeper make sense (§181). The Black Vulture's plumage (or lack thereof) likewise makes sense—although it is possible that we are overinterpreting the adaptive significance of the vulture's unfeathered head (§182). What can we say in this regard about the Wild Turkey, which, according to American mythology, Benjamin Franklin believed should be the U.S. national bird?

The avian emblem of the United States, the Bald Eagle, is not bald. As artist and humorist John Sill has noted, the bird has enough feathers on its head to stuff a pillow. Like the Black Vulture, however, the turkey is truly bald. Why? Could it have to do with sexual selection, as implied by Darwin (§182)? Probably not, for tom turkeys are just as bald in autumn as during the courtship season in spring. Besides, females are bare-headed, Darwin's implication to the contrary notwithstanding.

Here's a thought. Feathers are metabolically costly. Maybe turkeys have figured out what the rest of the bird world hasn't. They're huge and terrestrial; heat loss through the unfeathered head isn't nearly as severe for a turkey as for the diminutive, seafaring Dovekie, say. Maybe. Regardless, we've gone down the rabbit hole of adaptationist thinking (§182). Let's try a different tack.

The Wild Turkey is, by all accounts, an intelligent bird—so intelligent as to be possessed of what can only be termed "culture." In recent decades, the species has colonized the large cities of eastern, and to a lesser extent western, North America. The urbanization of the turkey is a real phenomenon, one that is believed to have been propagated not by genes, but rather by "memes." Memes? The term was a scientific one well before there were internet memes! Memes are traits that are transmitted culturally, not genetically. They may be adaptive, but they don't have to be. Could it be that turkeys have migrated to cities for the proverbial bright lights and night life? Could it be that they evolved baldness because it looks good? One thing's for sure: Turkeys hold séances (*tinyurl.com/turkey-séance*).

This is not a joke.

184 MEMES: THE EVOLUTION OF BEAUTY

⫷ ⫷ ⫷ ⫷ ⫷ ⫷ ⫷⟨⟩⟫ ⟫ ⟫ ⟫ ⟫ ⟫ ⟫ ⟫

American Goldfinch
Spinus tristis

MALE AMERICAN GOLDFINCHES, like 20-something American men, routinely molt into new plumages. In the case of *Homo sapiens,* it's the endless back-and-forth between bearded and clean-shaven. There's an adaptive explanation for this (§§181–183), some men will tell you: Beards are for cold weather, beardlessness for the warmer months. Uh-huh. You might as well apply adaptationist logic to the prohibition against wearing white after Labor Day. But what about male goldfinches, so different in late fall and early winter from how they appeared just a few months earlier?

Biologists have interpreted the male's radiant summer garb as a signal that he is fit, biologically worthy to combine his genes with a prospective mate's. Like human dreadlocks and Mohawks, the male goldfinch's breeding plumage is a bear to maintain. For starters, a lot of metabolic energy is required for feather growth; and keeping the plumage lustrous demands constant vigilance against the menace of lice, mites, ticks, and other feather parasites. What we humans see as beauty, the female goldfinch interprets as fitness, according to this interpretation.

In a genial but surprising recent book, Yale University ornithologist Richard O. Prum questions our human insistence that beauty is only in the eye of the human beholder. The thesis of *The Evolution of Beauty* is that birds, like humans, are capable of apprehending beauty. Birds appreciate color and pattern, music and dance, pleasure and sensuality.

The preceding is not to deny a role for adaptation, the workhorse of natural selection. But it opens our human minds to a significantly revised conception of the avian soul and spirit. Richard Dawkins, the biologist who invented the idea of the meme (§183), is an arch-adaptationist, but even he acknowledges the possibility of neutral or perhaps maladaptive memes— human religion, for example. In the original formulation, set forth in Dawkins's epochal book *The Selfish Gene* (1976), the author simply didn't go far enough. Dawkins didn't appreciate—nobody did at the time—the extraordinariness of avian culture, cognition, and imagination.

185 MAGPIE FUNERALS

Black-billed Magpie
Pica hudsonia

THE FRIENDS OF the deceased arrive with much clamor. Not all cultures wail publicly for their dead, of course, but many do. After a while, the formal ritual commences. A mourner respectfully places an object—a green strip of something—near the place where the body lies; then she performs a rehearsed nod or gesture, briefly achieving physical contact with the corpse. Another mourner takes her turn. Each of the bereaved repeats the ritual. Once the bands of green have been stacked, they are just as quickly removed. The memorial service is over.

Anthropologists have long recognized that funeral rites are a human universal. All cultures practice them. Even our proto-human ancestors buried their dead. Mourning the dead is one of the things that make us human. It is also one of the things that make magpies magpies. The ritual described above is practiced by Black-billed Magpies. (The green strips are blades of grass, plucked with care by comrades of the fallen bird.)

Magpie funerals weren't formally reported in the Western scientific literature until surprisingly recently, but they are well attested in the traditions of indigenous peoples. The Black-billed Magpie is in the family Corvidae, comprising such well-known birds as ravens, crows, and jays. These corvids have long been regarded, with equal parts admiration and frustration, as pranksters or tricksters. It's almost as if they consciously delight in what they're doing.

They probably do. Western science recently documented self-awareness in magpies, and native cultures have known about corvid cognition all along. The Yup'ik people of Alaska give the name "cella," denoting "consciousness" or "awareness," to the Canada Jay, a magpie relative.

Birds do amazing things that we humans cannot. They migrate thousands of miles; guided only by instinct, they build intricate nests; they swim and dive and even frolic in polar seas where we would surely die. But we're also belatedly coming to appreciate that their minds aren't all that different from our own.

186 NUTCRACKERS NEVER FORGET

Clark's Nutcracker
Nucifraga columbiana

REMEMBER MAPS? TODAY we ask Siri, but it wasn't so long ago that we traversed Milwaukee, say, or Memphis, by means of a big ole foldup laminated or polyethylene map. In London, whose street system is more labyrinthine than any city in the Americas, the black-cab drivers don't use maps. Neither do they resort to Siri. They simply know their way around. London cabbies are the human equivalents of Clark's Nutcrackers.

Like the Black-billed Magpie (§185), the nutcracker is a corvid. Thus it is possessed of advanced cognitive capability. Perhaps even approaching human levels of intellective achievement? No, it's the other way around. In one important respect, the Clark's Nutcracker easily surpasses the mental ability of *Homo sapiens*. This dashing inhabitant of western mountains is gifted with powers of memorization that can only be described as superhuman.

In late summer and autumn, nutcrackers store, or cache, thousands of seeds that they will recover in the months ahead. Winters are long and the snowpack deep in the Rockies and Sierra Nevada, but the nutcrackers know the exact location of every seed: 10.242 meters, 47.29 degrees east of north of that seed; then 12.901 meters, 106.03 degrees west of north of that seed over there; and so forth and so on, all across their winter home range. Although nutcrackers presumably don't think in terms of vectors with magnitude and direction (but who knows?), they are as successful as any human surveyor or geocacher.

How do they do it? The London cabbies suggest an answer. In order to obtain proper licensure, they must demonstrate mastery of "The Knowledge," the map of London's lanes, ways, crescents, circuses, terraces, and more. In a study of black-cab drivers preparing for the exam, it was shown that their brains actually increase in mass while they are learning to navigate the city. Same with nutcrackers and other seed-storing birds: The dorsomedial cortex of their brain, responsible for memory, is greatly enlarged in such birds.

A final thought. The dorsomedial cortex is responsible for another function: awareness of self—and of others.

187 PLACE AND PURPOSE: RANDOM WALK

<<< <<< <<< <<< <<< <<< <<<>>> >>> >>> >>> >>> >>> >>>

Steller's Jay
Cyanocitta stelleri

IN SPITE OF MOUNT RUSHMORE, the Black Hills of South Dakota are one of the most sublime natural features on the continent. Way out on the Great Plains, the Black Hills are an island of pine and granite in a sea of tallgrass prairie. The formation isn't an island in the literal sense, but that's what it is—formally, scientifically—for the ecologists who study where and why organisms occur on this Earth.

In the mid-1960s, ecologists Robert H. MacArthur and E. O. Wilson set forth a rigorous "theory of island biogeography" that, in nonrigorous language, can be said to have two main features: (1) It explains the distribution of plants and animals; and (2) it allows a sizable role for chance, or randomness, in how organisms are distributed in space and time. The first feature of MacArthur and Wilson's theory is conceptually agreeable. So we'll turn our attention to the second!

Plunk yourself down in the middle of the Black Hills, and it's easy to imagine that you're deep in the heart of the Rockies. Pygmy Nuthatches chatter from the edges of campgrounds; American Dippers ply the rapids in Spearfish Canyon; Flammulated Owls hoot in the ponderosa pine forests. Canada Jays are widespread. But Steller's Jays are not. Which, when you pause to think about it, is odd.

Whereas Canada Jays are generally scarce in the southern Rockies, Steller's Jays are ubiquitous. It is impossible to miss the latter species—boisterous, common, and easily identified. So why aren't they in the Black Hills? It's even weirder when you consider that Steller's Jays, unlike Canada Jays, are given to periodic "irruptions" well beyond the Rockies. (Irruptions are irregular, large-scale dispersal events.) If sedentary dippers, completely restricted to rushing mountain streams, found their way to the Black Hills, why didn't Steller's Jays?

They didn't. Go back to the second part of MacArthur and Wilson's theory. It's chance. It's random. Perhaps Steller's Jays *should* be there. But they aren't.

188 PLACE AND PURPOSE: THE BALANCE OF NATURE

≪≪ ≪≪ ≪≪ ≪≪ ≪≪ ≪≪ ≪≪◇≫ ≫≫ ≫≫ ≫≫ ≫≫ ≫≫ ≫≫

Evening Grosbeak
Coccothraustes vespertinus

THE THEORY OF island biogeography (§187) is dynamical. It is all about growth and turnover and change. It admits some amount of stability, but the truly exciting part of the theory is its emphasis on instability. The theory, in its proper and dynamical form, is a powerful antidote to the popular and erroneous conception of the balance of nature. Keep that idea in mind, please, as we delve into the ecology of the Evening Grosbeak.

Piranhas. Flying pigs. The motorcycle gang. All those epithets and more—they're terms of endearment, really—have been applied to these hearty, greedy, and gregarious lovers of sunflower seeds. Fill a feeder full of black oil or striped sunflower seed, and it will be depredated by a roistering flock of Evening Grosbeaks. But you have to be in the right place. And time.

In the early 1980s, Evening Grosbeaks were frequent winter visitants at feeders in the eastern states. By the 2000s, they were rare at best. For a few years in the mid-2010s, they staged a mini-comeback. Now go back more than a century. The record isn't as clear, but one thing is certain: Evening Grosbeaks massively invaded the East around the turn of the 20th century. The event was decades in the making.

The Evening Grosbeak is a finch. Finches are famously nomadic. They get around. For at least 150 years, the population dynamics (§§101–107, 139) of *Coccothraustes vespertinus* have been characterized by instability, chaos, and change. That's not to say that its population swings have been entirely random or stochastic (§§106, 187). For example, the widespread planting of box elder trees may have triggered the species' invasion of the East in the late 1800s and the early 1900s. (Evening Grosbeaks like box elder fruits, or samaras, almost as much as they like sunflower seeds.) Outbreaks of forest insects, including non-native species introduced by humans, may be another contributing factor.

In any event, the Evening Grosbeak is in a condition of long-term and probably perpetual imbalance. So are almost all bird species.

189 PLACE AND PURPOSE: INTRODUCED SPECIES

⋘ ⋘ ⋘ ⋘ ⋘ ⋘ ⋘◇⟫ ⟫ ⟫ ⟫ ⟫ ⟫ ⟫

Ring-necked Pheasant
Phasianus colchicus

T HE COCK PHEASANT, strutting across the snowy meadow, is a thing of beauty. If you were to put the entire collection of a major art museum—all the jade and jasper, all the topaz and gold—in one place, the result would be an adult male Ring-necked Pheasant. It is impossible not to admire the perfection of the bird. Yet certain birders are contemptuous of the species itself, *Phasianus colchicus*. It's an interloper, an invader, a "bad" bird.

The pheasant's scientific name commemorates an ancient nation or nationality in Asia. The kingdom of Colchis is long gone, but its pheasants live on. Through the ages, they made their way west across Europe to Britain and then on to America—eventually reaching Hawaii. They have conquered the Western world.

The preceding is revisionist history. The pheasants themselves had nothing to do with it. The Ring-necked Pheasant's success story is one of human agency. We don't have to throw our hands up, as we do in so many other attempts at explaining avian ranges (§§187–188). Pheasants are here because we deliberately stock them—for hunting and aesthetics. For once, we have a fully satisfactory explanation for the status and distribution of an "American" bird species.

The pheasant isn't supposed to be here, many birders will tell you, and yet we humans put it here. In the late 20th century, it was common for birders to expunge introduced species from their life lists. The purist's life list was proudly identified by the acronym NIB, for "no introduced birds."

It was a fantasy, a throwback to an old way of thinking about the proper categories for the objects and phenomena of this world. You could get away with it in the past century, with its persistent myth about the balance of nature (§188), with its insistence on deterministic explanations of biological processes (§187)—despite what biologists really told us! No longer. We have come to recognize that, for better or for worse, we are living in the Anthropocene epoch. The rules have changed.

190 PLACE AND PURPOSE: THE ANTHROPOCENE EPOCH

⋘ ⋘ ⋘ ⋘ ⋘ ⋘ ⋘◇⋙ ⋙ ⋙ ⋙ ⋙ ⋙ ⋙

Bald Eagle
Haliaeetus leucocephalus

THE CALL ISN'T particularly loud, but it is far-carrying, a cackling series, rising quickly in pitch and amplitude, then trailing off. Where *is* the big bird? You scan the tall trees, shrouded in freezing fog. Nothing. You hear it again, the sound of wildness, of freedom, a certain defiance. This could be Alaska's Inside Passage. You joke with your companion that you're half-expecting a glacier to calve any moment now.

Not here. Not in this sprawling city park in the heartland. Regardless, you're hearing a Bald Eagle, the U.S. national bird. You tap the sighting into the eBird app, and carry on.

A few minutes later, the two of you come upon a flock of passerines—chickadees, a couple kinglets, and a creeper—in some shrubbery at the periphery of the zoo. The zoo! Fiddlesticks, or the equivalent, your companion mutters. That Bald Eagle wasn't in the park. It was one of the captive birds in the zoo. You scratch the entry from your eBird app, and carry on.

It is self-evident to any card-carrying birder that an eagle in a cage doesn't count. Such a bird is disqualified, unworthy, for the patently obvious reason that it isn't wild. Perhaps. But what of its wild counterpart?

That bird may have been reared in a hack tower, an artificial nest site. If it wasn't, its mother or grandmother might well have been. It feeds on stocked fish in a reservoir impounded by a ginormous concrete dam. When it commences breeding early next year, the nest will be monitored by volunteers, studied by scientists, and protected by law enforcement. In all likelihood, the bird wouldn't be here at all if it weren't for the U.S. Endangered Species Act. The species was destined for extinction until humans intervened.

A wilderness mythos permeates the American psyche. Would we lose something of our national soul and spirit if we discarded it? Or would we awaken to a new conception of our own place and purpose in nature's realm?

191 SHIFTING BASELINES: AMERICA'S MOST ABUNDANT BIRD

≪≪ ≪≪ ≪≪ ≪≪ ≪≪ ≪≪ ≪≪◇≫ ≫≫ ≫≫ ≫≫ ≫≫ ≫≫

Passenger Pigeon
Ectopistes migratorius

SOME AMERICAN BIRDERS don't put introduced pheasants on their lists (§189)—because they're not "supposed" to be here. The vast majority won't count a captive Bald Eagle (§189), instantly disqualified, unworthy. Fewer still would tick the Passenger Pigeon off their lists. The only way to encounter a real Passenger Pigeon is to examine a museum specimen. The species is extinct.

The last Passenger Pigeon, named Martha, died in the Cincinnati Zoo on or around September 1, 1914. Reports of wild birds, viewed with suspicion then and now, persisted for a while. So did the hope for rediscovery, for chancing upon a hitherto undetected wild flock. By the mid-20th century, though, everybody agreed that the pigeon was gone forever. But not forgotten.

The recent centennial of the passing of Martha received considerable notice—not only from bird and nature lovers, but also from the broader public. Why? "For one species to mourn the death of another is a new thing under the sun," said Aldo Leopold in "On a Monument to the Pigeon," the most convicting work of the great essayist.

Leopold, writing in 1947, anticipated the modern conservation biologist's concern for shifting baselines, the continual resetting of a society's understanding of and relation to the natural world. In popular parlance, this is the problem of the "new normal." The Passenger Pigeon was the most abundant bird on the continent, with single flocks exceeding one *billion* individuals. We do well to remember what we have lost.

According to Leopold: "To love what was is a new thing under the sun, unknown to most people and to all pigeons. To see America as history, to conceive of destiny as a becoming, to smell a hickory tree through the still lapse of ages—all these things are possible for us, and to achieve them takes only the free sky, and the will to ply our wings."

Are we capable of transforming Leopold's act of imagination into meaningful conservation initiatives? The jury is still out on that one.

192 SHIFTING BASELINES, TAKE 2

Red Junglefowl
Gallus gallus

WHAT IS THE most abundant bird on the continent? In formulating your response to the question, try to avoid scanning an inch higher to the name of the species for this lesson. No fair! You might as well be instructed *not* to think about an elephant . . .

Anyhow, yes, the Red Junglefowl, known to all as the chicken, is the most numerous bird—and indeed the most abundant vertebrate—in North America. The U.S. population alone is nine billion, close to 30 chickens for every citizen. Most of them are imprisoned in ghastly indoor chambers, but countless millions roam free. A self-sustaining population in South Florida has been well established for centuries.

You won't find an entry for *Gallus gallus* in your *Nat Geo* field guide. The species is omitted from the continental checklist of the American Birding Association (ABA), the authority for all birders who keep lists. Your eBird checklist may well allow Helmeted Guineafowl and Indian Peafowl, two species that aren't on the ABA checklist; but probably not the Red Junglefowl. No, that would cross a line. Why is that?

Go back a century to Anna Botsford Comstock's magisterial *Handbook of Nature Study* (1911), and the chicken is the first species account. Then comes the pigeon, a species that didn't qualify for the Christmas Bird Count (§195) until the late 1970s. Next: the "Canary and the Goldfinch," treated in tandem, followed by the robin and the bluebird. Do you see it, the gradual transition from feral to wild? There is no clear breakpoint, no unambiguously demarcated boundary between birds that count and those that do not. Comstock was a pedagogical genius. And a realist.

Consider this. All across the heartland, the rooster's lusty *cock-a-doodle-doo* is the essence of the new day, as authentically American as apple pie. How is that not a part of who we are as a people? In what possible sense can the Red Junglefowl be said not to count? What do we value anyhow?

193 OUR HUMAN VALUES: THE GOOD

Eastern Bluebird
Sialia sialis

THE BIRDHOUSES IN the park's day-use area are distributed in a curious fashion: two right next to each other, then a gap of 100 meters, then another tight pairing, then another wide gap . . . What we have here is a "bluebird trail," ringing the day-use area, extending back along the park entrance, and running the length of a gravel maintenance road—40 birdhouses altogether. A spatial ecologist would have a field day with the configuration of bluebird boxes in this park, simultaneously clumped and hyperdispersed.

It's easy to understand why bluebird lovers would disperse boxes evenly across the landscape. Bluebirds are territorial. They want their nests to be spread out across the landscape, not randomly, but in a manner so as to maximize each pair's territory size. That's the essence of hyperdispersion, the reason the boxes are regularly spaced at 100-meter intervals. But why the pairing?

Bluebirds and Tree Swallows vie for nest boxes, and the aggressive swallows are every bit as competitive as the bluebirds. They don't tolerate conspecifics as next-door neighbors, but they're indifferent to bluebirds. Do the math: 40 evenly spaced birdhouses = 40 Tree Swallow pairs; 20 evenly clumped pairs of boxes = 20 swallow pairs + 20 bluebird pairs.

Bluebird lovers are clever. They are devoted. They are dues-paying members of every manner of bluebird society. And they prompt the question: Why do bluebirds enchant us so?

Because they are beautiful. Because they are native. Because they are (somewhat) monogamous and (relatively) good parents. Because they are fragile. Bluebirds are evicted from their boxes by mean birds like Tree Swallows. They devour injurious insects (in the same way as Tree Swallows, likewise native and beautiful, but never mind). They are the bluebirds of happiness, and harbingers of spring. The perfect sky is a bluebird sky; the perfect day, a bluebird day. And even if we've forgotten every other scene in Victor Fleming's setting of *The Wizard of Oz*, we still remember Judy Garland exulting in bluebirds over the rainbow.

Bluebirds touch something deep inside ourselves. Bluebirds are virtuous. Whatever that means.

194 OUR HUMAN VALUES: THE BAD

⋘ ⋘ ⋘ ⋘ ⋘ ⋘ ⋘ ⟨⟩ ⋙ ⋙ ⋙ ⋙ ⋙ ⋙ ⋙

Mute Swan
Cygnus olor

THE COLD WATERS of THE old millpond twinkle in the solstice sunlight. The original watermill is but a memory, yet the pond's swans hang on. You know in your head that the Mute Swan is a "bad" bird, but your heart gets the better of you right now. The two adults, "married" for as long as you've been coming here, are plainly majestic. No wonder humans brought them to this place long ago.

In the early going, they were uncontroversial. The swans were a source of civic pride, a positive good. They were living art. But they proved to have a dark side: The Mute Swans were also aggressive and proprietary, given to bouts of ominous hissing at passersby. A neighbor went so far as to accuse one of assault! Around the same time, wildlife biologists began to suspect them of far worse, of crimes against the environment.

The rap sheet on *Cygnus olor* is long indeed: Mute Swans outcompete native waterfowl, they overgraze aquatic vegetation, they foul lakes and ponds, they frighten pet owners, they may even be an air safety threat. Like the Ring-necked Pheasant, the Mute Swan is an introduced species (§189). But whereas pheasant populations tend to wink out unless they are restocked, Mute Swans are highly invasive. They quickly establish and just as quickly overrun the landscape—from urban parks and bustling marinas to quiet back bays and fragile coastal saltmarshes. Hence the guilty verdict against the species. Their punishment: euthanasia, sterilization, and translocation.

Not so fast.

Mute Swans have as many defenders as detractors. They are gorgeous, every bit as worthy as a mural or fountain or garden or gazebo. An emerging management strategy seeks to restrict swans to public parks and other venues with high visibility while stopping the species' broader invasion in its tracks. So the millpond Mute Swans are okay—just as long as they stay put. It's a fine compromise, but will it work? Time will tell.

195 OUR HUMAN VALUES: THE UGLY

≪≪ ≪≪ ≪≪ ≪≪ ≪≪ ≪≪ ≪≪◇≫ ≫≫ ≫≫ ≫≫ ≫≫ ≫≫ ≫≫

Double-crested Cormorant
Phalacrocorax auritus

IT'S THE MORNING of the Christmas Bird Count (CBC), a daylong survey of all the birds within a circle 15 miles in diameter. The CBC is the longest-running large-scale ecological survey in history, and it's conducted almost entirely by amateurs. For today's CBC you find yourself in the flat lowlands of the lower Mississippi River drainage, and your first assignment is to count the herons, ducks, and other aquatic species that mass at and in the general vicinity of a catfish farm. *Three Double-crested Cormorants. Ten more. Two hundred. Hundreds more.* Your final tally, a mix of exact counts ("77 perched on that tower") and quicker approximations ("330 flying over, 10x estimates"), exceeds 5,000 cormorants, a record high for your CBC sector.

Double-crested Cormorants have been increasing everywhere in recent decades. Like Brown Pelicans (§139), they are the beneficiaries of restrictions on pesticide use and a more general reversal of the environmental degradations of the first two-thirds of the 20th century. Their numbers may have been given a boost, too, by aquaculture—for example, catfish farming here in the lower Mississippi River valley.

Cormorants and humans are in conflict. It's simple. Both species like catfish. And catfish farmers are freaking out. Here and elsewhere they have succeeded in procuring permits to kill cormorants. The case against the cormorants is flimsy, but that doesn't matter. "It's the economy, stupid." That changes everything. And it doesn't help the cormorants' cause that they're . . . well, they're not as virtuous as bluebirds (§193), not as stately as swans (§194).

Cormorants are hulking and clumsy, jet black with strange, staring aquamarine eyes and sickly orange dewlaps (or gular pouches). They grunt and belch. They defecate prolifically, with predictable offenses against the human olfactory system. Worst of all, cormorants steal from catfish farmers. They arouse little sympathy. A recent monograph is titled *The Devil's Cormorant*.

Birds are diverse in every way imaginable—in color and pattern, in song and call, in behavior and ecology. Is it any surprise that we humans respond diversely—emotionally, aesthetically, even ethically—to all that avian variety?

196 ETHICALNESS

<<< <<< <<< <<< <<< <<< <<◇>>> >>> >>> >>> >>> >>>

Barred Owl
Strix varia

WATCHING BIRDS CAN BE a bit like visiting an art gallery, a chiefly aesthetic undertaking. Now extend the analogy a bit further. Art galleries are considerably more than pretty pictures and satisfied patrons. Behind the scenes, curators and archivists care for the collections and choose objects for public display; marketing specialists and philanthropy officers tend to fund-raising and budgeting—and sometimes painful decision-making. It is much the same in our engagement with the world of birds. Perhaps inevitably, the bird lover is led toward an ethical conception of bird appreciation.

In many instances, the ethical dimension of birding is a matter of established case law. It is okay to cull Mute Swan populations, many would say, because the species is introduced (§194). It is likewise acceptable to destroy cormorants, even though they are native, because they allegedly steal from fishermen—and, besides, they are so ugly (§195). And who would argue against nest-box provisioning for the bluebird of happiness (§193)?

The preceding is a caricature. Killing cormorants and swans is highly controversial. And although the actions of bluebird aficionados are inarguably well-intentioned, the priorities and interventions of such persons have received some scrutiny. But if you want to delve deep into situational avian ethics, you need look no further than the conflict between Barred and Spotted owls.

We humans love owls. We loved owls even before *Harry Potter*. We build owl boxes, we bait owls with mice, we rehabilitate them when they are injured, we keep them as pets. Harm an owl? An art lover might as well slash the canvas of a Rembrandt.

We love owls, but Barred Owls don't love Spotted Owls. The former are both native and aggressive, and they fight—literally fight—with Spotted Owls. The latter are threatened and declining, and expanding populations of Barred Owls are making things worse. If the matter were purely ethical, there would be an easy answer: Kill invading Barred Owls for the sake of imperiled Spotted Owls. And that is indeed the recommendation of the scientific community. But there's more to the matter than ethics, isn't there?

197 MORALITY

Northern Pintail
Anas acuta

THE DRAKE PINTAIL is taken down with a single shot. The bird hits the water with a soft plop, a black Lab fetches the carcass, the hunter stashes his trophy in a sack. This was a clean shot by a properly licensed hunter who wouldn't dare exceed his daily bag limit. In every regard, the man is an ethical hunter. Now take it a step further. In every regard, modern hunting is an ethical enterprise. Directly and indirectly, hunters cull the herd; they improve habitat; they promote local economies; they feed their families and perhaps their neighbors' families as well. Or so the argument goes.

The cold, hard evidence is shaky. Hunters stock field and stream with non-native biota; their prey flourish in fragmented habitats of dubious ecological value; they have failed at efforts to cull exploding deer populations. The popularity of hunting is waning steadily across the continent, with a corresponding decline in economic impact. And although malnutrition is a stubborn social ill in the United States, our supermarkets and soup kitchens are not exactly overflowing with inexpensive cuts of choice venison.

But what of the actions of the individual hunter? Surely, they are ethical? Maybe they are. But are they moral?

The hunter is a sportsman, his pintail a trophy. He plays by the rules. And so we persist in our evasion of the moral dimension of hunting. Is it immoral for a moral animal like a human to kill a nonhuman animal? Birds aren't the mindless automatons we once thought they were, a point made convincingly in recent books by Richard O. Prum (§184), Jennifer Ackerman, and Noah Strycker. It's one thing—perhaps—to kill an animal for food or research or human safety. But to do so for sport?

We haven't gotten to the point that hunting in America is a moral crisis. Not yet. But if there's anything that American history has taught us, it is this: Times change.

198 WHAT'S IN A NAME? NOMENCLATORIAL POLITICS

Long-tailed Duck
Clangula hyemalis

"OLDSQUAWS, OR LONG-TAILED DUCKS, as I should prefer to have them called, are lively, restless, happy-go-lucky little ducks, known to most of us as hardy and cheery visitors to our winter seacoasts, associated in our minds with cold, gray skies, snow squalls, and turbulent wintry waves." So wrote Arthur Cleveland Bent in his two-volume *Life Histories of North American Wild Fowl* (1923, 1925), itself an entry in the ornithologist's massive encyclopedia of the continent's birdlife.

Bent would get his way, but not until long after his death in 1954. According to a decree in 2000 by the American Ornithological Society (AOS, §§26–27), the standard English name of this sea duck was upgraded from Oldsquaw to Long-tailed Duck. Let's not beat around the bush: The name was changed for reasons of political correctness. The former name of the duck was a remarkably efficient epithet, achieving ageism, racism, and sexism in one fell swoop, in the space of a mere eight letters.

Bent's unease notwithstanding, the name appears to have been unobjectionable to the ornithologists of yesteryear. Oldsquaw was poetical, a nod to the species' mirthful chatter. One of Bent's correspondents supplied "the best description of it as *ow-owdle-ow* and *ow-ow-owldle-ow* with a Philadelphia twang; that is with a short *a* sound in the *ow*." Did we lose something in exchanging Oldsquaw for the admittedly rather clinical "Long-tailed Duck"? Thanks to the Principle of Priority (§29), we still have *Clangula hyemalis,* pure poetry, powerful and evocative. And we've gained something. We've advanced the AOS's stated goal to "connect a vibrant community of ornithologists throughout the Americas . . . to meet the ever-changing needs of ornithology and ornithologists."

Political correctness gets a bad rap. One wishes it were given a different name. What is it, after all, but a signal of good manners and goodwill, an acknowledgment of respect and esteem, the affirmation of another person's dignity? The AOS made the right call on this one.

199 WHAT'S IN A NAME? CULTURAL IMPERIALISM

⋘ ⋘ ⋘ ⋘ ⋘ ⋘ ⋘◁▷≫ ≫ ≫ ≫ ≫ ≫ ≫

Brewer's Blackbird
Euphagus cyanocephalus

A CCORDING TO THE most entrenched creation myth of all time: "The LORD God formed every animal of the field and every bird of the air and brought them to the man to see what he would call them; and whatever the man called every living creature, that was its name." This is the legend of Adam, of course, but it eerily foreshadows the nomen-clatorial authority of the American Ornithological Society (AOS, §§26–27). Whatever the AOS calls every bird species, that is its name.

Until the AOS changes its mind. Which happens with gratifying frequency. The AOS, guided by its mission to anticipate and address the needs of con-temporary ornithology, is forever messing with bird names. We just heard the story of how the Long-tailed Duck got its name (§198). Here's another: Van Remsen, one of the most influential ornithologists alive, proposes to change the Inca Dove to the Aztec Dove. The former, according to Remsen, is a "com-pletely misleading, nonsensical, embarrassing name that should not be per-petuated." (The species occurs way to the north of the old Inca empire.)

Thank goodness for the inoffensive, standard English name given to *Euphagus cyanocephalus,* the Brewer's Blackbird. Talk about playing it safe. This bird's name commemorates Thomas Brewer, a dead white male educated at Harvard. At least he was an American and an ornithologist. The bird's scientific name was conferred by Johann Wagler, a German herpetologist—and dead white male. Why are honorific, or patronymic, names so pervasive in ornithology?

In a gentle but hortatory commentary in *Birding* magazine in 2017, Frank Keim contrasts the scientific approach with that of the Yup'ik people of Alaska (§185). Yup'ik bird names are efficient, descriptive, and, most of all, highly scientific. And they are never, ever, patronymic. According to Keim, "The practice is simply alien to the Yup'ik people, which tells you something about the mind-set of their culture. And ours."

Keim's critique is fair. But there's just one thing. Times change (§197). People change. Cultures change.

200 WHO KNEW?

⋘ ⋘ ⋘ ⋘ ⋘ ⋘ ⋘◁▷⋙ ⋙ ⋙ ⋙ ⋙ ⋙ ⋙

Eastern Screech-Owl
Megascops asio

NEW YEAR'S EVE. A few minutes before midnight, and the little owl is singing steadily. The primary song of the Eastern Screech-Owl is lovely, a wavering glissando that falls in pitch. This is going to be your last bird of the year. The clock strikes 12, the owl lets loose another descending whinny, and you have your first species of the new year.

You haven't seen the bird. You don't even want to. The starry night is so perfect. Besides, the screech-owl is properly appreciated as a voice in the night woods, unseen, equal parts spooky and serene.

Eastern Screech-Owls have made their homes in this heavily visited city park for as long as you've been birding. You've heard the species on countless occasions here; the park's checklist calls *Megascops asio* a common permanent resident. It doesn't matter. The sound of the screech-owl is a blessing, every bit as bewitching as when you first heard it.

Really? That's an owl? In the big city? Right here? Does anybody else even know about this?

We hear an owl, for the first time or the 5,000th, and we say or whisper or think its sacred name. So it is in every avian encounter (§§1–3). Then we embark on any of the infinite number of journeys the human mind can lead us along (§§4–197). And when all is said and done, the bird is still a name, just a name (§§198–199), yet so much more, a new creation, reborn, remade, let loose, set free. So are we, unshackled at last from old ways of thinking.

We were drawn to birds in the first place by their beauty. We were sustained by the majesty and pageantry of their dawn choruses and hemispheric migrations. And we were buoyed—we still are, we evermore shall be—by their promise to delight and surprise and amaze us. We may not have realized it at first, but we know it now: We are madly and wonderfully and perfectly in love with birds.

A NOTE ABOUT THE GEOGRAPHIC
AND TAXONOMIC SCOPE OF THIS BOOK

⋘ ⋘ ⋘ ⋘ ⋘ ⋘ ⋘◇⋙ ⋙ ⋙ ⋙ ⋙ ⋙ ⋙

THE GEOGRAPHIC AMBIT of this book corresponds more or less to what birders know as "The ABA Area," defined as Canada, the United States, and, in a strange quirk, the French territory of Saint Pierre and Miquelon—all 93 square miles thereof! References to "our area" or "our region" thus refer to the United States and Canada. That said, the narrative occasionally sneaks well south of the U.S. border—just as it wanders from time to time into the realms of physics, sociology, and so forth. Birds, like birders, have little use for boundaries.

All but two of the species featured in this book are ABA "Code 1" species, meaning they are widespread and easily found. The two exceptions are the Passenger Pigeon (§191), probably the most abundant bird in our area until the mid-19th century, and the Red Junglefowl (§192), unquestionably the most abundant bird at the present time. What this means is that there is a bit of a bias toward the avifauna of the American and Canadian heartlands; that's because rarer birds (ABA Codes 2–5) are better represented along the edges, and especially the corners, of the continent.

The taxonomy in this book follows that of the American Ornithological Society (AOS). AOS taxonomy is forever in the process of revision. Once a year, species are split (and sometimes lumped), linear sequence is shuffled, genera are reassigned, and more. That's true of the AOS itself! Until recently, the organization was the AOU (American Ornithologists' Union); then it was "lumped" (or merged) with the Cooper Ornithological Society. Some people don't like all these changes, but the rest of us take heart in an exhortation of the late Stephen Hawking : "Intelligence is the ability to adapt to change."

In any event, the ever-changing taxonomy of North American birds is kept up-to-date at the AOS website; visit *checklist.aou.org/taxa,* which, amusingly, retains an older nomenclature (*aou.org*). Or if you want just the current names of the ABA Area avifauna, bop on over to the ABA's constantly updated Listing Central website: *listing.aba.org/aba-checklist.*

AN ANNOTATED CHECKLIST OF
THE BIRD SPECIES IN THIS BOOK

≪≪ ≪≪≪ ≪≪≪ ≪≪≪ ≪≪≪ ≪≪≪ ≪≪◇≫≫ ≫≫≫ ≫≫≫ ≫≫≫ ≫≫≫ ≫≫≫ ≫≫≫

T HE ENTRIES IN a human family tree do not ordinarily appear in alphabetical order. Instead they are placed in such a way as to indicate biological relatedness. If Adam and Zander are brothers, they occur next to each other; if Lara and Layla are second cousins once removed, they appear relatively distant from one another on the family tree.

In an analogous manner, a list of bird species may be ordered according to evolutionary relationships. As we saw in §32, "The ABCs (not) of checklist order," such orderings typically appear in a linear sequence which provides a partial overview of the biological organization that informs so much of our appreciation of birding and ornithology. A list by itself masks key groupings (genera, families, orders) of species, so it is customary to insert them at key breakpoints in the enumeration.

This listing of the 200 species in *How to Know the Birds* is very simple, showing family associations and nothing more. The intent is to give the reader a general feel for the linear sequence of the birds of the United States and Canada. This may or may not be a good thing, but many birders eventually memorize large swaths of the full checklist of the birds of their region! For greater taxonomic detail, see the AOS's annually updated online checklist: *checklist.aou.org/taxa*.

FAMILY ANATIDAE: Geese, Swans, and Ducks

These are the familiar waterfowl of lakes, rivers, and seacoasts. Most are large-bodied, and all are able swimmers. Some quack and honk, but others sound very different.

☐ 107. Snow Goose, *Anser caerulescens*—Population dynamics: Keystone species
☐ 138. Canada Goose, *Branta canadensis*—The upside of human-modified landscapes?
☐ 194. Mute Swan, *Cygnus olor*—Our human values: The bad
☐ 171. Tundra Swan, *Cygnus columbianus*—"Good birders don't wear white"
☐ 125. Wood Duck, *Aix sponsa*—"Molt is messy"
☐ 62. Cinnamon Teal, *Spatula cyanoptera*—The logic of migration: A tale of two teals
☐ 141. Northern Shoveler, *Spatula clypeata*—Paved with good intentions
☐ 83. Gadwall, *Mareca strepera*—Whither the field notebook?
☐ 34. American Wigeon, *Mareca americana*—Go to the head of the class

☐ 6. Mallard, *Anas platyrhynchos*—(Many) birds have distinctive colors
☐ 197. Northern Pintail, *Anas acuta*—Morality
☐ 18. Green-winged Teal, *Anas crecca*—ID birds by microhabitat
☐ 101. Canvasback, *Aythya valisineria*—Population dynamics: The duck factory
☐ 46. Redhead, *Aythya americana*—Duck music
☐ 22. Ring-necked Duck, *Aythya collaris*—The value of local experience
☐ 140. Lesser Scaup, *Aythya affinis*—Deal with the devil
☐ 198. Long-tailed Duck, *Clangula hyemalis*—What's in a name? Nomenclatorial politics
☐ 98. Bufflehead, *Bucephala albeola*—Bird nests: If you build it, they will come
☐ 108. Common Goldeneye, *Bucephala clangula*—Rethinking the breeding season: The pair bond
☐ 78. Hooded Merganser, *Lophodytes cucullatus*—A modest proposal
☐ 163. Common Merganser, *Mergus merganser*—On the origins of knowledge: Remote sensing
☐ 26. Red-breasted Merganser, *Mergus serrator*—By any other name
☐ 157. Ruddy Duck, *Oxyura jamaicensis*—Things birders do: Big Days

FAMILY ODONTOPHORIDAE: New World Quail

Together with the next family, these constitute the upland gamebirds. They trend in browns and grays, are mostly round-bodied, and favor terrestrial habitats.

☐ 44. Northern Bobwhite, *Colinus virginianus*—How to read the music of birdsong
☐ 93. Gambel's Quail, *Callipepla gambelii*—Baby birds: Early bloomers

FAMILY PHASIANIDAE: Upland Gamebirds

Generally larger than quail, the birds in this diverse group are perhaps best known for the extraordinary courtship displays of the males.

☐ 192. Red Junglefowl, *Gallus gallus*—Shifting baselines, Take 2
☐ 189. Ring-necked Pheasant, *Phasianus colchicus*—Place and purpose: Introduced species
☐ 155. Ruffed Grouse, *Bonasa umbellus*—Things birders do: Listing
☐ 183. Wild Turkey, *Meleagris gallopavo*—Memes: The evolution of culture

FAMILY PODICIPEDIDAE: Grebes

Expert divers and lovers of fish, grebes are usually seen in deep water both inland and coastally. Recent research establishes that they are related to flamingos and pigeons.

☐ 169. Pied-billed Grebe, *Podilymbus podiceps*—The Prime Directive: Field ID
☐ 132. Eared Grebe, *Podiceps nigricollis*—America's flightless bird
☐ 52. Western Grebe, *Aechmophorus occidentalis*—Night shift

FAMILY COLUMBIDAE: Pigeons and Doves

Most birds in this family are small-headed, big-chested, and of medium build overall. Look for them walking unobtrusively around the ground, and listen for their cooing vocalizations.

☐ 66. Rock Pigeon, *Columba livia*—Flying blind

☐ 103. Eurasian Collared-Dove, *Streptopelia decaocto*—Population dynamics: Fecundity

☐ 191. Passenger Pigeon, *Ectopistes migratorius*—Shifting baselines: America's most abundant bird

☐ 9. Mourning Dove, *Zenaida macroura*—Shape matters

FAMILY CUCULIDAE: Cuckoos

The bird that famously says *cuckoo!* is a Eurasian species that rarely strays to our area. But we've got the iconic roadrunner, huge and terrestrial. Cuckoos tend to be long-tailed and lanky overall.

☐ 64. Yellow-billed Cuckoo, *Coccyzus americanus*—Life history theory: Flappy fliers fly at night

☐ 147. Greater Roadrunner, *Geococcyx californianus*—The legacy of BirdChat

FAMILY CAPRIMULGIDAE: Nightjars

These cryptic birds "jar" the night with their spooky vocalizations. The family name is an odd one, meaning "goatsucker," another name for these nocturnal birds.

☐ 97. Common Nighthawk, *Chordeiles minor*—Bird nests: Nontraditional

FAMILY APODIDAE: Swifts

The vast majority of sightings of species in this family are of birds on the wing; swifts land only to roost and tend their highly concealed nests. Their bodies are tubular, their wings long and arced back.

☐ 84. Chimney Swift, *Chaetura pelagica*—eBird: Just Do It

FAMILY TROCHILIDAE: Hummingbirds

They glitter and sparkle; they hover on impossibly fast wingbeats; they're the smallest of birds. And their closest relatives are the swifts. Who'da thunk?

☐ 67. Ruby-throated Hummingbird, *Archilochus colubris*—Migrants powered by hyperphagia

☐ 23. Anna's Hummingbird, *Calypte anna*—Timing is everything

☐ 74. Rufous Hummingbird, *Selasphorus rufus*—Migration toggle switch

FAMILY RALLIDAE: Rails and Coots

These aquatic omnivores have a penchant for well-vegetated wetlands. Rails (including the Sora) hide in the cattails; coots often come out into the open. Their calls are explosive and vulgar.

☐ 164. Virginia Rail, *Rallus limicola*—On the origins of knowledge: Scientific collecting

☐ 49. Sora, *Porzana carolina*—What is birdsong?

☐ 32. American Coot, *Fulica americana*—The ABCs (not) of checklist order

FAMILY GRUIDAE: Cranes

These relatives of the rails and coots stand proud and tall; look for them in grain fields and shallow marshes, and listen for their evocative bugling as they fly high overhead.

☐ 54. Sandhill Crane, *Antigone canadensis*—A beautiful bird

FAMILY RECURVIROSTRIDAE: Avocets and Stilts

Look for these classy shorebirds in hypersaline environments: alkaline lakes, coastal lagoons, and sewage treatment ponds. They are large and boldly patterned, with fine, long bills.

☐ 153. American Avocet, *Recurvirostra americana*—Ornithological society meetings

FAMILY CHARADRIIDAE: Plovers

Run . . . pause . . . run . . . That manner of locomotion characterizes this family of shorebirds. The typical plumage pattern is brown above and white below with a prominent black breast band.

☐ 123. Semipalmated Plover, *Charadrius semipalmatus*—An inconvenient truth
☐ 75. Killdeer, *Charadrius vociferus*—Now what?

FAMILY SCOLOPACIDAE: Sandpipers

The birds in this speciose family exhibit relatively little plumage variety but great morphological diversity. Many are tremendous migrants, winging their way each year from the high Arctic to south of the equator.

☐ 68. Sanderling, *Calidris alba*—Fallout!
☐ 19. Least Sandpiper, *Calidris minutilla*—ID by physiological ecology
☐ 118. Short-billed Dowitcher, *Limnodromus griseus*—Molt migration
☐ 39. American Woodcock, *Scolopax minor*—The Catch-22 of unseen birds
☐ 30. Wilson's Snipe, *Gallinago delicata*—Splitting species in two
☐ 127. Spotted Sandpiper, *Actitis macularius*—How the sandpiper got his spots
☐ 57. Solitary Sandpiper, *Tringa solitaria*—Spring has sprung
☐ 173. Willet, *Tringa semipalmata*—The kids are alright
☐ 45. Greater Yellowlegs, *Tringa melanoleuca*—Learn bird vocalizations online
☐ 88. Wilson's Phalarope, *Phalaropus tricolor*—¡Viva la revolución!

FAMILY ALCIDAE: Auks

Restricted to northern hemisphere waters, these penguin-like birds breed in dense colonies on rocky seacoasts. Away from the nesting colonies, they are strictly marine, often occurring well out at sea.

☐ 85. Common Murre, *Uria aalge*—eBird: A lifetime of memories

FAMILY LARIDAE: Gulls and Terns

Everyone knows a gull, or "seagull," but identification at the species level can be difficult.

Terns, separated from gulls by bill shape and a particularly distinctive mode of foraging, also can be challenging to ID.

☐ 165. Laughing Gull, *Leucophaeus atricilla*—On the origins of knowledge: Digital photos
☐ 69. Franklin's Gull, *Leucophaeus pipixcan*—"Vis mig"
☐ 122. Ring-billed Gull, *Larus delawarensis*—A false dichotomy
☐ 15. Herring Gull, *Larus argentatus*—Individual variation
☐ 128. Forster's Tern, *Sterna forsteri*—With a little help from my friends

FAMILY GAVIIDAE: Loons

With bills like daggers, loons terrorize the fish fauna of deepwater habitats like lakes, lagoons, and reservoirs. They are famous for their midsummer wailings, but most encounters are with silent birds on migration and in winter.

☐ 13. Common Loon, *Gavia immer*—Seasonal variation

FAMILY PROCELLARIIDAE: Shearwaters and Petrels

Along with the related albatrosses, these are the ultimate oceanic (or "pelagic") birds, asea for months or more at a time. They are called "tubenoses," so-named for extensions on their bill that process saltwater into freshwater.

☐ 110. Sooty Shearwater, *Ardenna grisea*—Rethinking the breeding season: Summer or winter?

FAMILY PHALACROCORACIDAE: Cormorants

These expert anglers have increased overall in recent years, to the point now that they are considered by some to be nuisances. They combine all-black plumage with colorful bare parts.

☐ 195. Double-crested Cormorant, *Phalacrocorax auritus*—Our human values: The ugly

FAMILY PELECANIDAE: Pelicans

There are huge birds, and then there are pelicans. If you're looking at a bird with an absolutely ridiculous bill, it's likely a pelican. Ungainly on land, these birds are supremely gifted aerialists.

☐ 89. American White Pelican, *Pelecanus erythrorhynchos*—Bird observatories
☐ 139. Brown Pelican, *Pelecanus occidentalis*—What goes down, must come up?

FAMILY ARDEIDAE: Herons and Egrets

A tall bird stands motionless at the edge of a lake or marsh, then suddenly jabs its bill at the water, pulling out a fish or frog. Odds are, you've just seen a bird in this family. Most have awful, but oddly arresting, calls; many nest in dense, messy, foul colonies in trees.

☐ 106. Great Blue Heron, *Ardea herodias*—Population dynamics: Luck of the draw
☐ 148. Great Egret, *Ardea alba*—Birding listserv(e)(r)s
☐ 109. Snowy Egret, *Egretta thula*—Rethinking the breeding season: Emptying the nest

☐ 151. Green Heron, *Butorides virescens*—Join the club

☐ 172. Black-crowned Night-Heron, *Nycticorax nycticorax*—Slackers

FAMILY CATHARTIDAE: New World Vultures

These garbage collectors of the bird world eat anything—as long as it is dead. The deader the better: Stillborn livestock and roadkill are especially favored. Their plumage is entirely black, their heads unfeathered and grotesque.

☐ 182. Black Vulture, *Coragyps atratus*—Adaptationism

☐ 76. Turkey Vulture, *Cathartes aura*—Confirmed!

FAMILY PANDIONIDAE: The Osprey

This large piscivore is a raptor—but so distinct from others that it gets its own family. Ospreys catch food more in the manner of a Brown Pelican than a hawk or an eagle!

☐ 60. Osprey, *Pandion haliaetus*—The logic of migration: Resource availability

FAMILY ACCIPITRIDAE: Hawks and Eagles

These are the true hawks, or birds of prey, chiefly terrestrial hunters of mammals and birds. They vary in size from quite large to surprisingly small. All have hooked beaks, and the color brown is a recurring theme in this family.

☐ 152. Golden Eagle, *Aquila chrysaetos*—Bird festivals

☐ 166. Northern Harrier, *Circus hudsonius*—How we learn: Screen time

☐ 91. Cooper's Hawk, *Accipiter cooperii*—Breeding systems: territoriality

☐ 190. Bald Eagle, *Haliaeetus leucocephalus*—Place and purpose: The Anthropocene epoch

☐ 177. Red-shouldered Hawk, *Buteo lineatus*—Schrödinger's hawk

☐ 71. Broad-winged Hawk, *Buteo platypterus*—Check the weather before you go out!

☐ 56. Swainson's Hawk, *Buteo swainsoni*— "FOS"

☐ 3. Red-tailed Hawk, *Buteo jamaicensis*—(Most) birds are (fairly) easy to ID

FAMILY TYTONIDAE: Barn Owls

Known as "man birds," or variants thereof, in many cultures, the birds in this family appear pensive and soulful. Our one species is simply the Barn Owl, a ghostly thing that, even in this day and age, has a way of finding its way to old silos and other outbuildings.

☐ 158. Barn Owl, *Tyto alba*—Things birders do: Big Years

FAMILY STRIGIDAE: Typical Owls

Round-bodied and blockheaded, owls are in many ways the nocturnal equivalent of the family Accipitridae. Most have muffled wingbeats, an adaptation for hunting silently at night. Nearly all are cryptically patterned in browns and grays.

☐ 200. Eastern Screech-Owl, *Megascops asio*—Who knew?

☐ 51. Great Horned Owl, *Bubo virginianus*—He says, she says

☐ 90. Burrowing Owl, *Athene cunicularia*—Breeding systems: Coloniality
☐ 196. Barred Owl, *Strix varia*—Ethicalness

FAMILY ALCEDINIDAE: Kingfishers

The "fisher" part refers to their piscivorous proclivities, the "king" part to their impressiveness. Kingfishers sit unobtrusively on snags over the water's edge—until they splashily and conspicuously snag a fish near the water's surface.

☐ 28. Belted Kingfisher, *Megaceryle alcyon*—Scientific names: Love and logic

FAMILY PICIDAE: Woodpeckers

A mostly black-and-white bird hitches up a tree, bracing itself with stiff tail feathers. Woodpecker! The males (and some females) of all our species show splashes of red or, more rarely, yellow on the head.

☐ 135. Red-headed Woodpecker, *Melanerpes erythrocephalus*—The perils of portable toilets
☐ 50. Red-bellied Woodpecker, *Melanerpes carolinus*—What the woodpecker says
☐ 179. Yellow-bellied Sapsucker, *Sphyrapicus varius*—Fuzzy math
☐ 10. Downy Woodpecker, *Dryobates pubescens*—Massive parallel processing
☐ 143. Hairy Woodpecker, *Dryobates villosus*—The good book
☐ 162. Northern Flicker, *Colaptes auratus*—On the origins of knowledge: Stable isotopes
☐ 27. Pileated Woodpecker, *Dryocopus pileatus*—Standard English names

FAMILY FALCONIDAE: Falcons

These emblems of raptorial power and majesty were recently shown to be unrelated to the hawks and eagles. They're still powerful and majestic, but they're actually more closely related to parrots and songbirds. Falcons' pointed wings are distinctive in flight.

☐ 20. American Kestrel, *Falco sparverius*—Watch birds fly
☐ 36. Peregrine Falcon, *Falco peregrinus*—Other approaches: Systematics

FAMILY TYRANNIDAE: Tyrant Flycatchers

The "flycatcher" part is obvious: These birds catch flies (and other airborne insects). The "tyrant" part refers to the pugilistic tendencies of many species, especially the kingbirds. All perch upright, and many American species are decidedly drab.

☐ 99. Ash-throated Flycatcher, *Myiarchus cinerascens*—Resource limitation: No room at the inn
☐ 133. Great Crested Flycatcher, *Myiarchus crinitus*—Lights out!
☐ 81. Western Kingbird, *Tyrannus verticalis*—A challenge for ornithology: Habitat bias
☐ 136. Eastern Kingbird, *Tyrannus tyrannus*—The dark side of green energy?
☐ 144. Olive-sided Flycatcher, *Contopus cooperi*—The birder's library
☐ 154. Western Wood-Pewee, *Contopus sordidulus*—Bird records committees
☐ 120. Eastern Wood-Pewee, *Contopus virens*—The "basics" of molt
☐ 113. Willow Flycatcher, *Empidonax traillii*—Habitat degradation
☐ 70. Least Flycatcher, *Empidonax minimus*—Layover

☐ 131. Gray Flycatcher, *Empidonax wrightii*—Canary in a coal mine?
☐ 170. "Western" Flycatcher, *Empidonax difficilis*—What we don't know
☐ 37. Eastern Phoebe, *Sayornis phoebe*—After the spark

FAMILY LANIIDAE: Shrikes

A chiefly Old World family, these "butcher birds" have the gruesome habit of impaling their prey on thorns and barbed wire. Look for shrikes in open country with perches—especially ones with thorns!

☐ 156. Loggerhead Shrike, *Lanius ludovicianus*—Things birder do: Chasing

FAMILY VIREONIDAE: Vireos

These generally cryptic forest mites are hard to spot; and even when glimpsed, they are hard to identify. They were once known as greenlets, arguably a superior moniker. Know the songs, given frequently, even incessantly, and often distinctive.

☐ 134. Warbling Vireo, *Vireo gilvus*—Cats indoors!
☐ 77. Red-eyed Vireo, *Vireo olivaceus*—A summer project

FAMILY CORVIDAE: Crows, Jays, and Company

Some of our most familiar birds—magpies, jays, and ravens—are members of this family. They are medium to large, with strong legs and fairly long bills. Many are renowned for their intelligence.

☐ 187. Steller's Jay, *Cyanocitta stelleri*—Place and purpose: Random walk
☐ 87. Blue Jay, *Cyanocitta cristata*—eBorg
☐ 186. Clark's Nutcracker, *Nucifraga columbiana*—Nutcrackers never forget
☐ 185. Black-billed Magpie, *Pica hudsonia*—Magpie funerals
☐ 111. American Crow, *Corvus brachyrhynchos*—Is hunting bad?
☐ 8. Common Raven, *Corvus corax*—Size matters

FAMILY ALAUDIDAE: Larks

These are the birds made famous in English Romantic poetry. Only one species is widespread in North America, and it is only an average songster. Larks are ground lovers, flourishing in some of the bleakest habitats on the continent.

☐ 5. Horned Lark, *Eremophila alpestris*—A common but unfamiliar bird

FAMILY HIRUNDINIDAE: Swallows

Think of these as "swifts lite"—impressively aerial, but not as extreme as swifts. Mixed-species flocks forage over lakes, and perch shoulder to shoulder on wires.

☐ 115. Purple Martin, *Progne subis*—Habitat redux
☐ 55. Tree Swallow, *Tachycineta bicolor*—The greatest show on Earth
☐ 130. Northern Rough-winged Swallow, *Stelgidopteryx serripennis*—Into the fire

☐ 80. Cliff Swallow, *Petrochelidon pyrrhonota*—How many birds were there?
☐ 150. Barn Swallow, *Hirundo rustica*—Let me Google that for you

FAMILY PARIDAE: Chickadees and Titmice

Active and inquisitive, these little energy balls may be found in deep forests, as well as suburbs and even major cities. Their calls are harsh and chattering, their songs loud and ringing.

☐ 4. Black-capped Chickadee, *Poecile atricapillus*—Avian diversity
☐ 21. Tufted Titmouse, *Baeolophus bicolor*—Location, location, location

FAMILY AEGITHALIDAE: Long-tailed Tits

Only one member of this Old World family has reached the western hemisphere. The Bushtit is tiny and hyperactive; flocks seem to materialize out of thin air, then disappear just as quickly. Birdfeeders are defenseless against these "suet piranhas."

☐ 92. Bushtit, *Psaltriparus minimus*—Breeding systems: "It's complicated"

FAMILY SITTIDAE: Nuthatches

These oddly ovoid forest songbirds have the distinctive habit of walking upside down on the larger branches and boughs of old trees. Their chisel-like bills remind us of woodpeckers, but their broad tails do not.

☐ 129. Red-breasted Nuthatch, *Sitta canadensis*—Out of the frying pan
☐ 16. White-breasted Nuthatch, *Sitta carolinensis*—If it walks like a duck . . .

FAMILY CERTHIIDAE: Treecreepers

Tree huggers, literally. Look for them circling up the trunk of a tall tree. Exemplars of convergent evolution, treecreepers are extraordinarily similar in plumage and morphology to the unrelated Neotropical woodcreepers.

☐ 181. Brown Creeper, *Certhia americana*—Adaptation

FAMILY TROGLODYTIDAE: Wrens

It hardly seems fair to call these exuberant songsters "troglodytes." All are brown or brownish, with longish bills and cocked tails. Habitat is important for identification, and their songs are out-of-this-world awesome.

☐ 104. Rock Wren, *Salpinctes obsoletus*—Population dynamics: Find your own niche
☐ 79. House Wren, *Troglodytes aedon*—How many birds are there?
☐ 112. Marsh Wren, *Cistothorus palustris*—Habitat destruction
☐ 48. Carolina Wren, *Thryothorus ludovicianus*—Make recordings of birdsong

FAMILY POLIOPTILIDAE: Gnatcatchers

They're so small that a gnat is about all they can manage! All are long-tailed and basically blue-gray. Like many micro birds, they are exceedingly active.

☐ 102. Blue-gray Gnatcatcher, *Polioptila caerulea*—Population dynamics: Source and sink

FAMILY CINCLIDAE: Dippers

An aquatic songbird! Like all dippers, our one species is always found in and around—usually *in*—rushing rivers and streams. They are expert swimmers and divers, and their song is incredible.

☐ 17. American Dipper, *Cinclus mexicanus*—A colorless, shapeless, amazing bird

FAMILY REGULIDAE: Kinglets

We have two species, the tiny Ruby-crowned Kinglet and the teeny-tiny Golden-crowned Kinglet. They are spheroid, olive, and constantly on the go.

☐ 174. Golden-crowned Kinglet, *Regulus satrapa*—Bare-naked birding: See better
☐ 35. Ruby-crowned Kinglet, *Regulus calendula*—Other approaches: Taxonomy

FAMILY TURDIDAE: Thrushes

This diverse group is well-represented across the globe. The spot-breasted young are often easy to study during the summer months. The adults are excellent songsters.

☐ 193. Eastern Bluebird, *Sialia sialis*—Our human values: The good
☐ 61. Swainson's Thrush, *Catharus ustulatus*—The logic of migration: Wing morphology
☐ 25. Hermit Thrush, *Catharus guttatus*—Learn "S&D"
☐ 2. American Robin, *Turdus migratorius*—A familiar bird

FAMILY MIMIDAE: Mimic Thrushes

It's not that they mimic thrushes in appearance. Rather, they mimic thrushes—and everything else—in their vocalizations. Many of the birds in this family routinely incorporate other birds' songs in their own repertoires.

☐ 161. Gray Catbird, *Dumetella carolinensis*—On the origins of knowledge: Bird banding
☐ 168. Northern Mockingbird, *Mimus polyglottos*—How we learn: Me time

FAMILY STURNIDAE: Starlings and Mynas

Most members of this Old World assemblage are plump and glossy. The adults are intelligent, sociable, and vocal. The European Starling, introduced to America in the 19th century, has been fantastically if problematically successful here. Several mynas, also introduced, may be found in the wild, especially in Florida.

☐ 105. European Starling, *Sturnus vulgaris*—Population dynamics: Run for your life

FAMILY BOMBYCILLIDAE: Waxwings

No matter how many times you see a waxing, you just have to take another look. Waxwings are spectacular. They are also fascinating behaviorally: nomadic, gregarious, frugivorous in winter, insectivorous in summer, and, in an odd twist, apparently lacking a song.

☐ 1. Cedar Waxwing, *Bombycilla cedrorum*—Spark bird!

FAMILY PASSERIDAE: Old World Sparrows

Like New World Sparrows, they're mostly brown and gray. Their songs, simple to human ears but actually quite rich, are completely unlike those of New World Sparrows. The two species in our area were introduced in the 19th century.

☐ 121. House Sparrow, *Passer domesticus*—Two for the price of one

FAMILY MOTACILLIDAE: Pipits and Wagtails

Look for them in open country, and listen for their distinctive flight calls. Most are long-tailed and sleek of build. One species, the American Pipit, is widespread in our area; the others require some searching and luck.

☐ 86. American Pipit, *Anthus rubescens*—eBird: It takes a (global) village

FAMILY FRINGILLIDAE: Finches

All birds wander to some extent, but the finch clan is especially prone to nomadism. Grosbeaks, siskins, and particularly crossbills frequently stage massive "irruptions" hundreds to thousands of miles in extent. Finches favor forested districts, and some are irresistibly drawn to feeders.

☐ 188. Evening Grosbeak, *Coccothraustes vespertinus*—Place and purpose: The balance of nature
☐ 53. House Finch, *Haemorhous mexicanus*—A touchy subject: Hearing loss
☐ 178. Red Crossbill, *Loxia curvirostra*—Paradigm shift
☐ 96. Pine Siskin, *Spinus pinus*—Bird nests: Classic
☐ 184. American Goldfinch, *Spinus tristis*—Memes: The evolution of beauty

FAMILY CALCARIIDAE: Longspurs

Long thought to be New World Sparrows, the birds in this grouping were recently assigned their own family. After the fact, it all makes sense—for they differ greatly in everything from how they walk to what their flight calls sound like. Breeding males are snazzy, females and young less so.

☐ 33. Lapland Longspur, *Calcarius lapponicus*—Do the checklist shuffle

FAMILY PASSERELLIDAE: New World Sparrows

Perhaps more than any other family, the New World Sparrows are your classic LBJs (little brown jobs)—although many are quite beautiful. They have conical bills, and most sing splendidly.

☐ 40. Spotted Towhee, *Pipilo maculatus*—The absolute best way to learn birdsong
☐ 41. Eastern Towhee, *Pipilo erythrophthalmus*—Translating birdsong into English
☐ 24. American Tree Sparrow, *Spizelloides arborea*—Local movements
☐ 117. Chipping Sparrow, *Spizella passerina*—The five seasons

☐ 142. Vesper Sparrow, *Pooecetes gramineus*—What we know

☐ 94. Lark Sparrow, *Chondestes grammacus*—Baby birds: Late bloomers

☐ 167. Savannah Sparrow, *Passerculus sandwichensis*—How we learn: Face time

☐ 82. Grasshopper Sparrow, *Ammodramus savannarum*—A challenge for ornithology: Birder bias

☐ 59. Fox Sparrow, *Passerella iliaca*—Leapfrog migration

☐ 7. Song Sparrow, *Melospiza melodia*—Pay attention to pattern

☐ 175. Swamp Sparrow, *Melospiza georgiana*—Bare-naked birding: See farther

☐ 47. White-throated Sparrow, *Zonotrichia albicollis*—Back to the basics

☐ 12. White-crowned Sparrow, *Zonotrichia leucophrys*—Age-related plumage variation

☐ 31. Dark-eyed Junco, *Junco hyemalis*—Lumping species into one

FAMILY ICTERIIDAE: The one and only Yellow-breasted Chat

For ages, this bird was in the wood-warbler family—even though ornithologists suspected that it didn't belong in that grouping. We now know that this large-bodied, long-tailed, yellow-breasted, freaky-sounding bird is simply a Yellow-breasted Chat, a taxonomic outlier, all by itself.

☐ 176. Yellow-breasted Chat, *Icteria virens*—Jekyll and Hyde

FAMILY ICTERIDAE: Blackbirds and Orioles

Some are black, or at least primarily blackish; but others are brilliantly orange and gold. Many of the birds in this diverse family combine strong bills and sturdy legs with glossy plumage and a compact body plan.

☐ 119. Bobolink, *Dolichonyx oryzivorus*—What is molt anyway?

☐ 43. Eastern Meadowlark, *Sturnella magna*—A musical score for birdsong

☐ 42. Western Meadowlark, *Sturnella neglecta*—Birdsong without mnemonics

☐ 116. Bullock's Oriole, *Icterus bullockii*—Inflection point

☐ 124. Baltimore Oriole, *Icterus galbula*—Juvenilia

☐ 38. Red-winged Blackbird, *Agelaius phoeniceus*—Birds are somewhat to exceedingly noisy

☐ 95. Brown-headed Cowbird, *Molothrus ater*—Baby birds: Parasites

☐ 199. Brewer's Blackbird, *Euphagus cyanocephalus*—What's in a name? Cultural imperialism

☐ 29. Common Grackle, *Quiscalus quiscula*—Scientific names: Rules and regulations

☐ 160. Great-tailed Grackle, *Quiscalus mexicanus*—Things birders do: Travel

FAMILY PARULIDAE: Wood-Warblers

These "butterflies of the bird world" delight nature lovers with their bright plumages, fidgety demeanor, and impressive migrations. Rather than warble, most species trill and twitter.

☐ 100. Ovenbird, *Seiurus aurocapilla*—Resource limitation: Floaters

☐ 137. Northern Waterthrush, *Parkesia noveboracensis*—We'll leave the light on

☐ 72. Black-and-white Warbler, *Mniotilta varia*—Radar ornithology

☐ 58. Orange-crowned Warbler, *Oreothlypis celata*—Migration timing: A paradox

☐ 180. Nashville Warbler, *Oreothlypis ruficapilla*—Two for the price of three

☐ 159. Common Yellowthroat, *Geothlypis trichas*—Things birders do: Patchwork

☐ 73. American Redstart, *Setophaga ruticilla*—Morning flight

☐ 126. Yellow Warbler, *Setophaga petechia*—Zugunruhe

☐ 14. Yellow-rumped Warbler, *Setophaga coronata*—Geographic variation

☐ 63. Wilson's Warbler, *Cardellina pusilla*—Why do birds migrate?

FAMILY CARDINALIDAE: The Cardinal grab bag

Tanagers, cardinals, grosbeaks, buntings, even the Dickcissel—this New World group is characterized by strong bills, colorful plumages, and generally arboreal habitats. With many exceptions!

☐ 114. Scarlet Tanager, *Piranga olivacea*—Habitat fragmentation

☐ 11. Northern Cardinal, *Cardinalis cardinalis*—Sex and gender

☐ 149. Rose-breasted Grosbeak, *Pheucticus ludovicianus*—Rare bird alerts

☐ 145. Lazuli Bunting, *Passerina amoena*—Details . . . details . . .

☐ 65. Indigo Bunting, *Passerina cyanea*—How do nocturnal migrants know where to go?

☐ 146. Dickcissel, *Spiza americana*—Old media, new media

ACKNOWLEDGMENTS

A COUPLE YEARS AGO, Susan Hitchcock and I struck up a friendship. We discovered that the two of us share an abiding fascination with the challenge of communicating ideas about birds and nature. We talked about questions of audience and outlook, of accuracy and authority, of outreach and effectiveness. Together we designed an idealized bird book for the present age, a manifesto for the modern bird lover. Our conversations and correspondence were stimulating, but, I have to be honest, I thought sort of academic. You see, I always assumed that someone else would write the book. So imagine my delight when Susan asked me to write *How to Know the Birds*. Thanks, Susan, for the opportunity. I'm still in pinch-me-I'm-dreaming mode.

Once the project took off, Moriah Petty became integrally involved in the book's production. A lot of Moriah's work was behind the scenes—so far behind the veil that even I wasn't always sure what was going on. What I do know, though, is that she gave the entire manuscript a thorough and thoughtful read. Moriah tells me she's not a scientist, but I can assure you that she has an eerie ability to troubleshoot stretches of text where the science was misleading, unclear, or otherwise off.

Peter Pyle is the consummate scientist, one of the leading ornithologists of our day, and I am grateful for the considerable care that he gave to the manuscript. Peter caught all sorts of infelicities—from outdated taxonomy to imprecise terminology to outright botcheries of scientific names. Something else: Peter brought a certain sensitivity to his review of the manuscript, helping me to get through to the reader in ways I would not have otherwise.

I met Noah Strycker when he was 17 years old, and he was so amazing that I frankly thought he was lying about his age. He has continued to amaze me ever since. Noah went to town on every single page, practically every single paragraph, in *How to Know the Birds*. If there are any errors in this book, they crept in *after* Noah read the manuscript. And you'd think I was lying if I told you how fast he worked.

I can't decide if Frank Izaguirre contributed more valuably to the little things or the big things that go into writing a book like this one. The little things: Along with Moriah, Peter, and Noah, he bailed me out with fact-checking, proofreading, and formatting. The big things: He contributed several of the central ideas that permeate the pages of *How to Know the Birds*. A tease to all the rest of you: Frank's first book is going to majorly affect the way we think about people and birds.

Russell Galen is my literary agent, emphasis on "literary." He understands the bird book genre better than anybody alive, and he has played a direct role in the genesis of the most important English-language field guides and other natural history works of the 21st century. Russell has significantly influenced the way we look at birds. I'm proud to be his client.

There's a saying in the birding community: "Ask Rick Wright." Rick is the reigning authority on the history and sociology of birding. I met him eons ago in an upper-level seminar on Virgil (that is *so* Rick Wright), and he has been expanding and enriching my conception of the sciences and the humanities ever since. Plus, he read an early draft of *How to Know the Birds* and set me aright on various key points.

Macklin Smith, too, read an early draft of *How to Know the Birds* and gently but forcibly backed me out of several dead ends. A professional rhetorician, Macklin has a special talent for navigating the tricky intersection of authorial intent and readerly reception. I hope I've picked up a thing or two from him in this regard.

A work like this one is more than just words on the page. The birding gods smiled on all of us involved in the production of this book when renowned wildlife artist John Schmitt came on board; his drawings skillfully convey so many of the key concepts in *How to Know the Birds*. Art director Sanaa Akkach brought her considerable aesthetic sense to bear on the grace and balance of word and image in this book. And Judith Klein, production editor, moved the project from final draft to copyedited and proofread perfection (or as near as it could be).

I have to say a word or three about the American Birding Association (ABA). For well over half my adult life, I've had a dream job with the ABA—not only because the work itself is intrinsically awesome and endlessly rewarding, but also because the ABA has been incredibly gracious and progressive in all matters involving work-life balance. I couldn't have written this book except in my capacity as a proud ABA'er. And I wouldn't have been able to devote nearly as much time to my family. Speaking of whom . . .

Hannah Floyd, who edits cereal boxes and billboards for the joy of it, managed to get her hands on the manuscript and make various corrections. She's still in middle school. Noah, watch out, you've got competition. Andrew

Floyd, also in middle school, cheered me on, at several junctures supplying me with original ideas for content; see if you can discern his contributions to the lessons on Bushtits, Chipping Sparrows, and especially Blue Jays. Kei Sochi was a faithful critic and champion throughout the project, giving me comfort when I needed comfort, encouragement when I needed encouragement, and, just as important, space when I needed space.

Finally, Jack Solomon and Paul Hess. They had nothing to do with this book. As far as I know, they haven't seen it till now. For once in my life, I didn't ask them for help. Because it was time to give them a rest. Jack and Paul have helped me along the way, in every manner imaginable, for close to 40 years. They've had everything to do with this book—its voice and vision, its ideas and content, its heart and soul. It is an honor to dedicate *How to Know the Birds* to Jack and Paul.

ABOUT THE AUTHOR

TED FLOYD IS an internationally recognized birding expert and Editor of *Birding* magazine, the award-winning flagship publication of the American Birding Association. He has written four books previously, including the *Smithsonian Field Guide to the Birds of North America*, and is the author of more than 200 popular articles, technical papers, and book chapters on birds and natural history. Floyd is a frequent speaker at bird festivals and ornithological society meetings. He and his family live in Lafayette, Colorado.

ABOUT THE ILLUSTRATOR

N. JOHN SCHMITT IS an internationally known bird illustrator who has contributed to numerous magazines and books, including *Raptors of Mexico and Central America*, *The Ripley Guide to the Birds of South Asia*, *Birds Asleep*, and *National Geographic Field Guide to the Birds of North America*. He has also worked extensively as a museum preparator and a field biologist. Schmitt lives and bird-watches in California's Kern River Valley.

INDEX

A CELEBRATION
OF OUR WINGED
WONDERS

In paint or pencil; black-and-white or
Kodachrome; high-speed shutters,
camera traps, or telephoto lenses,
National Geographic storytellers
bring you a magnificent book that
chronicles our expanding knowledge
and changing awareness of birds
over the past 130 years.

AVAILABLE WHEREVER BOOKS ARE SOLD
and at NationalGeographic.com/Books

NATIONAL
GEOGRAPHIC